W9-BFN-463

Lincoln's Admiral

Also by James P. Duffy

Hitler Slept Late, And Other Blunders That Cost Him the War
*Target Hitler: The Plots to Kill Adolf Hitler**
*The Assassination of John F. Kennedy: A Complete Book of Facts**
*Czars: Russia's Rulers for Over One Thousand Years**

* with Vincent L. Ricci

Lincoln's Admiral

The Civil War Campaigns of David Farragut

James P. Duffy

John Wiley & Sons, Inc.
New York • Chichester • Weinheim • Brisbane • Singapore • Toronto

To Patricia Duffy, O.P.

This text is printed on acid-free paper.

Copyright © 1997 by James P. Duffy
Published by John Wiley & Sons, Inc.

Frontispiece portrait of Admiral Farragut with signature courtesy of Hastings (N.Y.) Historical Society.

Library of Congress Cataloging-in-Publication Data

Duffy, James P.
    Lincoln's admiral : the Civil War campaigns of David Farragut / James P. Duffy.
        p.   cm.
    Includes bibliographical references and index.
    ISBN 0-471-04208-0 (cloth : alk. paper)
    1. Farragut, David Glasgow, 1801–1870.   2. Admirals—United States—Biography.   3. United States. Navy—Biography.   4. United States—History—Civil War, 1861–1865—Naval operations.   I. Title.
E467.1.F23D84   1997
973.7'5'092—dc20
    [B]   96-34986

Printed in the United States of America

10 9 8 7 6 5 4 3 2 1

Oh, never through all time shall be forgot
His last brave deed, now told by every lip,
When on he sailed, amid a storm of shot,
Lashed in the rigging of his staunch old ship.

—Anonymous
Harper's Weekly
September 10, 1864

Contents

Illustrations

Plates

Maps

Acknowledgments

So MANY PEOPLE HAVE HELPED ME in so many ways to research the material in this book that it is impossible to list them without inadvertently leaving some out. Therefore I have decided once again simply to express my appreciation to each of you as I did at the time when you gave me your assistance.

Having said that, I would like to extend special thanks to the following: Alice S. Creighton of the Nimitz Library at the United States Naval Academy; Michael Henderson of the Dauphin Island Park and Beach Board; Bob Gibson of the Confederate Naval Museum; Peter Harrington of the Anne S. K. Brown Military Collection, Brown University Library; Randy W. Hackenburg and Michael J. Winey of the U.S. Army Military History Institute; James Cheevers and William B. Cogar of the United States Naval Academy Museum; Mary L. Allison of the Hastings (N.Y.) Historical Society; and Tom Freeman, artist.

I must also recognize the special help given me by the always patient and always professional staff of the Millbrook (New York) Free Library, especially Lois Rigoulot, Nancy Rogers, and Jo Hausam, who worked ceaselessly to respond to my requests, and never seemed to tire of finding new sources of information.

Without the tireless efforts and extremely patient support of a wonderful editor, Hana Umlauf Lane, this book might never have been completed. For everything Hana did during the writing of this book, she has my gratitude and my appreciation.

Finally, I would like to thank my wife, Kathleen, and my daughters, Alexandra and Olivia, for their patience and support.

Prologue

AT 7:15 A.M. ON AUGUST 5, 1864, cannon shells from the heavy gun batteries of Fort Morgan began raining down on the eighteen-ship Union fleet. The Federal fleet was attempting to penetrate the minefield blocking the channel entrance to Mobile Bay. The objective was to isolate and close the harbor of Mobile, Alabama, the Confederacy's vital port and railroad center. Beyond the mines, known as torpedoes, the dreaded rebel ironclad *Tennessee* lay in wait to attack any Union ship that survived the torpedoes and the cannon bombardment. A fleet of armored gunboats reinforced the *Tennessee*.

The dense, acrid smoke coming from the barrage from the forts and the ships of both fleets was so thick that Union gunners feared hitting their own ships.

In the rigging of his flagship, the *Hartford*, high above the mantle of smoke, stood sixty-three-year-old Rear Admiral David Farragut. It was the only location aboard ship that afforded a panorama of the battle. He held a spyglass firmly in one hand, and a megaphone in the other. Bound securely to the mast, Farragut deftly directed the action of his fleet in what would be one of the most important naval engagements of the Civil War. He periodically raised the spyglass toward the bay, keeping a watchful eye on the *Tennessee* and her able commander and his old friend, Confederate admiral Franklin Buchanan. Had a rebel shell struck the *Hartford*'s mast, a prized target of every Confederate gunner, Farragut would have crashed to the deck, or been catapulted overboard.

1

Admirals du Pont, Farragut, and Porter. Courtesy of the Nimitz Library, U.S. Naval Academy.

The image of Farragut directing the battle from the rigging of the *Hartford* was quickly immortalized in an illustration titled "American Naval Officer Going into Action" in *Frank Leslie's Illustrated Newspaper.* The notoriety bolstered a reputation that was quickly outstripping those of all previous American naval officers other than the legendary John Paul Jones.

1

A Lifetime of Service

JAMES GLASGOW FARRAGUT—he later changed his first name to
David—was born on July 5, 1801, on a farm near Campbell's Station
in Knox County, Tennessee, a dozen miles southwest of Knoxville.
James's father, Jorge (Anglicized to George) Anthony Magin Farragut,
had immigrated from his ancestral home on Minorca, one of the
Balearic Islands off the east coast of Spain. The Farragut family had
a long history of close military and civilian ties to Spanish royalty.
George had been born in September, 1755, on an estate bestowed on
the Farragut family by King James I of Aragon. It was awarded in
recognition of the services of Don Pedro Farragut, who helped drive
the Moors from Majorca and Valencia in the thirteenth century. Following his tenth birthday, George abandoned his formal schooling in
Barcelona and went to sea aboard a merchant ship plying the trade
routes of the Mediterranean.

By 1773 the young, adventurous sailor became bored with the
routine of Mediterranean life, which consisted of visiting the same
ports over and over, and ventured to the New World as captain of a
merchant ship. On a brief stop at New Orleans in 1775, Farragut
learned that the American colonies had revolted against Great Britain.
Inspired by the idea of a people rising en masse to gain their independence from a foreign power, he sailed to Port-au-Prince, Haiti,
where he exchanged his cargo of commercial goods for muskets, cannon, and ammunition. By the time he arrived at the Charleston, South
Carolina, harbor in early 1776, the American Revolution had become

3

a full-fledged war, and his ship and its precious cargo were well received.

George Farragut sought and received an appointment as a first lieutenant in the North Carolina Navy. He commanded a war galley in the valiant yet unsuccessful defense of Savannah, and then a shore battery in the defense of Charleston. When the latter fell to the British on May 12, 1780, Farragut was taken prisoner.

Released in a prisoner exchange a short time later, Farragut joined a privateer out of Philadelphia, but soon found himself ashore after a musket ball shattered several bones in his right arm during a battle with a British warship. Although a surgeon managed to save the arm from amputation, the resulting handicap prevented George from finding duty on either a warship or a privateer. Instead, he joined a Continental Army cavalry company and participated in the campaign against British general Cornwallis's army in the Carolinas. By the end of the war he had risen to the rank of major.

As with so many veterans of the American Revolution, Farragut's selfless service left him near poverty. Despite the limited use of his right arm, he turned to the work he knew best and spent the next seven years at sea, devoting most of that time to the lucrative West Indies trade. His sailing days ended in 1790 when an old friend, William Blount, governor of the Southwest Territory, invited him to Knoxville and appointed him a major of militia. The next several years were consumed in fighting the Creeks and Cherokees over disputed land boundaries. During this time, George was the recipient of several land grants in Knox County for his services during the Revolution.

In 1795 the forty-year-old George Farragut married Elizabeth Shine, ten years his junior. Elizabeth came from a North Carolina family of some reputation and position. Descendants of an Irish immigrant, Elizabeth's father and uncle had both served as officers in the Revolution. During the first five years of their marriage, George and Elizabeth lived in a house George built with his own hands on Emmerson Street in Knoxville. Their first son, William, was born there. By the close of the century, George had sold off several parcels of land he had acquired, and had purchased the 600-plus-acre farm near Campbell's Station on which his son James was born.

The Tennessee farm remained their home until the sea once again beckoned to George. The summons came from another of Farragut's old friends, William Charles Claiborne. President Thomas Jefferson had appointed Claiborne governor of the new Territory of Orleans, which was a portion of the vast region acquired from France that was known as the Louisiana Purchase. In 1807 the Farragut family, along with all their portable possessions, sailed down the Holston, Tennessee, and Ohio rivers, and finally the Mississippi, to New Orleans. The voyage, made in a large, flat-bottomed riverboat, took over two months.

In New Orleans, Governor Claiborne obtained an appointment for George Farragut as a naval sailing master, as well as commander of a gunboat patrolling the Mississippi River. Farragut soon became friendly with another sailing master, David Porter Sr., whose son was a naval officer. In late spring of 1808, the elder Porter fell ill from sunstroke while fishing, and was taken into the Farragut home, where Elizabeth nursed him. His condition, complicated by consumption, which had already taken a severe toll of his health, worsened, and he died while in Elizabeth's care. In a strange turn of fate, Elizabeth, who herself had been stricken with yellow fever while caring for him, died the same day, June 22, 1808. Elizabeth Farragut and David Porter Sr. were both buried two days later in the same cemetery.

A few months after his father's burial, Commander David Porter Jr., who had taken command of the New Orleans naval station three days before his father's death, visited the Farragut home. In gratitude for the kindness shown his dying father, Porter offered to take one of George's sons into his own home and train him as a naval officer. James was eight years old at the time. Awed by the impressive uniform worn by Porter, and a little envious of his older brother William's recent appointment as a midshipman, James quickly accepted the offer. The Farragut children had been scattered to the homes of friends following the death of their mother. George, who was having difficulty finding someone to care for them while he worked, agreed to the arrangement. Residing in New Orleans with the Porters was made palatable for the little boy because James could still visit his father and sisters often.

James's separation from his father was made permanent in June of 1810, when Porter was reassigned to duty in Washington, D.C. He now had a new family, and his childhood would be anything but normal. When Porter introduced James to Secretary of the Navy Paul

Hamilton, the nine-year-old expressed his desire for an appointment as a midshipman. Hamilton, who took an immediate liking to Farragut, agreed to make the appointment as soon as the boy reached the age of ten. As it turned out, Hamilton's promise was fulfilled by a commission dated December 17, 1810, six months before Farragut's tenth birthday. One reason for the early appointment as midshipman may have been the navy secretary's desire to fill all available warship berths as war clouds thundered across the Atlantic.

Great Britain had been at war with revolutionary France since 1793, when Napoleon drove British forces from Toulon. The conflict regularly spilled over to involve ships of neutral nations. Friction arose between the United States and Great Britain as a result of the British government's policy of having Royal Navy warships stop American merchant ships on the high seas, or in neutral harbors. British naval officers would then board the merchantmen with press gangs, and remove any seamen suspected of being a British subject. Often these sailors would be American citizens who, for whatever reason, could not provide adequate proof of their citizenship at the time. Hundreds, if not thousands, of sailors were taken from American merchant ships in this way. This method of manning British warships blatantly disregarded the rights of foreign citizens. Despite efforts by American diplomats to avoid war with Great Britain, British arrogance held sway. When Britain stationed two frigates near the entrance to New York Harbor in February 1811, war was not far off. Despite protests, the British warships stopped all merchantmen leaving New York, taking as prizes of war those bound for French ports, and impressing American sailors who were unable to prove they were not British citizens.

In May 1811, Commodore John Rodgers was ordered to assemble a squadron to patrol the coast and protect American merchant ships from British assaults. David Porter was assigned to command the thirty-six-gun frigate *Essex*, and to join Rodgers's squadron. In early August, Porter and Farragut, the latter resplendent in his new midshipman's uniform, boarded the *Essex* at Norfolk. Soon after, the frigate set sail to join the Commodore's patrol.

On June 18, 1812, President James Madison signed a declaration of war against Great Britain. Midshipman Farragut, not yet eleven years old, went to war as an officer in training. Much of the War of

1812 was conducted at sea, between the mighty Royal Navy and the tiny and inadequately equipped United States Navy. The *Essex*, with the daring and resourceful Porter in command, saw more than her share of action, and young Midshipman Farragut received a comprehensive education in seamanship and the art of war at sea. During the first four months of the war, the *Essex* sailed the Atlantic from Bermuda to Newfoundland. She captured eight merchantmen and the first British warship taken in the conflict, the twenty-gun sloop-of-war *Alert*.

David Porter's reputation as a naval commander grew as a result of the *Essex*'s successes. Following this first war cruise, the *Essex* lay in the Delaware River being provisioned. Porter, with Farragut in tow, visited his wife at the Porter homestead in nearby Chester, Pennsylvania. During that visit they read in the *Philadelphia Democratic Press* that Porter and his ship had been challenged to a one-on-one duel by Sir James Yeo, captain of the British frigate *Southampton*. Yeo named the date and place the ships were to meet. Porter responded immediately. With his young protégé at his side, he rushed back to his ship and set sail for the open sea. When the *Southampton* failed to appear, the *Essex* returned to her anchorage to await further orders.

Orders arrived soon, and on October 28, 1812, the *Essex* slipped past the Royal Navy cruisers blockading the harbor and sailed out into the Atlantic. She headed for the Cape Verde Islands and a planned rendezvous with the forty-four-gun frigate *Constitution* and the eighteen-gun sloop-of-war *Hornet*. Together they were to form a squadron under the command of Commodore William Bainbridge. The commodore sent Porter instructions to prepare his ship for "a long cruise." As she set off, the *Essex* proudly and defiantly flew her banner proclaiming "Free Trade and Sailor's Rights."

Bainbridge's squadron was to sail the South Atlantic in search of British merchant ships, and destroy or capture as many as possible. Once they accomplished this, they were to sail down the east coast of South America, around Cape Horn, and into the Pacific Ocean. There they were to do as much damage as possible to the as yet unmolested British whaling fleets.

But the rendezvous never took place, because the *Constitution* and the *Hornet* had a successful engagement with two British cruisers, which they seized and returned to the United States for use by the navy. Consequently, taking full advantage of instructions to operate at his own discretion should the rendezvous not occur, Porter cruised the South Atlantic for the next few weeks, where he captured several British merchantmen. One particularly satisfying prize was the ten-gun Royal Navy packet *Nocton*, which was discovered to be carrying $55,000 in British specie. The coins were placed in a secure location aboard the *Essex*, to be used to help defer the costs of her cruise. An American crew was placed aboard the packet, along with a dozen British sailors who were paroled in return for their services, and she sailed north for the United States. Unfortunately, she was captured by a British warship near Bermuda and returned to His Britannic Majesty's service.

Life aboard the *Essex*, especially for Farragut and the twelve other midshipmen, comprised long periods of boredom and routine duty occasionally broken by furious pursuits of enemy merchant ships, some successful, others less so. Years later, Farragut would recall this cruise, and the lessons he learned from studying how Porter handled his ship and crew, always aware of the dangers of allowing boredom or disease to reduce the ship's efficiency. Porter's reputation as a captain who looked after the health and well-being of his men was well earned, and Farragut learned the value of this concern. It meant a fit and efficient ship, and the generally unquestioning loyalty of her crew.

Captain Porter kept a watchful eye on his young protégé, whom he took to calling by his middle name, Glasgow. This by no means meant that Farragut received special treatment from the ship's commander. On the contrary, Porter was determined that his education be complete, including punishment for misdeeds, which were actually few. On one such occasion, Porter discovered the boy chewing tobacco, a habit he personally disliked. Farragut attempted to conceal the tobacco by keeping his mouth closed, but the telltale black liquid seeped from the corner of the boy's mouth. Without a word, Porter clamped his hand over Farragut's mouth, forcing him to swallow the tobacco. It was a lesson well learned, for throughout his long life Farragut never again used tobacco in any form.

It was during this long and dangerous cruise that Farragut decided to honor Captain Porter by changing his first name to David. Hardly anyone called him James anyway, and most of the officers and crew preferred to follow Porter's lead in calling him Glasgow. Changing his first name had little immediate effect, for the crew and officers continued calling him Glasgow throughout the *Essex*'s long cruise.

Several failed attempts to rendezvous with Bainbridge's squadron, along with reports from neutral Portuguese merchantmen that British warships were extremely active in the area, convinced Porter that the time had arrived to sail for the Pacific. On January 26, 1813, Porter turned south and the *Essex* prepared for the 2,500-mile journey that would take them through the dangerous waters off the coast of Tierra del Fuego and into the Pacific.

On February 13 the *Essex* approached the entrance to the Strait of Le Maire and for almost three weeks battled furious seas, howling gales, and bitter cold. More than once the ship was nearly driven onto nearby rocky shoals. The *Essex* was badly battered by the sea and the winds in what Farragut described as "dreadful weather." It was, he later wrote, "the only instance in which I ever saw a regular good seaman paralyzed by fear at the dangers of the sea." As water crashed over the *Essex* and rushed down her hatchways, several of the men dropped to their knees and prayed what they expected to be their last prayers. This beating of the ship and men went on almost continuously, day after day, night after night. At long last, the ordeal ended on March 5, when the ship finally rounded the long, narrow finger of South America and entered the South Pacific Ocean. The gales subsided and the seas settled from their fury. The crew quickly set about making badly needed repairs to the *Essex*. Porter turned north and sailed along the coast of Chile.

The cruise of the *Essex* in the South Pacific was a historic one. Until her arrival, the only American ships in those waters were twenty-three whalers. Most were unarmed, since they had sailed prior to the outbreak of the war. The twenty British vessels in the region were heavily armed, since their government had been at war for almost twenty years. Also plaguing the American ships were several Peruvian privateers, who were little more than licensed pirates. One of these, the fifteen-gun *Nereyda*, had captured and sent into port as prizes, several American whalers. Flying a British flag to allow himself to get close to the privateer, Porter deceived the Peruvian captain long enough to effect his capture and the release of the crews of two

American whalers held aboard her as prisoners. The guns and ammunition of the *Nereyda* were dumped overboard, and the ship sent home with a message to the Spanish viceroy at Lima, threatening naval bombardment of coastal towns if Peruvian attacks continued. This effectively halted the Spanish-instigated seizures of American ships.

During the next few weeks the *Essex*, accompanied by a small fleet of captured British whalers and American whalers released from Peruvian ports, wreaked havoc on British commerce in the Pacific. One of the whalers was turned into a war cruiser when she was outfitted with an assortment of twenty guns taken from the British ships. Captain Porter christened her the United States Ship *Essex Junior*, and placed Lieutenant John Downes of the *Essex* in command. Porter had no difficulty manning his small fleet from among the many American sailors who had been illegally pressed into British service and were rescued by the *Essex*.

A few days after the fleet celebrated July 4, 1813, off the coast of Peru, the *Essex Junior* parted company with the *Essex* and sailed south for Valparaíso, Chile. She convoyed four captured British whalers, which were now the *Essex*'s prizes. These were the *Montezuma*, the *Catharine*, the *Hector*, and the *Policy*. Also in the convoy was an American whaler, the *Barclay*, which had been recaptured from Peruvian privateers. Downes's mission in Valparaíso was to make the best deal he could for the sale of the British whalers and request safe refuge in the port for the *Barclay*. He was then to meet Porter at the Galápagos Islands. Chile had revolted against Spain, which had been nominally an ally of Great Britain since British troops drove Napoleon's forces out of Spain. The Chileans had set up their own government. The newly independent Chile made clear its intention to maintain friendly relations with the United States.

This event proved to be the high point of Midshipman Farragut's early career in the navy, for he was chosen to be the prize master of the *Barclay*. This meant, in effect, that he was, at twelve years old, the commander of the ship and her crew. The latter was made up of men drawn from the crew of the *Essex*. Being selected to command the *Barclay* was "an important event in my life," Farragut later wrote. "I felt no little pride at finding myself in command at twelve years of age."

Also aboard the *Barclay* was her captain, Gideon Randall. Porter had decided that Randall would be responsible for the navigation of the ship, while Farragut would control the crew and issue all necessary orders. The captain reluctantly agreed to this arrangement, having no other option except to lose all influence over the future of his vessel. Randall was clearly an unhappy man when the trip to Valparaíso began. He would have preferred to return to whaling, taking his chances with British ships and privateers on the open sea.

Once the *Essex* was out of sight, and the *Essex Junior* and the four prizes had pulled slightly ahead, Randall attempted to intimidate the thin young boy with the aquiline nose who had been put in charge of his ship. He made his move when Farragut issued the order to fill the topsail so as to catch up with the *Essex Junior*. Randall immediately bellowed that he would shoot any man who obeyed the order. The sailors hesitated, waiting to see who would win the confrontation. Farragut realized this was the first test of his command abilities, and "mustered up my courage," as he later wrote. He repeated his order. To this, the crusty old captain repeated his warning, proclaiming he "had no idea of trusting himself to some damned nutshell." To demonstrate his sincerity, Randall said he was going below to get his pistols.

With Randall momentarily off the deck, Farragut called one of his trusted crewmen to his side and repeated his order concerning the topsail. The man responded with a crisp and loud "Aye, aye, sir," making it clear where his allegiance was placed, and enabling the boy to shore up his courage. Farragut then sent word below to Randall that if he appeared on deck armed he would be thrown overboard. Captain Randall judiciously accepted the threat as real, and left his pistols where they were stored. Farragut had met the first test of his command head on, and had won. The rest of the journey to Valparaíso was made peacefully.

While in Valparaíso, Downes learned that three British warships had sailed from the Atlantic into the Pacific with orders to attack and sink the *Essex*. These were the forty-gun frigate *Phoebe* and two sloops-of-war, the *Cherub* and the *Raccoon*, each carrying twenty-four guns. After hearing this, Downes left Valparaíso as quickly as possible and joined Porter on September 30, 1813, in the Galápagos Islands, where he delivered the bad news. Actually, the timing was just right. The best intelligence available to Porter told him that only one British whaler remained at large in the South Pacific. His toll on enemy commerce had been devastating, and it was time to leave the scene and return to the South Atlantic, where he would attempt to link up with Commodore Bainbridge's squadron.

Leaving the remaining prize ships behind with small crews to protect them, the *Essex* and the *Essex Junior* sailed for the Chilean coast, arriving at Valparaíso on February 3, 1814. The Americans were greeted even more cordially than before, with the officers invited to a round of social events. Believing the British warships would not arrive for some time, Porter invited the local Chilean dignitaries to a ball aboard the *Essex* on the evening of February 7. The event was a huge success, but the following morning, as the decorations were being taken down, the *Essex Junior*, which had sailed from the harbor before daybreak, signaled the arrival of two vessels.

The *Essex*'s signal gun was quickly fired to bring aboard the crew members who had gone ashore, and the ship was prepared for action. A short time later the frigate *Phoebe*, accompanied by the sloop *Cherub*, sailed into the harbor. The second sloop, *Raccoon*, continued north for the Columbia River with orders to disrupt the American fur trade centered there.

As the *Phoebe* entered the harbor, she swung toward the two American vessels, which were anchored close together. The *Essex Junior* was astern of the *Essex*. In a daring display of seamanship, the huge frigate slipped between the two Americans, coming within ten or fifteen feet of the *Essex*. Aboard the American warship, every man was at his station. Boarders waited with their cutlasses and pistols at the ready, and cannons stood fully loaded, with powder boys alongside each, holding slow-burning matches.

Aboard the *Phoebe*, Captain James Hillyar watched as his ship closed on the enemy. He stood on the rear gun, in plain sight. Dressed in a regulation pea jacket and standing nonchalantly, Hillyar appeared a fine specimen of a sea captain confident in the handling of his vessel. With all eyes on him, the British officer called to the American ship, "Captain Hillyar's compliments to Captain Porter, and hopes he is well."

Porter watched with suspicion as the British ship closed in. Although it was true they were in a neutral port, Hillyar's reputation for violating neutral territory was widely known. Porter quickly responded, "Very well, I thank you; but I hope you will not come too near, for fear some accident might take place which would be disagreeable to you."

Hillyar replied that if his ship did make contact with the *Essex*, it would be purely accidental. "Well," called Porter, "you have no business where you are. If you touch a rope-yarn of this ship, I shall board you instantly." The threat was real, but the opportunity was lost as the *Phoebe* gradually pulled away. She had gotten so close that her jib boom had swung over the *Essex*'s forecastle, but miraculously it had touched nothing.

It was ironic that these two captains should come together to battle each other. Years earlier, in the Mediterranean, the two had been close friends, with Porter a frequent visitor at Hillyar's home on Gibraltar. Now they were avowed enemies, anchored in a neutral port, waiting to sail into open waters and fight to the death.

The *Phoebe* and the *Cherub* dropped anchor not far from the American ships. The captains visited each other ashore, and Hillyar assured Porter he had no intention of violating Chilean neutrality. It took a few days for the replenishing of provisions for the British warships. That completed, they sailed from the harbor and cruised off the coast, waiting for their prey. Porter made several attempts to get Hillyar to agree on a single-ship action, but each met with failure. It soon became clear that Hillyar was biding his time, evidently waiting for additional Royal Navy ships before entering combat with the *Essex* and her smaller cohort.

Porter knew he stood little chance of battling both the *Phoebe* and the *Cherub* at the same time. His guns, more than sufficient at short range, were no match for the long-range guns of the British, and the position of the harbor eliminated the possibility of rushing past them into the open sea. He was stuck where he was, and the situation would only worsen if Hillyar received reinforcements.

Porter's predicament remained static until March 28, when a furious wind swept down the mountains behind the city, and ripped the *Essex* from her anchorage. Whipped by the winds, the ship set sail for the sea, Porter hoping to pass the British ships while they were engaged in securing themselves from the gale. Unfortunately, nature was against him. The *Essex* was pounded by the wind, and almost went over on her side. Despite strenuous efforts by her crew, she began to come apart. First her maintopmast was carried away, along with several crewmen. This loss eliminated any hope Porter had of escaping, for without this vital section of mast he could never outrun the *Phoebe*.

Turning back, the *Essex* attempted to regain the relative safety of the port, but the winds prevented her from doing so, and Porter was forced to anchor in a section of the east side of the harbor, still within the traditional three miles internationally recognized as the extension of neutrality. Hillyar decided not to recognize this boundary, not when his enemy was badly crippled and lay nearly defenseless. Had the *Phoebe* come closer, the *Essex* would not have been defenseless, but the majority of her guns were thirty-two-pound carronades, which had a devastating effect on a ship's hull at short range, but were virtually useless at long range. As the *Phoebe* stood out of range, the only guns the *Essex* could bring to bear on her were six long-range twelve-pounders. Against this, a broadside from the *Phoebe* could comprise thirteen long-range eighteen-pounders, one long-range twelve-pounder, and one long-range nine-pounder. Aside from being crippled in her ability to maneuver, the *Essex* was a sitting target for a ship that only had to remain out of range of her guns.

The *Essex* was in a desperate situation as the two enemy ships bore down on her. On board, everything was prepared for attack. Midshipman Farragut, as busy as every man aboard *Essex* preparing for the coming battle, later recalled, "I well remember the feelings of awe produced in me by the approach of the hostile ships; even to my young mind it was perceptible in the faces of those around me, as clearly as possible, that our case was hopeless."

A few minutes before 4:00 P.M. the British ships commenced firing. This first clash ended a half hour later, when the *Phoebe* and *Cherub* withdrew to make repairs caused by the enthusiastic firing of the Essex's three long-range guns, which had been moved to her stern and made more maneuverable.

The *Essex* was badly damaged in this first brief confrontation, with the loss of many men. Porter realized it was not possible to stand and fight the enemy; they simply remained out of range of his most destructive guns and pounded him mercilessly. His only hope of success was to get close enough to the *Phoebe* to board her. It was a dangerous move, to come under the very broadsides that had raked his ship from a distance, but there was little else he could do, short of surrendering.

Their repairs completed, the British ships returned for the kill. Hoping to get close enough to use his carronades and possibly board her, Porter used the only sail he had left, the flying jib, cut his anchor cable, and set his sights on the *Phoebe*. Just as he got her within range, Hillyar slipped his cable and literally backed off. This cat-and-mouse tactic, played out with a badly crippled cat and a powerful mouse, continued for several hours. As this struggle continued, the decks of the vastly outgunned *Essex* became awash with blood, and were left a splintered mess, made even worse each time cannon fire raked the ship. The majority of the crew were killed or wounded, with the survivors having to fight amid the mass of dismembered bodies and flesh that had earlier been their shipmates. Thousands of people crowded the coast to watch, many in dismay, as the badly crippled *Essex* tried repeatedly to close on her enemy, only to have that enemy pull back each time.

Porter soon recognized that the fight was hopeless. The frigate would continue to move out of range, and continue to dismantle the *Essex* with her cannon fire, until not a man was left alive. The last straw for him was the sight of flames shooting up from the hatchway and reaching toward what was left of the magazine. While he himself was determined to fight to the death, he did not want to take with him the lives of the many wounded men who would surely drown when the *Essex* went down. With great exertion he turned the sinking ship toward shore in an effort to get as close as possible, thereby enabling those few men left unwounded to help the wounded ones reach the safety of the beach. The struggle came to nothing, for suddenly a heavy gust of wind again blew down from the mountains and pushed what remained of the *Essex* around and back toward the open sea.

From the shore, thousands of pairs of eyes watched in awe and horror as the burning and virtually out-of-control ship was pitched and twisted, almost completely at the mercy of the sea and wind. Using what little control he had, Porter attempted to bring what was left of her guns to bear on the enemy. The British kept backing away from the *Essex*, holding a position that remained out of range of her carronades, and firing broadside after broadside at her. Each time the American swung around, the sailors manning her long-range guns fired on the *Phoebe* and the *Cherub*, to the amazement of the crews of those ships. And still, enemy cannon fire continued to rake her, flames raged everywhere, and splintered wood from her decks and rails flew through the air, wounding as many on board the *Essex* as did the British cannons.

For young midshipman Farragut, this was a moment of thrilling terror. During the battle, which lasted two and a half hours, he acted as captain's aide, carrying messages throughout the ship for Porter. He served as a gunner when that position was opened by death or wounds, and even as powder boy when needed. At least twice, amid the slaughter and destruction around him, Farragut was nearly killed himself. Once, when he was descending the wardroom ladder in pursuit of badly needed gun primers, a gunner nearby was struck in the face by a British eighteen-pound shot and his body flung against the boy's. Both crashed down the ladder, the larger man lying atop the younger. Farragut's head struck something, and he was momentarily knocked unconscious. When he came to, he realized that had the gunner's body landed more directly on him, he would have probably been crushed. He struggled out from under the headless corpse and proceeded with his mission.

A short while later, Farragut was standing alongside Quartermaster Francis Bland, who was at the ship's wheel. Farragut suddenly saw an enemy shot coming straight for them. He yelled for Bland to jump out of the way, then leaped against the older man in an effort to shove him away from the danger. Unfortunately the young midshipman was a fraction of a second too late, for the shot ripped Bland's right leg from his body, and tore through Farragut's coat. He helped the gravely bleeding Bland below, but the surgeons were so badly overworked, trying to cope with the many wounded men, that he bled to death before they could get to him.

At around 6:00 P.M., Porter sent word for the commissioned officers to meet with him on deck to discuss, among other things, how best to continue the fight. The *Essex* was slowly being consumed by flames, and smoke choked the men who manned the few remaining guns, making it almost impossible for them to see the enemy. Bodies of their comrades floated in the waters around the ship, some burned beyond recognition. It was clear to everyone on board, as well as to those watching from the enemy ships and from the shore, that the gallant ship was doomed. Captain Porter was prepared to take a vote among his remaining officers on the issue of surrender, but even that was not to be accomplished, since there was only one officer besides himself who was still capable of functioning. All the others had been severely wounded or killed. With this officer, Lieutenant Stephen Decatur McKnight, Captain Porter decided that only by surrendering could he prevent the *Essex* from sinking and taking the wounded men with her. Her hull had been shot through with so many holes that water was literally pouring into her.

Before hauling down his colors, and thus announcing his surrender to the enemy, Captain Porter told all those physically capable of doing so to jump overboard and swim to the beach. At that moment, the *Essex* was about three-quarters of a mile from the shore. As enemy shot poured in around him, Porter yelled over the din to Midshipman Farragut to find the ship's signal book and drop it over the side before the enemy came aboard. Locating the valuable book, Farragut did as ordered, watching it slip away beneath the waves, out of reach of the British. Then, with adrenaline still pumping through his body, and recognizing that the fight was lost, Farragut joined another boy midshipman in throwing overboard all the small arms they could find. They would at least keep this booty from the hands of British sailors.

At twenty minutes past six, approximately two hours and twenty minutes after the fearful fight had begun, Captain David Porter ordered the colors struck. Whether it was the blinding smoke or the rush caused by the battle isn't known, but even after the colors had come down, the British warships kept up their deadly firing for another ten minutes, killing four more men aboard the *Essex*. Porter surrendered his sword to the British naval officer who boarded the *Essex* for that specific purpose.

The following morning a tearful, not yet thirteen-year-old Midshipman Farragut was taken as a prisoner aboard His Britannic Majesty's frigate *Phoebe*. As he was being escorted to the steerage where the prisoners were to be held, Farragut saw a British midshipman about his own age holding a pig, and shouting, "A prize, a prize." The pig, named Murphy, was a pet of the *Essex*'s crew. Refusing to abdicate to the humiliation he was beginning to feel as a prisoner, Farragut approached the lad and demanded that he hand over the pig. The British midshipman refused, claiming the pig was his prisoner. A struggle ensued as both boys tried to seize the squealing pig. British sailors, drawn by the struggle, soon formed a circle around the two boys and agreed that they should fight each other and the winner be awarded custody of the pig. Farragut was the undisputed victor of this episode of pugilistics, and walked away with Murphy under his arm, and some of his personal dignity restored.

A short time later he was invited to join Captain Hillyar and his prisoner, Captain Porter, for breakfast in Hillyar's cabin. Hillyar saw the discomfort the boy felt in the presence of the man who had destroyed his ship and defeated his captain, and tried to console him by telling him in a kindly way, "Never mind, my little fellow, it will be your turn next perhaps," meaning that the next time Hillyar and Farragut met, the British captain might be his prisoner.

On the verge of tears, and fighting back the emotions that swept over him, the boy responded that he hoped so, and quickly left the cabin.

What remained of the crew of the *Essex* and the *Essex Junior*, 132 men and officers out of 255, were paroled and returned to the United States aboard the *Essex Junior*, after her guns had been removed. According to official British reports, the lopsided battle had also resulted in a disproportionate number of casualties. On board the *Phoebe*, which had received eighteen twelve-pound shots below her waterline, four men were killed and seven wounded. The *Cherub* reported one killed and three wounded. In all, some seven hundred eighteen-pound shots had been fired at the *Essex*. The American ship, crippled even before the battle had begun, had fired her twelve long-range guns seventy-five times. Both British warships were badly damaged in the encounter, and required extensive repairs before they returned to service. The *Essex*, or what remained of her, sank just outside the Valparaíso harbor.

In later years, Farragut, who never faltered in his enthusiastic support for Porter, would acknowledge errors his captain had made at Valparaíso.

"In the first place. I consider that our original and greatest error was in attempting to regain the anchorage; as, being greatly superior to the enemy in sailing qualities, I think we should have borne up and run before the wind. If we had come in contact with the *Phoebe*, we should have carried her by boarding."

And so, before his thirteenth birthday, Midshipman David Farragut had participated in the most eventful cruise of an American warship up to that time, had received his baptism under fire in one of the most famous naval engagements of the war, and was among those survivors who, on their return to New York Harbor, were welcomed as heroes.

In his report on the Battle of Valparaíso, Captain David Porter commended the conduct of his officers, and singled out several of them by name, including Farragut, for having "exerted themselves in the performance of their respective duties." He added that he regretted that Farragut was "too young for [the] promotion" he deserved.

Sailing on the *Essex* with Porter was the best education a young future sea captain could receive. Porter was a superb seaman and an outstanding captain, and throughout his long career Farragut never forgot the lessons he learned aboard that ship. Among them was how to use a well-trained crew to board a larger and more powerful enemy ship and bring her flag down in defeat. Porter constantly drilled his crew in the arts of boarding and hand-to-hand combat. Crewmen on the *Essex* exercised daily with muskets and "single-sticks," which were substitutes for broadswords and cutlasses, the actual weapons being too dangerous for practice drills.

Later in life, Farragut recalled this invaluable training, claiming "that I have never been on a ship where the crew of the old *Essex* was represented, but that I found them to be the best swordsmen on board. They had been so thoroughly trained as boarders, that every man was prepared for such an emergency, with his cutlass as sharp as a razor, a dirk made by the ship's armorer from a file, and a pistol."

When his parole expired, Farragut was assigned to another ship, but the war ended before he could see additional action. Shortly after the peace with Great Britain, President Madison declared war on Algeria, and Farragut was assigned to the flagship of Commodore Bainbridge, the ship of the line *Independence*. He served as aide to the ship's commander, Captain William M. Crane. No longer under the watchful eye of his mentor, Captain David Porter, who was appointed one of three naval commissioners in Washington, David Farragut was now on his own. Although Porter would continue to take an interest in his young protégé's career, Farragut's future was essentially in his own hands.

The years following the War of 1812 and the war against Algeria offered little in terms of advancement for naval officers. The navy had too many lieutenants and captains, and postings aboard warships were few and far between. But it was a time of education for a young midshipman destined to reach the heights in his naval career. One of the lessons he learned during this time, which Farragut considered of utmost importance, came while he was stationed aboard the ship of the line *Washington*, on which he sailed in the Mediterranean from 1816 to 1818. The ship's commander, Captain John Orde Creighton, was a noted martinet who was determined that his vessel be a "crack ship," something he accomplished by abusing the men and officers under his command. While the *Washington* was maintained in perfect order, with all brightwork glistening and the decks constantly scrubbed clean, it was an unhappy ship. Instead of infusing his men with the desire to work hard and be proud of the condition of their ship, driving a crew the way Creighton did, Farragut saw, only resulted in their slothfulness when out of sight of an officer.

"My experience," he later wrote about the use of discipline and abuse to produce a "crack ship," "instead of making me a proselyte to the doctrine of the old officers on this subject, determined me never to have a 'crack ship' if it was only to be attained by such means." Farragut could not help but compare the leadership styles of men such as Creighton with Porter, who never forgot the considerations of his crew, and therefore commanded a well-run vessel whose crew was totally devoted to their captain.

During this three-year cruise, Farragut spent time ashore in Tunisia, where he suffered sunstroke, the effects of which remained with him the rest of his life. Because it affected his vision, he was never able to read or write more than one page without stopping to rest his eyes and recover from the weakness the strain of reading produced.

Another important lesson Farragut learned during these years stemmed from an experience he endured in the summer of 1820, when he received orders to return to the United States to take the examination for promotion to lieutenant. Earlier he had been made acting lieutenant of the brig *Shark*, and was, in fact, at eighteen, that ship's commanding officer. Now he finally had the opportunity to achieve promotion to the rank permanently.

Upon arriving at Gibraltar, he found no American naval vessels sailing for the United States, and was forced to take passage on a merchantman, the *America*. Also on board were two invalided sailors who were returning home.

The voyage proceeded without incident until, just a few days' sail from the U.S. coast, a suspicious-looking brig appeared on the horizon. With the weather perfectly calm, neither ship could make much speed, but the brig soon broke out her oars and quickly approached the merchantman. Everyone on board was convinced the approaching vessel was a Caribbean pirate ship, and they feared what would happen to them once the pirates came aboard. Their fears were well founded, because the waters of the Caribbean and the nearby Atlantic were infested with ruthless pirates who had no regard for the lives of passengers and crews of captured vessels.

The *America*'s captain and crew were paralyzed with fear as the unknown vessel neared them. The brig then put a boat in the water, which headed straight for the *America*. Farragut realized the captain and crew had no intention of putting up any resistance to the approaching boat, even though everyone aboard the ship would be killed, and perhaps tortured first, if pirates boarded her. As the boat drew closer they begged Farragut to remove his uniform for fear their own fate would be even worse if the pirates found a naval officer on board. The eighteen-year-old midshipman not only refused to disguise his rank, but immediately took command of the ship. He called the crew and passengers together and asked if they would help defend the ship against boarders. Only the two young navy sailors stepped forward; the rest, according to Farragut, were "alarmed at the idea of resistance, although they had no hope of mercy by surrendering." Shamed by the bravery of the crippled sailors, several members of the crew joined Farragut, and together they prepared to use whatever items were available to attempt to sink the boat that almost immediately pulled alongside the merchantman.

"Do you come as friend?" Farragut shouted down to the boat.

"Yes," came the reply in good English.

Farragut then invited the officer who had responded aboard, but directed him to leave his arms in the boat. The man did as instructed.

It soon became obvious that these were not pirates, for the man identified himself as "Mr. Smith" of Baltimore, and his vessel as a Colombian brig-of-war. Smith offered to supply Farragut with anything his ship required. The midshipman thanked him, took several letters Smith wished mailed in the United States, and watched as the brig sailed away.

Impressed by the different reactions of man-of-war sailors and merchant sailors to impending danger, Farragut expressed the opinion that "men trained to arms will never fail, if properly led." Throughout the rest of his naval career, Farragut never forgot this lesson, that good training and leadership are essential ingredients in producing good fighting men. The *America*, with her captain once more in command, resumed her voyage to the United States.

After so many years of his young life spent at sea, Midshipman David Farragut arrived in Washington, D.C., on November 20, 1820, feeling like a "stranger in my native land, knowing no one but Commodore Porter and his family."

Ordered to New York for his lieutenancy examination, Farragut was confident of his abilities as a sailor, having been commander of a brig-of-war, but was less confident of his mathematics. It was his weakest subject, something that was quite understandable as he had gained little formal schooling other than that provided aboard naval warships. After all, he had gone to sea at the age of nine. What he had not considered was how much personal feelings might influence his passing or failing the examination.

A few days before the scheduled examination, Farragut evidently got into a heated quarrel with a Captain George Washington Rodgers over the charges of drunkenness that had been brought against Rodgers's friend and fellow captain, Christopher Raymond Perry. Farragut had known both as ships' commanders in the Mediterranean. Rodgers made a veiled accusation that Farragut had spread rumors concerning Perry's drinking problem, something the midshipman denied. Farragut refused to discuss the matter with Rodgers, telling him that if Perry had anything to say to him he should do so personally and not send intermediaries.

Unknown to Farragut, Rodgers, the man whom he had insulted, shared quarters with Captain Samuel Evans, an influential member of the Naval Board of Examiners. Rodgers had evidently told Evans of his encounter with Farragut. At his examination, Captain Evans openly demonstrated his dislike for the midshipman, and the two got into a quarrel. Needless to say, Farragut did not pass the examination. But when he took the examination again, the following year, he passed.

Between examinations, Farragut took up residence in Norfolk, awaiting assignment. There he made the acquaintance of Susan Caroline Merchant, with whom he quickly fell in love and whom he secretly harbored a desire to marry once he had achieved a respectable rank and pay level.

Passing the examination did not bring automatic promotion, nor did it automatically bring assignment to a warship. Farragut had to wait until May 1822 before he was assigned to a ship, the twenty-eight-gun frigate *John Adams*. Most of the following two years were spent in the Caribbean chasing pirates who regularly attacked American merchantmen.

Pirate attacks in the Caribbean had become so common, and the loss of cargoes and lives so great, that the country was in an uproar over the situation. In response, Commodore Porter stepped down from his post as navy commissioner, and formed what became known as the Mosquito Fleet to fight the pirates. Along with regular warships, the fleet included eight fast-sailing Chesapeake Bay boats, each mounting three guns and a crew of thirty-one men, and drawing less than seven feet of water. These were to be used to follow the pirates into the shallow streams and creeks in which they hid from pursuing American and British warships. The fleet also included five unusually large rowing barges, and a swift sidewheeler that had been a Jersey City ferryboat, but which now boasted three guns.

The islands of the West Indies contained thousands of waterways in which the shallow-draft pirate vessels found sanctuary from pursuing warships, but Commodore Porter planned to put a stop to that. Twice before, expeditions had been launched to halt the Caribbean pirate trade. The first, in 1819, had failed miserably, and had cost the life of the expedition's commander, Commodore Oliver Hazard Perry, who died of yellow fever. In 1822, Commodore James Biddle met with a bit more success, capturing or sinking over two dozen pirate vessels, but he remained frustrated by the ability of the pirates to slip from his grasp, disappearing into the shallow creeks and streams along the island coasts with which only they were familiar. Now it was Porter's turn.

Two events of great personal satisfaction occurred during the two years Farragut spent chasing pirates in the West Indies. The first was the assignment of his older brother, Lieutenant William Farragut, to the fleet. The two had not seen each other for thirteen years. The second was a visit he made to New Orleans to visit his sister, whom he had not seen for an even longer period. The visit was friendly but strained, since the two were virtually strangers. It was then he learned that his father had died several years earlier. As it happened, the vessel on which he took passage up the Mississippi River to the Crescent City also carried the first bricks used in the construction of Fort Jackson, which would play a critical role in his life nearly forty years later.

Returning to the Mosquito Fleet, Farragut, still waiting for his promotion to lieutenant, was given command of one of the bay boats, the *Ferret*. The Mosquito War, as it became known, was extremely successful in sinking pirate vessels and capturing hundreds of pirates. As a result, piracy all but vanished from the West Indies. Most of Farragut's time was now spent escorting merchant vessels throughout the area. With the decline of piracy, these cruises became less dangerous, although the greatest danger of all, yellow fever, never subsided.

Having driven most of the pirates off the seas, the Mosquito Fleet was soon reduced in size and scope. Toward the end of July 1824, the *Ferret*, Midshipman David Farragut commanding, was ordered to leave its base at Key West and sail to Washington for reassignment. As with most of the ships that had been fighting the war against the pirates, the *Ferret* had suffered from the effects of yellow fever. Although the reports are unconfirmed, it is believed that Farragut himself suffered two bouts of the deadly disease. A third and worst yellow fever attack struck him five days after leaving Key West, within sight of Washington. As a result he was hospitalized for several weeks in Washington.

At the end of August, with his doctor forbidding a return to the West Indies for the sake of his health, Farragut was released from the hospital. He immediately rushed off to Norfolk, to fulfill plans he had made during the years he had spent hunting pirates in the Caribbean: he asked Jordan Merchant for the hand of his third daughter, Susan Caroline. The wedding took place on September 2, 1824, at Trinity Church in Portsmouth, Virginia. Following the wedding, the couple traveled to Washington and spent several weeks at the home of Commodore Porter and his wife. The Porters were then residing on a 110-acre estate located about one mile north of the White House, in a beautiful mansion Porter had built, called Meridian Hill.

Unknown to the Porters or the Farraguts, that autumn would be the last happy time for the Porters. Later that year, after recovering from his own bout with yellow fever, Commodore Porter returned to resume command of the Mosquito Fleet. At the beginning of November 1824, he was informed that a Lieutenant Platt, commanding officer of the schooner *Beagle,* had been briefly imprisoned by the Spanish authorities at Fajardo, on the east coast of Puerto Rico, while attempting to locate pirated American goods believed to have been hidden in the town. It was evident that the town's mayor had conspired to keep Platt from finding the plunder.

Outraged over this insult to the United States Navy, and perhaps cognizant of what might happen if the incident went unpunished, Porter decided an apology from the mayor of Fajardo was in order. On November 14 he landed near the city's fort with two hundred armed men drawn from the crews of three naval vessels anchored in the harbor. He sent a message to the mayor requesting him to join him at the landing site and apologize for his actions, or face the consequences of his armed force invading the town. Faced with overwhelming might, the mayor offered no resistance. The same afternoon he visited Porter and expressed his regret over the incident both to the Commodore and to Lieutenant Platt.

Although Spain made no protest over the incident, the United States Navy did not take Porter's actions lightly. The commodore was brought up on charges of conduct unbecoming an officer. Although information concerning the origin of these charges is less than clear, it would appear that rival officers were behind them. Porter was found guilty, and sentenced to six months' suspension, even though the court-martial attributed his actions to "an anxious disposition on his part to maintain the honor and advance the interest of the nation and of the service."

An indignant Porter resigned from the navy. He then served for four years with the Mexican navy, returning to the United States in 1829. Offered his old post by President Andrew Jackson, Porter refused, explaining that he could not associate with the men who had punished him for defending the flag. Jackson understood and agreed with Porter's position. Anxious not to lose his service to the nation, the President appointed him to several diplomatic posts. Commodore Porter died in 1843, while serving as Minister to Turkey. He had been a brave sailor and the best tutor and mentor a young boy destined for a naval career could have had.

Following their honeymoon at Meridian Hill, David and Susan Farragut made Norfolk their home. It was the first home Farragut had known since joining the navy fourteen years earlier. Although little is known about their domestic life, there is no doubt that the Farraguts were forced to lead a frugal existence. As a midshipman, Farragut's pay was nineteen dollars per month and one meal per day. After passing the lieutenant's examination, his compensation had been increased to $20 per month and two meals per day. This was not much money for a young couple to live on, even in 1824. Added to this burden was Farragut's decision to contribute to the support of his two sisters, Nancy and Elizabeth, both of whom lived with foster families in Louisiana. His earlier visit to New Orleans had helped reestablish relations with what remained of his family. This was a voluntary obligation he took on without request from either sister.

Farragut remained a midshipman until the beginning of the following year, receiving his promotion to lieutenant on January 13, 1825. At twenty-three he was unusually old for a midshipman. The age difference between Farragut and most other midshipman had caused him some embarrassment, and occasionally some discomfort. Although he had been as old as some of the officers on board a ship, and might have had even longer time in the service, he had been forced, because of his rank, to continue to mess in steerage with the other midshipmen, many of whom were young boys. Farragut attributed at least part of the responsibility for the long delay in receiving a lieutenancy to the remarks Captain Porter had included in his report of the battle at Valparaíso. Porter had written that Farragut was

Rear Admiral David G. Farragut in an undated
photo. Courtesy of the National Archives.

too young to receive the promotion his actions during the battle deserved. "I never appeared," Farragut commented much later in his
life, "to get any older in the eyes of the government or my commander, and consequently had to contend inch by inch, as opportu-
nities presented, with men of riper age and apparently more entitled
to the places sought."

The promotion, late though it might have been, brought with it
something the struggling young couple badly needed, an increase in
pay. As a lieutenant on active duty, Farragut was entitled to forty dollars a month and three meals per day. Unfortunately he was in Norfolk awaiting assignment, and because that wasn't considered active
duty, he was actually only on half pay.

Financial relief finally arrived on August 9, 1825, in the form of orders instructing Lieutenant Farragut to join the company of the newly constructed forty-four-gun frigate *Brandywine*. Named for a famous Revolutionary War battle, the ship's first assignment was the transportation of a famous Revolutionary War hero, the Marquis de Lafayette. Lafayette was returning to France following a much heralded and successful visit to his adopted nation.

Upon returning to the United States in May 1826, Farragut found his wife had been suffering from neuralgia during his absence. He requested and received a leave from the navy so he could take her to New Haven, Connecticut, where he sought the help of a Yale College professor, Dr. Eli Ives, who specialized in treating this painful affliction of the nerves. There is no record indicating whether Dr. Ives was able to help Mrs. Farragut. The neuralgia would leave the young wife partially disabled for the remainder of her life.

During the four months the Farraguts lived in New Haven, David availed himself of the many lectures conducted by Yale professors. He found this especially enjoyable because the effects of the sunstroke he had suffered in Tunisia continued, as they would the remainder of his life, to prevent him from enjoying extended periods of reading. The future admiral recorded that a favorite lecturer was Professor Benjamin Silliman, who occupied the college's chair of chemistry and mineralogy.

In October 1826, the Farraguts returned to the Norfolk area, where he was assigned to duty aboard the receiving ship *Alert*. During this tour of duty, which kept him stationed in Norfolk, Farragut started a school to further the education of the many young boys who were serving in the navy, and who, "with very few exceptions, did not know their letters." Having suffered himself from the lack of basic schooling during his own formative years in the navy, he was determined that these boys, many of whom would go on to become naval officers, should learn to read and write. This school, which earned Farragut "one of the few, the very few, compliments I ever received from the Navy Department or its head," was the precursor of the shipboard schools that led to the establishment of the Naval Academy at Annapolis.

Farragut's assignment aboard the *Alert* at Norfolk afforded him the opportunity to remain close to Susan, and to care for her during her long periods of painful attacks of neuralgia.

But David Farragut was a lieutenant in the United States Navy, and sooner or later he was bound to return to the sea. Orders to do just that arrived on October 15, 1828, when Farragut was assigned to the brand-new eighteen-gun sloop *Vandalia,* which was being sent to duty off the South American coast. Construction of the ship had just been completed, and she was being fitted for her duty when Farragut arrived at the Philadelphia Navy Yard. The *Vandalia* sailed for the Brazil Station on December 18. The highlight of this cruise, which lasted one year, was the presence of the *Vandalia* in the harbor at Buenos Aires, Argentina, during May 1829. During that month the city, and with it the country, succumbed to the revolutionary forces of the famed Juan Manuel de Rosas. Leading an army built around his following of gauchos, the extremely popular Rosas brought down the dictatorship of General Lavalle. Rosas would rule Argentina until 1852.

Suffering from increasingly failing eyesight, Farragut was relieved of duty and ordered to return to the United States at the end of December 1829. The voyage home lasted fifty days. His journey was made aboard a merchantman since no warships were sailing for Norfolk at the time. When he arrived home in February 1830, Farragut was dismayed to find his wife bedridden by her neuralgia and another undiagnosed ailment, which might have been arthritis. Fortunately, Farragut was again stationed at Norfolk, where he was able to look after Susan's needs. With his wife's health steadily deteriorating, and his own eyesight in need of attention, Farragut requested and received a leave of absence in the summer of 1832 in order to seek help from doctors in Philadelphia. But there is no record that either of the Farraguts received much assistance with their medical problems in Philadelphia before they were forced to flee the city a few weeks later, when a cholera epidemic broke out.

In December of 1832 he returned to duty and was assigned as first lieutenant, the equivalent of the modern executive officer, aboard the sloop *Natchez,* which was identical to the *Vandalia.* The *Natchez* spent the first three months of 1833 anchored off Charleston, South Carolina, waiting to enforce federal actions that might be ordered against that state in the wake of an "Ordinance of Nullification" she had passed against federal tariff rates. Many people expected the state to go into open rebellion, but a settlement of the tariff issue was finally worked out, and the *Natchez* returned to Norfolk.

On May 8, 1833, the *Natchez*, with First Lieutenant David Farragut aboard, left Norfolk and sailed for the Brazil Station, returning Farragut to the locales of his earlier cruise. He remained on the *Natchez* until March 7, 1834, when he was given command of the ten-gun schooner *Boxer*, which arrived from her station in the East Indies. Her own officers and crew were relieved of duty and returned to the United States as passengers aboard another vessel, while their ship remained on the Brazil Station. Although it was Farragut's second command, the first having been the bay boat *Ferret*, serving in the Mosquito Fleet, it was his first command of an actual warship.

Unfortunately, his first true command was not destined to last long, for after refitting and three months' duty with the fleet, Farragut was ordered to take the *Boxer* to Norfolk, where she was to be decommissioned. Arriving home in late July, Farragut found his wife's condition had worsened. He often had to carry her from room to room because she was too weak to make these brief journeys. Now came a four-year wait for orders; although this meant half pay, it afforded him a prolonged period in which to care for Susan. His devotion to his ailing wife made an impression on friends and associates, and increased the esteem in which people who knew the young naval officer held him.

Four years waiting for orders may seem like a long time, but it was not unusual for the period. The navy's system of construction of new warships and repair of existing ships was riddled with contractor corruption. As a result, during the late 1830s, there were more American warships of the larger variety, ships of the line and frigates, laid up for repairs than on sea duty. That left an unusually large number of qualified and experienced officers without duty. Many of these men were forced to find temporary employment elsewhere, such as serving on merchant ships, because they only received half pay while they were waiting for orders.

To while away the many long hours of idleness, Farragut began making repairs to his home, some of which were badly needed following his long absences. He soon acquired a proficiency in carpentry rivaled only by professionals. During this time Susan's health appeared to stabilize, but did not improve in any meaningful way.

Orders for sea duty finally arrived on April 10, 1838. He was ordered to duty aboard the frigate *Constellation*. Farragut joined her shortly before she sailed for the Mexican coast as part of an American fleet sent to Tampico to look after U.S. interests there while Mexican and French forces engaged in what turned out to be a brief war. On August 8 he was given command of the eighteen-gun sloop *Erie*. The war situation grew worse when a revolution broke out among the Mexican forces, and the *Erie* was required to sail up and down the Mexican coast, removing American citizens and funds to safety.

During this time Farragut received a valuable lesson concerning the vulnerability of a powerful fort to naval bombardment when he watched a French fleet attack and nearly reduce to rubble the proud and ostensibly impregnable fortress near Veracruz, the Castle of San Juan de Ulloa. Inspecting the castle shortly after its Mexican defenders capitulated, he estimated that had they not surrendered, the place would have been totally destroyed in a few more hours. Viewing the damage, Farragut could see that virtually any structure could be leveled by ships standing offshore engaged in a steady bombardment that not only did material damage, but forced the fort's gun crews to abandon their guns and seek safety from the rain of shot and shell.

In January 1839, Farragut relinquished command of the *Erie* to Commander Joseph Smoot, and sailed for New Orleans, where he spent two weeks visiting his sister Nancy. Making his way home overland, he arrived in Norfolk to find that his wife's health had deteriorated further. He spent the remainder of that year and the next in or near Norfolk in order to provide Susan with as much comfort as possible. On December 27, 1840, Susan Farragut died following three days of violent spasms. In his grief over her passing, he wrote that she had led a life "of unequaled suffering, which she bore with a resignation and patience unparalleled for sixteen years, setting an example, to all sufferers, of calmness and fortitude under the severest afflictions."

Returning to duty the following February, he was assigned as executive officer on the seventy-four-gun ship of the line *Delaware*, which was then refitting for sea duty at Norfolk. On September 27, 1841, a few days before the *Delaware* sailed as lead ship of a squadron bound for the Brazil Station, David Farragut was promoted to commander. He was now forty-one years old, and had been a lieutenant for sixteen years. His new pay grade exceeded two hundred dollars per month while at sea.

On June 1 of the following year, Commander Farragut was given command of the sixteen-gun sloop-of-war *Decatur*, also on the Brazil Station. Her former commanding officer, Commander Henry Ogden, had fallen ill and was forced to return home for convalescence. The *Decatur* and her new commanding officer spent several months in and around Buenos Aires, during which Farragut was a regular guest of Governor Juan Manuel de Rosas, at both his official residence and his country home outside the city.

Farragut's command of the *Decatur* ended on February 18, 1843, when the ship, which had been at sea for a long time before he took command, returned to Norfolk for refitting. Her officers and men were relieved of active duty pending reassignment. The navy continued to suffer from a shortage of functioning ships because so many were laid up for repairs. The fact that many more senior commanders sought the limited number of available ships meant Farragut was going to remain in Norfolk waiting for assignment for an extended period. This gave him the opportunity to resume a social life. He soon met and fell in love with Virginia Dorcas Loyall, eldest daughter of a well-to-do and highly respected Norfolk citizen, William Loyall. Following a short courtship, they were married at Christ Church in Norfolk on December 26, 1843.

The following April, Farragut was back on active duty, this time as executive officer of the *Pennsylvania*. At 120 guns and 3,241 tons, she was the largest ship in the United States Navy, and one of the largest in the world. Because she was assigned as the receiving ship at Portsmouth Navy Yard, the newlyweds would not be separated by a long sea voyage.

On October 12, 1844, Virginia gave birth to a boy, whom the couple named Loyall Farragut. As the Farraguts were living on board the *Pennsylvania* at the time, Mrs. Farragut had gone to her father's home on East Main Street in Norfolk to prepare for the birth. It was there that Loyall was born. At forty-three years of age, Commander David Farragut had finally become a father. For the remaining years of his life he would be completely devoted to Loyall, who was a constant source of pride. As the time of his own death neared, Farragut entrusted his papers and records to Loyall, leaving him the duty of writing the admiral's first biography, a homage the faithful son executed with great commercial success.

At the request of the commanding officer of the Norfolk Navy Yard, Commodore Jesse Wilkinson, Farragut was transferred there in October 1845 to serve as his executive officer. To be requested by Wilkinson was an honor, for it showed great faith in Commander Farragut, who would be responsible for the day-to-day operations of the vast yard. During this duty at Norfolk, Farragut dictated to an assistant a book of memoirs of his life to that time. Badly handicapped by his sunstroke-damaged eyes, and able to write only a few pages at a time, he found the only way he could complete the book was through the use of dictation. The work was titled *Some Reminiscences of Early Life, by D. G. Farragut, A Captain, The United States Navy.*

In 1846, when war loomed with Mexico over the question of annexation of Texas by the United States, Farragut made several requests for sea duty in the Gulf of Mexico. He cited, as reasons for consideration, his knowledge of Spanish, in which, along with French, Italian, and Arabic, he was thoroughly conversant. He also emphasized his experience in Mexican waters during past cruises, especially his presence when the French took the Castle of San Juan de Ulloa, which had since been rebuilt and served as the primary defense of the important Mexican city of Veracruz. He hoped to participate in taking the castle with United States naval forces, using his knowledge of the area and the fortress and her batteries. For some unknown reason, perhaps because of the great number of similar applications being made by other officers, his requests either went unanswered, or he received only perfunctory acknowledgments, but no action.

Finally, in February 1847, he was given command of the sloop-of-war *Saratoga*, then stationed at Norfolk. Through great effort he was able to put together enough men to man the ship, although many were cooks and servants from other vessels. Racing as quickly as possible to the scene of action, he was greatly disappointed to arrive off Veracruz on April 26 to find the American flag flying over the castle. It had surrendered to U.S. Army forces under the command of General Winfield Scott, with the navy squadron of Commodore Matthew Perry playing only a subordinate and minor role.

Farragut's disappointment was twofold. Not only had he earlier, on his own initiative, submitted a detailed plan for the conquest of the castle by naval forces that Perry had ignored, but he had hoped to play an important part in that action. In addition, Farragut hoped that a spectacular and successful naval engagement, such as the taking of this famous fortress, would aid in correcting a shortcoming he believed hurt the navy, the absence of any admirals. Farragut had become part of a faction of younger officers and civilian friends of the navy who strongly advocated the creation of the rank of admiral. Many in Congress believed that the rank smacked of royalty, perhaps because so many European monarchs also held the rank of admiral in their own navies. As a result, the U.S. Navy was not permitted to commission any officer above the level of captain. Among the disadvantages of having no admiral was that when the navy engaged in a joint action with a foreign fleet, United States vessels had to subordinate themselves to foreign command, because the leadership of a combined force traditionally was given to the highest-ranking officer. Virtually every other country with a substantial navy had the rank of admiral. U.S. Navy officers referred to as commodores were actually captains who had received this purely ceremonial rank in recognition of their having commanded squadrons of ships, thus placing them in command of captains of individual vessels.

Farragut injudiciously voiced his disappointment over Perry's failure to take advantage of what he considered a great opportunity to win glory for the navy. When his words were repeated to Commodore Perry, the older man was angered, and bad blood soon existed between the two. As punishment, the *Saratoga* was placed on blockade duty for an extended period, and not permitted to take part in any of the engagements of the war. At one point, Perry attempted to rebuke his junior officer for what he termed neglect of duty for failing to stop and search a British steamer that had arrived with a Mexican Army general aboard. When Farragut rightly pointed out that the U.S. Army was in charge of the port, and had assumed all duties for halting and inspecting all incoming ships, Perry backed down. Regardless, word of the incident somehow reached the American press, where it was reported that Commander Farragut had been reprimanded by Perry for neglect of duty.

Frustrated over not being allowed to see action, Farragut requested to be relieved of command of his ship, but nothing came of it. Perry, it seems, was determined to keep him isolated from action. Even after yellow fever broke out aboard the *Saratoga* and Farragut himself was struck down by the disease, Perry forced the ship to remain on station weeks longer than any other vessel before allowing her to sail to Pensacola, Florida, where yellow fever victims received medical care.

Farragut's service on the *Saratoga* ended on February 19, 1848, when he turned control of the ship over to the Brooklyn Navy Yard. The cruise into Mexican waters had been, in his own words, "the most mortifying" service of his career.

During the next few years, Farragut served in various shore posts. Following a short return as executive officer of the Norfolk Navy Yard, the Farraguts, including Loyall, who was now three years old, were moved to Washington, D.C., where Farragut participated with several other officers in preparing a book of naval ordnance regulations. While in Washington he spent his free evenings attending lectures at the Smithsonian Institution, just as he had done so many years earlier in New Haven.

In April 1852, Farragut returned to the Norfolk Yard, where his chief duty was to conduct weekly lectures on gunnery for officers stationed there. Then his own long interest in the improvement of naval guns, and his work on the ordnance manual, led to a special assignment of a year's duration. At the request of the navy's chief of the Bureau of Ordnance and Gunnery, Commodore H. W. Morris, Farragut was placed in charge of a program to conduct endurance tests on various types of guns. Working at nearby Fortress Monroe, he also examined methods for improving the endurance of the guns in use aboard naval ships. Among the officers assigned to assist Farragut were two lieutenants who would play important roles in Farragut's Civil War campaigns, Percival Drayton and Henry Bell.

Farragut returned to the Norfolk Navy Yard when the program ended in August 1854. Following several weeks of detailed discussions in Washington, he was sent to San Francisco, California (the state had joined the Union four years earlier), to establish a Navy Yard to service naval vessels assigned to the Pacific Ocean. The Farragut family traveled to California by first taking a steamer to Nicaragua, which they crossed by a combination of wagons and small lake craft, then boarding a steamer on the Pacific coast for the final leg of the journey. They left New York on August 19, and arrived at San Francisco on September 14. It was an arduous trip through a beautiful, wild country they would not soon forget.

The site chosen for the navy's first repair and supply facility on the Pacific coast was Mare Island, a half-mile-wide, three-mile-long island in San Pablo Bay, some thirty miles from San Francisco. In less than four years a great navy yard was constructed under the personal supervision of the yard's commandant, Captain David Farragut. Farragut had been promoted to captain on October 8, 1855, thirteen months after arriving at Mare Island. On August 20, 1858, after four productive years, he left the Mare Island Navy Yard and returned east. The yard was a monument to his abilities as a commander and his talents for getting important tasks done, and was one of the high points of his career to date.

Through his performance in overseeing the construction of a navy yard equal to, or better than, the best yards the navy had on the East Coast, Farragut left an indelible impression on an extremely important and influential man in the naval service, Commodore Joseph Smith, chief of the Bureau of Yards and Docks. In just a few years, Smith would be instrumental in obtaining for Farragut the command that offered him the opportunity to demonstrate his abilities as a wartime fleet commander.

The Farraguts—David, Virginia, and Loyall, who was now a strapping fourteen-year-old—returned to Norfolk early in December 1858. Before their arrival, Captain Farragut had received orders from the secretary of the navy to take command of a newly constructed steam-powered sloop-of-war, the twenty-four-gun *Brooklyn*. The *Brooklyn* was a new type of ship, and one of the fastest in the navy. The introduction of steam engines had begun transforming the look of naval vessels, but because the engines remained less than completely reliable, ships of war like the *Brooklyn* were built with both a steam-driven screw and a full rigging of sails.

For the next two years, Farragut commanded the *Brooklyn*, spending a majority of that period in the Gulf of Mexico. On board a great deal of that time was Robert M. McLane, U.S. Minister to Mexico. At the time, Mexico was in the throes of a revolution. Supporters of Benito Juárez, who was the elected president, were fighting General Miguel Miramón, who had seized control of the government in Mexico City by military force. Since the United States recognized Juárez as the legal president, it was to him at his Veracruz headquarters that McLane presented his credentials when he arrived on the *Brooklyn*.

Farragut played an essential role in transporting McLane to various coastal cities to visit U.S. representatives, and in conveying Juárez himself so that the president could muster support among his countrymen.

On October 20, 1860, Captain David Farragut turned over command of the *Brooklyn* to Captain W. S. Walker. It was the last time that he would have command of an individual ship. Farragut returned to Norfolk following a brief visit to Loyall, who was attending a school in Poughkeepsie, New York.

While he had been away serving his country along the Mexican coast, the United States had been gradually splitting into opposing camps over the issues of slavery and states' rights. The election that year of Abraham Lincoln of Illinois had been the last straw for many southerners, and on December 20 the state of South Carolina voted to withdraw from the Union. Secession fever spread throughout the South, and Farragut soon found himself the object of interest to those forces determined to create a new nation out of the former Southern states. They recognized that this new nation would require its own navy, and who better to head it than a naval captain who was not only a southerner, but had nearly fifty years of experience?

2

"The Best Command in the Navy"

DAVID FARRAGUT WAS A SOUTHERNER BY BIRTH. Although he had not resided in his birth state since his childhood, the United States Navy Register continued to list him as a citizen of Tennessee. Norfolk, Virginia, was the only place that had served him as a hometown since he first joined the naval service a half century earlier. He had married two daughters of the Commonwealth of Virginia, and most of his friends and acquaintances, both on land and in the navy, were southerners. His own sisters lived near the great southern port of New Orleans, and his father was buried in southern soil. So, it was not without some justification that many of those who knew him, personally or by reputation, especially southerners, expected him to join the cause of the emerging Confederate States of America.

What they didn't realize was that for nearly fifty of his fifty-nine years, Farragut had served aboard ships that proudly flew the American flag. He had stood at attention when that flag had been saluted by ships of other great nations, and watched tearfully as she was taken down before the guns of a mighty enemy warship off Valparaíso. He had also watched with horror the devastation and misery caused by civil war in places like Argentina and Mexico, and knew that secession would lead the nation down the road to just such a war. When it came time for Farragut to take a stand, he did not feel the emotional and sentimental attachment to Virginia and the South that forced other men to renounce their oaths of allegiance to the Union. Many were sorely disappointed in him. Many men, including some who had been close to him, would never forgive him for that disappointment, even long after the war ended.

Norfolk was predominantly a navy town. Naval officers were almost always present at social functions, some on active duty in the nearby yards, others from ships visiting the yards, and still others, like Captain Farragut at the time, waiting for orders. A majority of them were southerners by birth, or by family connection through marriage to Southern women. As the news came that more states were debating secession, or had actually seceded, a number of these men began the practice of gathering at a Norfolk general store. They came to hear the latest news, and to discuss and debate its implications for themselves, their states, and their country.

The sentiment among most of these men was in favor of the South. Farragut was one of the few who held out hope that somehow the Union would be preserved. He told his fellow naval officers that he feared that secession would result in a bloody civil war, but for the most part they laughed at his dire prediction, and called him a "croaker."

Matters grew worse when a Virginia state convention gathered to discuss the issue of secession. Its members, mostly pro-Union men, were compelled by a mob to vote for a resolution supporting the right of a state to secede, and to lay down guidelines under which Virginia would be justified in seceding herself. The most important guideline stated that Virginia would be within her rights in seceding from the Union if the Federal government adopted military measures to recapture forts that had been occupied by militia forces of the seceding states. The implication was clear: If the government in Washington attempted to use the national army to take back possession of those forts, Virginia would secede. Of course, if the national government did nothing about the loss of those forts, it was obvious to anyone with a level head that more would be taken, along with navy yards and other Federal facilities located within those states.

Farragut revealed his inner conflict when he told several officers, "God forbid I should have to raise my hand against the South." But he also would not turn his back on the nation to which he had sworn allegiance, and which he had faithfully served for so many years.

Loyall Farragut later described his father's position at this time as having been that if the country were amicably divided, and such division was accomplished at the will of the people, both North and South, he would remain in Virginia among his friends and relatives. But, Loyall wrote, "he felt he owed his first allegiance to the United States government."

The confused situation in Virginia was demonstrated during the first week of April 1861, when the state convention soundly rejected a proposal to secede. Farragut was heartened by what he felt was a vote that accurately reflected the will of the people of Virginia. Then matters turned decidedly worse. On April 12, forces of the state of South Carolina attacked the small garrison of Federal troops stationed at Fort Sumter in Charleston harbor, after the commanding officer, Major Robert Anderson, refused a demand to surrender and evacuate the fort. Two days later the fort fell.

On the fifteenth, President Lincoln issued a proclamation calling for the formation of an army of 75,000 men, drawn mostly from state militias. The army's objective was to retake Fort Sumter and the other Federal facilities "seized from the Union" by rebel forces, and "to cause the laws to be duly executed."

The gauntlet had been thrown down by one side, and accepted by the other. The war of words was coming to an end, to be replaced by a war of shot and shell. Two days later the Virginia state convention approved, by a vote of eighty-eight to fifty-five, an ordinance of secession, and the streets of Richmond and Norfolk were crowded with soldiers of the state militia who had already begun parading in anticipation of the vote. There wasn't an American flag to be seen. As word of the vote spread, volleys of muskets were fired in the air in celebration.

The following day, Farragut arrived as usual at the store where he and his friends and fellow officers met. On his arrival he quickly understood that he was no longer welcome in their company. Most had already submitted their resignations to the Navy Department, although a few might have done so with some regret. It was made clear to him that if his loyalty remained with the Federal government, he would no longer be welcome in Norfolk. He told the group that he believed President Lincoln's actions were justified, and that "I can live somewhere else." He also told the assembled former navy officers, "You fellows will catch the devil before you get through with this business."

Virginia Farragut in 1869. Courtesy of the Hastings (N.Y.) Historical Society.

As he rushed back to his home on Duke Street, Farragut could sense the growing level of violence in the city. Undisciplined militiamen roamed the streets firing their weapons and playing at searching out traitors. He knew it might be only a matter of hours before the great navy yard, stripped of its defenses by the resignation of so many officers, would be the target of the rebellious forces. He was determined to leave the city before the yard was attacked, to prevent from being called on to fire guns at the citizens of Norfolk.

Upon arriving home, he related to his wife what had occurred, and told her the time for the decision they had already discussed had come. He explained that his decision to "stick with the flag" would in all likelihood mean a prolonged separation from her family, one that could last for years. Whether she left with him or stayed to be with her family was her decision to make. Without hesitation she chose to leave and accompany her husband to whatever fate awaited him.

That evening, amid rumors that Farragut would soon be arrested, and following tearful farewells to members of the Loyall family, David, Virginia, and Loyall Farragut quietly slipped away from the little frame house that had been their home. Traveling with them was one of Virginia's sisters, Mrs. R. P. Ashe, and her two young children. Mrs. Ashe was going as far as New York City, where she had booked passage on a ship that would return her to San Francisco and her husband. Mrs. Ashe and her children had been visiting the Loyall family.

They boarded a steamer headed for Baltimore, and not a moment too soon, for the Virginia state forces were already moving batteries to vital points along the shore to give them control over the harbor. On April 20, with state militiamen forcing their way into the Norfolk Navy Yard, the aged Captain Charles Stewart McCauley, commander of the yard, made a failed attempt to destroy the installation and the warships in it by putting the place to the torch. The loss of the multimillion-dollar facility to the rebels raised a public outcry against the sixty-eight-year-old McCauley, effectively ending his career.

Arriving at Baltimore on the afternoon of April 19, the Farragut party found the city in chaos. Earlier that day, Southern sympathizers had attacked Pennsylvania and Massachusetts militia units making their way to a railroad station to board a train to Washington, where they were to help defend the city against a rumored attack by rebel forces. Four militiamen and twelve civilians were killed in the melee. Finally, city police stepped in and held back the crowd to allow the soldiers to board their train.

Farragut's original plan had been to take the railroad from Baltimore to Philadelphia, and then continue by coach to New York City, but arsonists had destroyed the railroad bridge over the Susquehanna River, severing the connection to Philadelphia. The captain was lucky enough to be able to find passage north on a canal boat. With more than three hundred people crowded on the boat, many of them refugees like the Farraguts, it was not a pleasant voyage. From Philadelphia the little party continued on as planned to New York.

"Admiral Farragut's Home, Hastings-on-Hudson." Courtesy of the Hastings (N.Y.) Historical Society.

Having seen Mrs. Ashe and her children off aboard the San Francisco steamer, the Farraguts spent a few days in the city, which was preoccupied with war preparations. From there they moved north to Westchester County, New York, and settled into a rented six-room cottage in the picturesque little riverside village of Hastings-on-Hudson. The village would remain his home throughout the war.

Now, a few months short of his sixtieth birthday, Captain David Farragut waited patiently for his government to call on his services. At five foot six and one-half inches and weighing about 150 pounds, Farragut retained the athletic figure of his youth. But his age was showing in other respects. Years of exposure to the elements had turned his face leathery, and his previously black hair was quickly turning gray. A bald spot was increasingly consuming the crown of his head despite efforts to hide it by combing hair over it. His poor eyesight had contributed to making him nearsighted, yet he refused to wear eyeglasses.

Although many predicted a short, victorious war, Farragut agreed with General Winfield Scott's assessment that it would be a long, bloody conflict. He was convinced that the navy would need him, even if there was nothing for him to do at the moment. This in large part resulted from a shortage of warships: rebel forces had seized dozens of Federal warships tied to wharves or anchored in the harbors of Southern ports. On May 1, 1861, Farragut wrote to Secretary of the Navy Gideon Welles, informing him of his change of residence and explaining that his sudden departure from Norfolk had resulted from the fact that the position of a United States officer was "rendered uncomfortable" in that city by the secession of Virginia.

Time passed slowly for Farragut as he waited for orders. In mid-July he traveled to Washington and met with the assistant to the chief of the Bureau of Detail in the Navy Department, Captain Charles Henry Davis. Although there is no record of the subject of their conversation, it is likely that Farragut requested command of a fast ship in order to carry out a plan he had for capturing the *Sumter*, a notorious Confederate commerce raider that was causing great loss among ships bound for Northern ports. The *Sumter* was commanded by Captain Raphael Semmes, who would gain lasting fame as the captain of another rebel commerce raider, the *Alabama*. However, no assignment came directly from this meeting.

Farragut was in an unusual position. He was a Southern-born officer, married to a Southern woman, who had declared for the Union. The government bureaucracy, including that in the Navy Department, were unsure and generally distrustful of all southerners. There was a strong current of feeling against giving command of a Union warship to a southerner, no matter how loyal he claimed to be. But in time the government and country would turn to this quiet, rather unassuming man whose naval career, while not spectacular in the sense of great accomplishments, had demonstrated that he was a naval officer of uncommon courage, and a man who could be relied on to carry out virtually any task entrusted to him.

When the Civil War erupted, General Winfield Scott, hero of both the War of 1812 and the Mexican War, was the general-in-chief of the United States Army, a post he had held since 1841. Born in 1786, and inevitably described by contemporaries as "a year older than the federal constitution," Scott was far too advanced in age, and in poor health, to continue in his position during an active war. He recognized this himself more than did anyone else, and retired from active service in November 1861, giving Lincoln enough time to select a replacement.

While others were proclaiming that Jefferson Davis, President of the Confederacy, would be strung up from a lamppost before July, 4, 1861, and the Northern press was proclaiming "On to Richmond!" it was Scott who recognized that the war would last for at least several years, and submitted a plan for its successful execution. He proposed that the Confederacy be isolated from all outside contacts and supplies, and virtually starved into submission. A great strategist who husbanded his own resources and relied on maneuvering rather than on the grand stroke, Scott urged a naval blockade of the entire Confederate coast along the Atlantic and the Gulf of Mexico. He recommended that General George McClellan, who would replace him later in the year, use between 60,000 and 80,000 soldiers stationed along the Mississippi River from Cairo, Illinois, to the Gulf coast to close that river to enemy use. They would be supported by gunboats patrolling the river. When word of his plan leaked out, Scott's critics in the press jeered. Instead, they urged quick action against the Confederacy, something the Union was not then capable of performing. They called Scott's proposal the Anaconda Plan, after the snake that wraps itself around its victim and gradually smothers it.

Although Scott's plan was never formally adopted, its basic concept eventually evolved as the strategy with which the Union successfully fought the war, with the addition of invasion forces to speed up the Confederacy's collapse. The first step in this evolution began when President Lincoln proclaimed a blockade of the South's Atlantic and Gulf coasts.

The unenviable task of sealing the enemy's ports fell to Lincoln's secretary of the navy, Gideon Welles. The fifty-eight-year-old, short, stocky Welles wore a huge white beard that made him look like a biblical prophet. He had been active in Connecticut politics for many years, earning a reputation first as an outspoken editorialist for the *Hartford Times and Weekly Advertiser*, then as an ardent supporter of the Jacksonian Democrats. He had served five years as the Hartford postmaster, a highly political post awarded for his support of John Niles, the *Hartford Times* publisher, who won a senatorial seat in 1835. During the presidency of James Polk he served as chief of the Bureau of Provisions and Clothing in the Navy Department. Welles had broken with the Democratic Party, to which he had been closely allied for so many years, and joined the new Republican Party over the issue of slavery. A supporter of states' rights, he abhorred the Southern attempt to expand slavery using that doctrine as a catalyst. Although he had no real naval experience to bring to the wartime post of secretary of the navy, Lincoln selected Welles in part because he perceived him as an honest man.

The navy Welles had inherited from his decidedly pro-South predecessor, Isaac Toucey of Connecticut, was in chaos. With war quickly approaching, Toucey had permitted over half of the navy's warships to remain on foreign stations, instead of bringing them home to bolster forces stationed at naval facilities in Southern states. Had this been done, it is likely that both the Norfolk and Pensacola navy yards, and the large quantity of resources stored in them, would not have fallen into rebel hands. In addition, some twenty-five percent of naval officers had resigned and "gone south," as it was described. A large number of Southern-born officers remained in the navy, but many Northern government officials distrusted their loyalty, even when, as in the case of Captain Farragut, they had abandoned homes and most of their possessions because of their loyalty.

Welles was faced with the need to rebuild the navy, or what was left of it, in order to carry out the President's order to block Southern ports to all traffic. He soon found himself locked in a power struggle with Secretary of State Henry Seward, who sought to control the Navy Department. Seward, a close friend of Lincoln's, thought nothing of bypassing Welles and going directly to the President to discuss naval issues.

Surrounded by men he did not trust, and faced with the rivalry of the powerful Seward, Welles turned to the only man he did trust, Gustavus Fox, a businessman from Massachusetts with extensive naval experience. Fox had been appointed a midshipman in 1838, and had served in various stations, including the Mexican War, before resigning as a lieutenant to enter the woolen manufacturing business. Highly regarded by those who knew him, with numerous powerful people among his friends, Fox had been called on by General Scott in February 1861, when he needed suggestions concerning the reinforcing

Gustavus Fox, Undersecretary of the Navy. Courtesy of
Anne S. K. Brown Military Collection, Brown University
Library.

of Fort Sumter before the rebellious South Carolina moved against
the island fort. Fox had quickly produced a plan for sending troops
and supplies to bolster the fort's small garrison, but it had been rejected by President Buchanan. However, the new Lincoln adminis-
tration sent Fox to Fort Sumter to meet with its commanding officer,
Major Robert Anderson, and to determine what was needed to defend the fort. When Fox returned to Washington, his original plan was
revived, and relief ships were sent south. Unfortunately, South Carolina forces compelled Fort Sumter's surrender before the relief force
arrived.

Welles nominated Fox to the new post of assistant secretary of the
navy, as soon as Congress approved its creation. Together, Welles and
Fox set about the job of building the navy to fight the war. Vessels of
all sizes and types were purchased or chartered and rapidly converted
to warships. When this system proved incapable of producing the
number required, a huge shipbuilding program was begun. Among

the new vessels built was a shallow-draft, steam-driven gunboat of Russian design that was ideally suited for close work in coastal waters and rivers.

Welles formed an advisory board to recommend the best way to use the navy's available resources to conduct the most effective blockade. The board's report on the Gulf Coast concentrated on two key areas: Mobile, Alabama, and New Orleans, Louisiana. With five paragraphs devoted to Mobile, and eleven pages to New Orleans, it was obvious that the board saw the latter as the most critical location on the Gulf. The report recommended that the capture of New Orleans be undertaken, but not until enough ships with sufficient armament could be assembled to contend with the two forts that dominated the Mississippi River south of the city.

Meanwhile, Captain David Farragut passed the time in Hastings-on-Hudson waiting. Impatient with inactivity, Farragut spent long hours wandering over the beautiful hills around the village, many with extraordinary views of the Hudson River. His strolls soon raised questions in the minds of local citizens. Some asked if he might be a Confederate spy sent to observe naval preparations along the river. Or perhaps he was a saboteur determined to destroy the aqueduct running from the Croton Reservoir to New York City, through which the city received most of its water supply. After all, they said, it passed just a few yards behind his rented cottage. People who had made little or no sacrifice in the Union cause carefully watched the comings and goings of a man who had lost nearly all his worldly possessions and many of his dearest friends in support of the Union.

The months dragged on for Farragut, but there was so little naval action during that period that he probably didn't feel he was missing much, although he awaited the mail each day in hope of receiving orders. When orders finally did arrive, in mid-September 1861, they were disappointing. He was instructed to proceed to the Brooklyn Navy Yard to participate in a retirement review board that was to pass judgment on every naval officer on the active list. It wasn't the kind of duty he wanted, and what made matters worse was that the board was under the direction of Commodore Hiram Paulding, for whom Farragut had little respect.

Meanwhile, a series of events in the Gulf of Mexico had both embarrassed the United States Navy and emphasized the importance of capturing New Orleans. In June the commerce raider *Sumter* had broken through the blockade and escaped Union pursuers to begin a noted and costly—for the Union—career on the open seas. She had been a bark-rigged steamer named *Habana* that happened to be at New Orleans when the war began. The Confederate navy bought her, fitted her out as a warship, and under command of Captain Raphael Semmes, she dashed past the blockading fleet at the mouth of the Mississippi River. On October 12 the iron-plated ram *Manassas* slipped out of New Orleans and attacked the Union steam sloop *Richmond*, causing so much confusion that four blockading vessels fled the scene. Two Federal ships, the *Richmond* and the *Vincennes*, managed to get stuck on a sand bar for several hours. Coming under enemy fire, the *Vincennes*'s commander hastily dumped his guns over the side in an effort to lighten the ship and release her from the bar.

The Northern press berated the ships' commanders, the navy in general, and Secretary Welles in particular following public disclosure of each episode.

It was painfully obvious to Welles and Fox that attempting to blockade the mouth of the Mississippi was not realistically possible. Besides, in addition to being the Confederacy's major commercial port, New Orleans was quickly becoming its center for naval construction, especially of the kinds of vessels that could guarantee the South continued control of the river. The only solution was to capture and occupy New Orleans and deny its assets to the government in Richmond. The question remained: How was it to be done, and who could do it? The conventional wisdom among Union military minds was to launch a combined army and navy assault down the river from Cairo, Illinois, which many believed could be more easily accomplished than to try to sail warships up the enemy-infested river one hundred miles from the Gulf to the city. A major obstacle to the southern route lay in the two powerful forts south of the city that dominated a tight turn in the river and effectively blocked the waterway to enemy vessels. In 1815, a British fleet had spent nine days, and expended over a thousand shells, in attempting to pass Fort St. Philip on its way to New Orleans. Since then, the second and more powerful Fort Jackson had been built across the river and a little south of Fort St. Philip. With the guns of these powerful forts focused on the same stretch of the river, most government officials and mili-

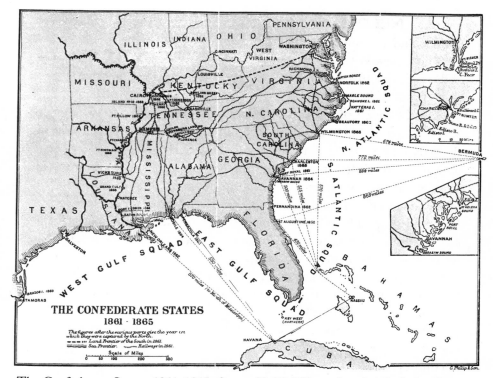

The Confederate States, 1861–1865. *Source:* H. W. Wilson, *Ironclads in Action* (Boston: Little, Brown, 1898). Used with permission.

tary leaders on both sides of the war considered that portion of the river impassable by invading ships.

Before the war, Fox had commanded merchant ships calling at New Orleans. He felt he knew the river well enough to recommend that the city be assaulted by a fleet moving upstream from the coast. The fleet would include transports carrying army troops to occupy the city once it fell to the navy. Fox's familiarity, though, did not take into account that the Confederate army had reinforced both Fort Jackson and Fort St. Philip. He was blinded by the great success experienced by the navy when a squadron commanded by Commodore Samuel Francis du Pont had outgunned the Confederate forts protecting the entrance to the harbor at Port Royal Sound, South Carolina, and captured them on November 7. In August, Commodore Silas H. Stringham had accomplished a similar feat, reducing the two forts at

Hatteras Inlet. These two victories proved that the old adage that ships could not successfully fight a fort was out of date. The introduction of the steam engine and its contribution to the maneuverability of warships had forever changed the equation in such a confrontation.

Fox believed that if the two forts at Hatteras and the two at Port Royal could be silenced by naval gunfire, then so could the two on the Mississippi River. But there were several factors he either chose to ignore, or failed to consider in his enthusiasm. One was the strength of the two river forts. No one in the Union camp had solid intelligence concerning the current status of either Fort Jackson or Fort St. Philip. The other was that the Union fleet would be virtually trapped in a river some seven hundred yards wide, reducing its ability to maneuver. Running past these two forts would be made more difficult by a series of barriers the rebels had erected across the river to prevent ships from rushing past. Adding to the difficulty was the fact that ships traveling up the river had to reduce speed as they approached the forts in order to negotiate the sharp bend in the river just above them. The conditions a fleet attacking these forts would encounter would be very different from those confronted by the fleets attacking the forts along the coast.

The victories at Port Royal and Hatteras persuaded Welles, with some prompting from Fox, to set aside the idea of attacking New Orleans from the north. It was, in any event, an army scheme with little real chance of success, since the invading force would have to travel hundreds of miles of enemy-controlled river. Instead, they would focus on capturing the city through the use of naval forces steaming upriver from the Gulf. To reinforce their conviction, they met with Lieutenant David Dixon Porter, who had just returned from duty with the Gulf Blockading Squadron. His ship, the steam frigate *Powhatan*, had been stationed near the mouth of the Mississippi. The two questioned Porter, who was the son of the famous commodore and stepbrother to Farragut, about the Mississippi Delta and the approaches to New Orleans. He proved to be an extremely observant man with a storehouse of critical information. When told of the plan to attack New Orleans from the south, Porter wholeheartedly endorsed the idea, adding only that he believed a bombardment of the forts by mortar boats was essential to their reduction.

The mortar boats Porter was recommending were different from other naval vessels. They were usually old sailing schooners that had been extensively converted for their new use, and were usually towed into position for action by either steamers or sailors in rowing boats. Each carried only a single gun, a thirteen-inch stubby cannon that resembled a seated frog with its mouth open. These fired an unusually heavy projectile, weighing some 285 pounds, that was usually equipped with a timed explosive device set to go off when it landed on its target. Though these mortars had only a short range, the size and weight of the shell and its explosive capacity had a devastating effect on a fort. Porter pledged that both forts would be rendered useless, if not completely destroyed, in forty-eight hours of bombardment by these guns.

Filled with enthusiasm, Welles and Fox went to Lincoln, who was quickly won over to the project. Next, General McClellan was advised of the proposal. At first he was critical of the idea, expecting that Welles and Fox would require fifty thousand army troops for the job, men he couldn't spare. When they explained it was to be a purely naval operation, and that it would require only about ten thousand soldiers to occupy the city and garrison its forts after they fell to the navy, McClellan agreed to provide the troops the navy needed.

A great deal rode on the success or failure of an attack on New Orleans: the navy could strike a blow that would have a crippling effect on the Confederacy, taking from it the South's largest city and most important port. Success would go a long way in erasing from the public's mind the earlier failures of the Gulf Blockading Squadron, when the *Manassas* had attacked and scattered Federal warships, and the *Sumter*'s escape into the open seas from New Orleans. Failure, on the other hand, might mean the total destruction of a large fleet of costly warships under the powerful guns of the river forts.

Naval planners expected that New Orleans itself would offer less resistance than would the forts. Because almost everyone, North and South, thought that when the time came for Union forces to attack New Orleans, the attack would originate from the north, most of the city's recently constructed defenses faced in that direction. The only important exception were the two forts. Because of this, naval planners expected the two forts to be the main obstacles to capturing the city from the south. While the Confederate navy and army were facing upriver watching for an invading fleet, the Federal fleet would attack through the back door, the mouth of the Mississippi River. The Union strategists believed the capture of New Orleans depended on first reducing the two forts. Farragut's daring and single-minded purposefulness would prove them wrong.

After months of anxious waiting, Farragut's time had come. The final and perhaps most important question remaining was the selection of the man who would command the fleet sent to take New Orleans. When the deed had been done, just about everyone involved claimed he had been the one to put forth David Farragut's name for this most important duty. The actual selection process was probably less grandiose, but did include recommendations from those who knew Farragut, or were familiar with his record. Secretary Welles reviewed a list of potential candidates. The obvious choices were Commodores du Pont, Wilkes, and Goldsborough, but all three were already on important duty and should not be moved. Then came a list of captains, some of whom were not on active duty at the moment, but were awaiting orders. One of the latter was Captain David Glasgow Farragut.

Most of the men on that list had fine if not distinguished careers. Farragut tended to stand out as an officer who was greatly admired by others. Commodore Joseph Smith, chief of the Bureau of Yards and Docks, strongly supported the selection of Farragut, describing him as bold and impetuous, "with a great deal of courage and energy." But could he lead a squadron into war? Smith responded that the answer would be "determined only by trial." Smith had been favorably impressed by Farragut's performance in building the Mare Island Navy Yard from nothing more than a barren piece of land in just four years. Fox claimed he was impressed by the speed with which Farragut had left Virginia when the state seceded, because it showed a man of unquestioned superiority and loyalty. Porter, whose rank prevented him from seeking the assignment for himself, something the overly ambitious officer would surely have done if he could, also supported the selection of his stepbrother, whom he knew to be a sound and reliable officer.

It was Secretary Welles, of course, who would make the final decision on who would command the fleet. He thought Farragut a fine, imaginative officer. During his earlier service in the Navy Department he had had the opportunity to hear Farragut describe how American naval forces could capture the fortress castle at Veracruz during the Mexican War. But Welles was looking for a man who already had a reputation as a great naval leader, and there was nothing really distinguishing about his career, except perhaps the longevity of it. Farragut's greatest accomplishment appeared to be the construction of the Mare Island facility, certainly not the type of assignment that would recommend a man for such an important wartime assignment as the taking of New Orleans. Welles was looking for a man with a reputation to match the great British commander Horatio Nelson. The problem he faced in reaching this goal was that the United States Navy had not been engaged in a great naval battle of the type from which a Nelson would emerge since the War of 1812, a half a century earlier.

Perhaps in the end it was not so much the selection of Farragut that won him the post, but the elimination of another man from the list of candidates before Welles. Lieutenant John A. Dahlgren, the inventor of the famous cannon called the Dahlgren gun, was, by a special act of Congress, commander of the Washington Navy Yard. This post would not normally be given to a mere lieutenant, but this particular lieutenant was different. He was President Lincoln's favorite naval officer. The President had been pressing Secretary Welles to find a vacant captaincy into which he could promote Dahlgren. Welles personally disliked Dahlgren, and saw the ambitious naval officer as a potential rival with direct links to the President as strong as, and perhaps stronger than, his own. He would certainly not want to give such an important assignment to a man who was sure to use the mission's success—if it was successful—to further his own career and influence.

So, in the end, and by whatever process, Captain David Farragut was the sole candidate to command a naval squadron on the most daring and important assignment yet conceived by the Navy Department during the Civil War. But would Farragut, a southerner, accept an assignment that was sure to cost many Southern lives? After all, members of his own family lived in or near New Orleans. It was an important question that had to be answered before he was offered the command. Other Southern officers who had remained with the Union had expressed their desire for posts that would not require them to engage in actual combat against their brethren. Would Farragut be one of them?

David Porter was given command of the mortar vessels he had so energetically maintained were needed for the successful reduction of the river forts. And as he was soon traveling to New York on business connected to the purchase of ships for conversion to that use, Welles instructed him to meet informally with his stepbrother to sound him out. The two met in Brooklyn's Pierpont House for what Farragut thought was a congenial reunion.

After a brief conversation covering personal matters, Porter went far beyond his instructions, as was his habit, and told Farragut he had been empowered to offer him "the best command in the Navy." He asked Farragut if he would accept a command that would send him deep into enemy territory. Farragut hesitated, then expressed a desire not to be sent to Norfolk to fight against his own in-laws and close friends. Porter told him he was not the man the Navy Department was looking for, if he was reluctant to carry out whatever duty was assigned him. He then proceeded beyond all bounds, telling Farragut that Norfolk was the target of the campaign for which he was being considered. Tortured by the conflict between fighting his own relations and keeping his oath to his country, Farragut agonized over his response to Porter's question. Finally he said he would accept such a command and conduct it with no hesitancy. Porter then revealed that the actual target was New Orleans. Farragut must have been greatly relieved that he was not being offered a command that would send him against the city that had been his home, and in which his own house was located. When they parted, Porter told Farragut he would hear from the Navy shortly.

The following day, Farragut received instructions to come to Washington for a conference. Upon arriving early in the morning on Saturday, December 21, he was met at the train station and taken to the home of Postmaster General Montgomery Blair, Navy Undersecretary Fox's brother-in-law. Blair had been taken into the navy's confidence concerning the proposed New Orleans expedition. Following breakfast, Fox outlined the project and asked Farragut if he thought the plan could succeed, to which the captain answered in the affirmative. Did he think he could accomplish the task of reducing the forts and taking New Orleans? Once again the reply was affirmative.

Fox told him he was to be given command of the squadron and was expected to succeed. Unable to hide his pleasure at the assignment, Farragut told the undersecretary, "I expect to pass the forts and restore New Orleans to the government, or never return. I may not come back, but the city will be ours." Handed a list of the vessels already committed to the project, Farragut remarked that he could run the forts with fewer ships. Although he was not enthusiastic about the inclusion of Porter's mortar boats, which he felt would only serve to advise the enemy of the approaching fleet and considerably and needlessly slow the operation down, he would accept them as planned.

Fox, and later Welles, when the former reported the results of the meeting to him, were both satisfied they had selected the right man. Fox was impressed by Farragut's enthusiasm for the project, and Welles by the modest self-reliance exhibited by Farragut, who nonetheless "saw himself equal to the emergency and to the expectation of the government."

Not everyone was pleased with the selection Welles had made. Some members of Congress questioned Farragut's loyalty, others his lack of demonstrated ability to lead a wartime squadron. But Welles knew he had made the right decision. He was determined to stand firm, and refused to be swayed by what he regarded as biased views by politicians, some of whom had their personal candidates for the important assignment.

Two days later a naval messenger arrived at the Hastings-on-Hudson cottage with instructions that Captain David Farragut prepare himself for orders to assume command of the Western Gulf Blockading Squadron.

The current commanding officer of the Gulf Blockading Squadron, Flag Officer William McKean, who was ill and awaiting relief from his command, was told that the squadron would be divided into two independent units. He would command the East Squadron centered on the Florida coast, and Farragut the West Squadron, covering the rest of the Gulf coast all the way to the Rio Grande.

During the second week of January 1862, Farragut received the following communication from Welles.

"Sir: You are hereby appointed to command the Western Gulf Blockading Squadron, and you will proceed to Philadelphia and report to Commodore Prendergast; and when the United States steam sloop-of-war *Hartford* shall be prepared in all respects for sea, you are authorized to hoist your flag on board that vessel." Further instructions would follow, before his departure.

Captain Farragut, soon to be Flag Officer Farragut, accompanied by his wife, Virginia, and their seventeen-year-old son Loyall, moved into Philadelphia's Continental Hotel while the *Hartford* was being readied for service. He received his final orders on January 20, 1862. In addition to other details, it instructed him to "proceed up the Mississippi River and reduce the defenses which guard the approaches to New Orleans, when you will appear off that city and take possession of it under the guns of your squadron, and hoist the American flag therein, keeping possession until troops can be sent to you."

On the twenty-third of that month, the USS *Hartford*, with the square pennant of Flag Officer David Farragut snapping in the cold breeze, left Philadelphia and steamed down the Delaware River toward the open sea.

3

"This Is No Time for Prayer"

THE USS *HARTFORD* WAS A BEAUTIFUL SIGHT as she glided down the Delaware River. A wooden-hulled sloop-of-war powered by steam engines and a full rigging of sail, she was 226 feet long, with a beam of forty-three feet, weighed 2,790 tons, and carried a compliment of twenty-two nine-inch smoothbore guns on her broadsides, and two twenty-pound Parrott rifles. Launched at Boston in 1858, the *Hartford* was a sister ship to the *Brooklyn*, which Farragut had commanded so ably during the Mexican civil war. His familiarity with this type of vessel proved extremely helpful, for the *Hartford* would be not only his headquarters, but his home while at sea for the rest of the war.

The *Hartford* dropped anchor at Hampton Roads, Virginia, on January 28, 1862, where the remainder of her crew were awaiting her arrival. It was one day after President Lincoln issued General War Order Number One, appointing February 22 "the day for a general movement of the Land and Naval forces of the United States against the insurgent forces." While there, Farragut wrote to his wife, Virginia, "You can better imagine my feelings at entering Hampton Roads as an enemy of Norfolk than I can. But, thank God, I had nothing to do with making it so."

Anticipating that the coming battle with the two river forts would result in many killed and wounded aboard his ships, Farragut decided to modify the frigate *Potomac* so she could serve as a hospital ship. This would mean that wounded, sick, and injured sailors and marines could receive quick professional medical care before they were transferred to a distant, land-based hospital. Explaining this decision, he wrote to Undersecretary Fox that the men under his command would be gratified to know that medical care was so readily available, for they all knew that "more men lose their lives from bleeding to death from want of early attention, than from the severity of their wounds." He wanted large quantities of tourniquets and other medical supplies to stock on the *Potomac*.

After a brief stopover at Havana, where he showed the flag and his impressive ship to several Confederate vessels and Spanish and French warships anchored at that neutral port, Farragut arrived at Ship Island, Mississippi, on February 20. Flag Officer McKean was there waiting for him, and the two made quick work of transferring several ships from McKean's to Farragut's command. A short time later, McKean left for his new base at Key West.

Dividing the Gulf Blockading Squadron into two separate commands, East and West, served two purposes. The first, and most obvious, was that each squadron commander could focus his attention on a smaller portion of the Confederate coast with better results expected from each command. The second was that it enabled Welles to send Farragut to the Gulf for the purpose of attacking New Orleans, without giving the enemy a hint of the intended goal. The subterfuge was only partially successful, since veteran sailors knew Farragut was not the kind of man to spend too many months sitting off the enemy's shores without taking some kind of real action against the Confederacy.

Ship Island was a natural jumping-off point for vessels heading up the Mississippi River. Named for its shiplike formation, the barren stretch of land, one hundred miles from the mouth of the Mississippi River and thirty miles south of Biloxi, Mississippi, had been used as a base by the Royal Navy during the War of 1812. It now served as the United States Navy's sole base along the Confederate-controlled Gulf Coast. With the same high-energy style he had used years earlier at Mare Island, Farragut immediately went to work preparing Ship Island for its role as the base for his invasion of Louisiana. Lieutenant George Dewey described the atmosphere on Ship Island after Farragut's arrival as being "surcharged with his energy." Dewey considered Farragut his ideal of a naval officer, "urbane, decisive, indomitable."

For the next few weeks Farragut worked on his detailed plans for the coming campaign. During this same period the other ships assigned to his squadron gradually began arriving at the island marshaling point. On March 18, Farragut sent a small party into Biloxi to raid the post office and obtain copies of local newspapers. These provided encouraging news about Union victories at Nashville, and at Fort Donelson on the Tennessee River. He continued gathering intelligence concerning the Mississippi River and its tidelands from the efforts of men assigned to his squadron from the Coast Survey, whom he sent out to locate and mark channels through which his larger ships could pass. Unlike most rivers, the Mississippi does not open to the sea at a wide mouth, but instead divides itself into a series of five outlets into the Gulf. These passes, as they are called, tend to become clogged with mud washing down the long river, and become so shallow that during peacetime dredging operations were under way almost continuously. Since the outbreak of the war, not much dredging had been done, so the passes were in unusually bad condition for the passage of large ships. The situation was exacerbated by the constantly shifting riverbed, which made identifying a permanent channel through the mud nearly impossible.

Farragut's instructions from Washington were based on the Navy Department's incorrect assessment that the water flowing through at least several of the passes was nineteen feet deep. This would allow for easy passage of all his ships, with the exception of the forty-gun frigate *Colorado*. A plan had been developed to lighten the *Colorado* by removing her guns and supplies, including water casks. When these measures failed to reduce the great warship's draft enough to get her into the river, her guns were distributed to other ships, and she was left at Ship Island.

On March 7, the first day of the two-day Battle of Pea Ridge, Arkansas, a pivotal fight for control of the Trans-Mississippi region, Farragut decided that the *Hartford* and the *Brooklyn* should enter the river and steam to the planned assembly point, a group of bleak little buildings squatting atop pilings driven into the mud, called Pilot Town. From there the infamous river forts were only thirty miles upriver. Using the information the government had supplied him, he selected the pass closest to Ship Island for his entry, Pass à l'Outre. Both ships drew approximately sixteen feet of water, and should have made the river entry without incident if the Navy Department's information had been correct. Unfortunately, the pass hadn't been used by large vessels for several months, and the endless flow of sediment down the mighty river had caused the mud barrier to reach a height that prevented the sister ships from entering. For three days the two warships struggled to penetrate the pass, each in turn finding herself stuck in the mud for several hours at a time.

Finally, with the *Brooklyn* grounded and unable to move under her own power for seventeen hours, a frustrated Farragut gave up the effort. With lines passed between the two ships, the *Hartford* strained her engines to pull the *Brooklyn* loose. After several hours of exertion the *Brooklyn* was finally freed, and both sloops steamed west. Despite a brief grounding of the *Brooklyn*, they succeeded in entering the river through the Southwest Pass. One by one the ships of Farragut's squadron arrived and made their way through the passes to the assembly point. Farragut sent several companies of sailors and marines from his gunboats ashore to occupy the dozen or so buildings at Pilot Town. Having accomplished this without incident, they immediately began converting the ramshackle buildings into hospitals and warehouses.

On March 18, Commander David Porter arrived at Pilot Town with his fleet of twenty mortar boats towed by seven steamers, and dropped anchor. Several of the steamers were sent downriver to help the larger Union warships cross the mud-obstructed Southwest Pass. Using one of his own gunboats, the *Winona*, Farragut returned to Southwest Pass and personally supervised the lightening and dragging of the seventeen-gun side-wheel steamer *Mississippi* and the twenty-three-gun sloop *Pensacola* over the mud bar.

With both ships stripped of every item that could be removed, including all coal not required for the passage, the steamers tugged and pulled for four days before getting the *Mississippi* across the mud. The *Pensacola* was another story. Her commander, Captain Henry W. Morris, attempted to ram his way through the pass, but accomplished little except to lock his ship securely in several feet of mud. Angered at Morris's refusal of help from his steamers, Porter swore he would offer no further help, relenting only after Morris humbled himself by personally requesting assistance in freeing his ship. It took nearly two weeks to free the *Pensacola*, then drag her inch by inch through the pass.

The Lower Mississippi. *Source:* H. W. Wilson, *Ironclads in Action* (Boston: Little, Brown, 1898). Used with permission.

Porter, who was apparently having second thoughts about not having sought command of the squadron for himself, began writing to Fox, complaining about the "old fogies" who were in charge of the larger ships. His envy of both Farragut's position as flag officer and his accomplishments revealed themselves in Porter's private communications, and would forever shadow his own deeds during the war. More letters were to follow, with Porter becoming increasingly critical of both Farragut and the other older captains of the fleet. In one letter he told Fox that Farragut's "administrative abilities are not of the first order." Later, when Farragut had proven himself and gained wide public recognition through his great victories, Porter might regret his comments, but until then he was using his direct line to Washington in an attempt to undermine the confidence of both Fox and Welles in the flag officer. Despite his letters of complaint, long after the war, when both of these men were dead, Porter brazenly claimed full responsibility for Farragut's selection as commander of the expedition. Twenty years after the fighting had ceased, Porter wrote two books about the war in which he described his role in the coming battles in glowing, self-aggrandizing terms.

Meanwhile, Farragut concentrated on the task ahead. He prepared detailed instructions for the captains of his ships, and spent much of his time visiting the ships themselves, giving heart to those who saw the job of reducing the river forts as insurmountable. The sixty-one-year-old flag officer's physical stamina impressed all who saw him, especially those who witnessed his morning ritual of turning a handspring on deck.

By the middle of April 1862, the fleet was fully assembled, including eighteen thousand army troops under the command of General Benjamin F. Butler. Butler's orders were to be prepared with troops sufficient to occupy whatever Confederate facilities or towns were taken in naval victories, including the city of New Orleans itself.

Aside from Porter's mortar schooner flotilla, Farragut's invasion fleet consisted of seventeen warships. The largest and most heavily armed were the four sloops-of-war, the twenty-four-gun *Hartford*, Commander Richard Wainwright (with Flag Officer Farragut and Fleet Captain Henry H. Bell aboard); the twenty-two-gun *Brooklyn*, Captain Thomas T. Craven; the 24-gun *Richmond*, Commander James

Alden; and the 23-gun *Pensacola*, Captain Henry W. Morris. Next in size was the sidewheeler *Mississippi*, with seventeen guns, Commander Melancthon Smith. Known as a steam frigate, the side-wheeler had a long, illustrious career, having served as Commodore Matthew Perry's flagship when he forced Japan to open her doors to foreign trade in 1853. She was followed by three screw corvettes, the *Oneida*, *Veruna*, and *Iroquois*. Each was slightly over one thousand tons and carried nine, ten, and seven guns respectively. Finally, at around five hundred tons, and carrying two guns each, were the gunboats *Cayuga*, *Itasca*, *Katahdin*, *Kennebec*, *Kineo*, *Pinola*, *Scotia*, *Winona*, and *Wissahickon*. Counting the guns removed from the *Colorado* and distributed among the other vessels, the squadron mounted 181 guns.

Porter's flotilla consisted of twenty mortar boats, mostly converted sailing schooners. Each was mounted with a thirteen-inch mortar, although most carried a second gun, either a thirty-two-pounder or a twelve-pound howitzer. Six of his seven gunboats were side-wheel ferryboats, the seventh a more traditional gunboat similar to those in the main fleet. Together, the seven steamers carried twenty-seven guns.

Farragut's fleet captain was, like the flag officer, a southerner by birth, and married to a woman from a leading Virginia family. Also like Farragut, Bell never hesitated for a moment in his loyalty to the Union. When his native state of South Carolina seceded, Bell wrote to the Navy Department and requested that the registry be changed to show him as coming from New York rather than from that secessionist state. Bell had distinguished himself in the mid-1850s in China, when a boat from his ship, the frigate *San Jacinto*, came under fire by Chinese troops manning forts controlling the Canton River. In retaliation, Captain Bell and Captain Andrew H. Foote of the nearby *Portsmouth*, a man who would also rise to prominence during the Civil War, led a force of marines and sailors in an attack on the forts, driving the defenders out in terror. They then blew the forts apart, reducing them to rubble.

While Farragut's squadron prepared for its passage upriver, Bell took one of the gunboats to reconnoiter the defenses of the two forts. Despite heavy fire, he gathered important information, not only about the forts themselves, but also about the condition of the obstruction the Confederates had stretched across the river to block the Union fleet. Bell made a second trip upriver, this time accompanied by Farragut himself, the flag officer being anxious for a look at the enemy before launching the attack.

Seventy-five miles below the city of New Orleans stood that city's main defenses against attack from the Gulf, Fort St. Philip and Fort Jackson. Located just below a sharp turn in the river known as Plaquemine Bend, the forts were generally believed to be sufficient defense for the South's most important city. The first fort an enemy ship sailing up the Mississippi River would encounter was Fort Jackson, standing on the left, or western, bank. Slightly to the north and across the river was Fort St. Philip. Together they formed a strong obstacle to any enemy fleet.

The older of the two was Fort St. Philip. Originally constructed by the Spanish governor of Louisiana, Baron de Carondelet, in 1792 as Fort San Felipe, it was the more formidable in appearance. In 1815 this single fort halted and, after a nine-day battle, drove off a Royal Navy fleet attempting to support a British army attack on New Orleans. The British warships had withdrawn after sending more than one thousand shells into the fort to no avail, and determining its reduction to be a hopeless cause. Farragut was fully aware of how well one fort had kept a large fleet from reaching New Orleans fifty years earlier. That knowledge is probably what convinced him of the folly of his orders to destroy the forts before proceeding upriver to New Orleans. It was no secret among the senior officers of his fleet that he would have preferred to simply run past the forts, isolating them from the support and supplies they received from the city.

Fort St. Philip had been expanded and strengthened since the War of 1812. The brick-and-earth wall facing the river contained no openings through which guns could be fired. Instead the Confederates relied on guns mounted *en barbette* that fired over the wall at the enemy. Her ramparts rose seventeen to nineteen feet above the river, and were twenty feet thick. As the Union squadron approached, St. Philip boasted some fifty-two guns in the main fort and two water-level batteries on each of her sides.

About seven hundred yards to the south, on the opposite bank, was Fort Jackson, the newer and more powerful of the two forts. Built between 1822 and 1832 as a defense against Spanish attack, she was named for the man who had first argued for the fort's construction,

General Andrew Jackson. Constructed as a star-shaped pentagon, her brick walls rose twenty-five feet above the river, and contained openings for casement guns facing directly toward the river. In the center of the star was a structure built to serve as a bomb shelter that could safely house five hundred men during a heavy bombardment. Fort Jackson boasted seventy-five guns.

At the time of Louisiana's secession from the Union on January 26, 1861, both forts had been long neglected, and were manned only by small garrisons commanded by an orderly sergeant, Henry Smith. On January 10 the forts were approached by a steamer arriving from New Orleans with a troop of Louisiana militiamen under the command of Major Paul E. Theard. When Theard demanded the surrender of the forts, Smith had little option but to comply. When the forts were transferred from the control of Louisiana forces to those of the Confederate government, work was begun to strengthen and improve them.

Over half the guns in both forts were twenty-four-pounders, along with a large number of thirty-two-pounders. These were considered small caliber for the job they were assigned, but since most Confederate officials expected New Orleans to be attacked from the north and not from the south, little concern was given to this situation. One other problem remained with the forts: the composition of their garrisons. Many of the men stationed in them were northerners who had been living in or visiting the New Orleans area when the war began. While some had been conscripted into the Confederate service at bayonet point, others had volunteered for service in the forts, expecting them to remain safe from Union attack. Many were foreigners, mostly German and Irish, who for the most part felt they had no part in the quarrel between the Northern and Southern states.

One man who was concerned about the defense of New Orleans was Confederate major general Mansfield Lovell. A former New York City deputy street commissioner, Lovell was born in Washington in 1822, where his father had been surgeon general of the United States Army. A graduate of the West Point class of 1842, Lovell served, as did so many other Civil War generals, in the Mexican War, where he was wounded twice. He had retired from the army as a captain of artillery in 1854, but his experience as an artillery officer was put to good use when he was engaged as an artillery instructor in the New

York City Guard, training militia troops in the use of the guns of Fort Hamilton. A strong supporter of states' rights, Lovell's sympathies were with the South when the secession movement began. He had been offered a commission by Confederate President Jefferson Davis at the urging of Generals P. G. T. Beauregard and Joseph E. Johnston. In October 1861, Davis had appointed him commanding officer of the Confederate troops guarding New Orleans, raising objections from some Southern-born officers who coveted the position for themselves. Once Lovell took command, Beauregard pointed out to him that despite popular opinion about an attack coming from upriver, powerful steamships could run past the river forts on their way to New Orleans. He recommended that the river itself be blocked, forcing any approaching enemy ships to stop while under the guns of the forts.

The responsibility for the defense of New Orleans was not Lovell's alone. The Confederate and state naval forces operated in the river independent of his command. Believing that a unified command was the best way to defend New Orleans, Lovell attempted to bring these naval forces under his command, but was rebuked in this by Davis himself.

Lovell had roughly three thousand men under his command, excluding the approximately one thousand troops who made up the garrisons of the two forts under the command of Brigadier General Johnson K. Duncan. Lovell's command had been stripped of its best soldiers for fighting elsewhere, and he was constantly battling to maintain the troops he had left against conscription by the Richmond government.

Lovell had spent the time since his appointment trying to convince both city officials and the Confederate government that the real threat to New Orleans was from the south. Because his authority did not give him control over civilians, he could not simply order local officials to make appropriate preparations for an attack from downriver. He undermined his own cause when he told the Louisiana governor that he regarded "Butler's Ship Island expedition as a harmless menace" to New Orleans.

One line of defense Lovell had successfully lobbied for was the construction of an obstruction blocking the river between the forts. Using mooring chains removed from ships tied up at New Orleans, forty-foot-long cypress trees were chained together and strung across the river, and secured with the use of ship anchors. A space was left open that would permit the passage of a single ship at a time. However, the amount of driftwood that flowed downriver was so great and accumulated so quickly that the obstacle was soon wrecked. It was later replaced by an assortment of demasted schooners. Perhaps the greatest impediment to the building and rebuilding of the river obstructions was the difference of opinion between Lovell and Duncan about the ability of the two forts to halt an attack by steam-powered warships. The commanding officer of the forts had what Lovell described as "undue confidence in the ability of the forts" to withstand such an attack, and to prevent an enemy fleet from reaching New Orleans.

As Farragut prepared for his attack, a fleet of Confederate war vessels assembled in the river just north of the forts. These included the ironclad *Louisiana,* with sixteen guns, the notorious ram *Manassas,* and an assortment of smaller vessels, including six riverboats from the Confederate river navy known optimistically as the River Defense Fleet. The River Defense Fleet was part of the Confederate Army, and functioned under a rather vague charter assigning it to the army commander of the military region in which it was operating at any given time. A few of the other vessels belonged to the Confederate Navy, while the remainder were part of the Louisiana State Navy. This integrating of army, navy, and state forces was further confused by the absence of a single naval officer with authority to command all these vessels. The River Defense Fleet was commanded by Captain John Stephenson, a Confederate Army officer who disliked naval officers and refused to obey the orders of the senior Confederate naval officer, Commander John K. Mitchell. Although the little fleet boasted almost forty guns, it offered the opportunity for little resistance to the Union warships. This was partly because it lacked unified command, and partly because most of the vessels were small wooden craft, and their crews were not well trained. The only exception was the *Louisiana,* but she was hampered by faulty engines since her construction had been completed. Unable to move under her own power, she had to be towed downriver from New Orleans and moored about a half mile north of Fort St. Philip.

Also on the river, above the forts, were a large number of fire rafts anchored to the riverbanks. These rafts were loaded with combustible material, usually dry wood covered with tar. The rebel plan was to release these fire boats into the river with their cargos burning, and allow the current to maneuver them among the Union ships, causing not only damage to the ships they were lucky enough to strike, but panic among the sailors on all the Union ships. It was hoped that this would result in the vessels being imprisoned in their own lines and those of the ships near them.

One man missing from the defense of New Orleans, and who might have made a difference in the outcome, was Commodore George Nichols Hollins. The sixty-three-year-old former U.S. naval officer had been responsible for defeating the Union blockade of the Mississippi River in October 1861, and, since December of that year, had been in command of Confederate naval forces in the upper Mississippi.

Hollins's fame and high regard among New Orleans's citizens and leaders was a result of a daring exploit that had driven away Union ships blockading the passes at the mouth of the Mississippi. Taking command of an odd assortment of mostly riverboats, he had sailed downriver from the city and, on October 12, 1861, had attacked the Union fleet stationed there. The center point of his fleet was one of the most unusual vessels to ever take part in naval war, the ram *Manassas*. She was originally a steam-powered seagoing tug built in Medford, Massachusetts, and known as the *Enoch Train*. Converted for war duty, her hull had been covered with iron plate one and one-half inches thick. Everything above the waterline had been stripped away, and she was covered with more plate. Her new shape resembled a huge cigar, which her builders believed would help deflect enemy shells. Less than three feet of the ram's rounded hull was above water, making her difficult to see. The *Manassas* was 143 feet long, drew only eleven feet, weighed 387 tons, and carried a crew of thirty-three. Except for the two smokestacks poking out of her center, the vessel's appearance, with the rounded top floating only slightly above the water, was of a huge turtle. Armed with only a single thirty-two-pounder that was hidden beneath a trapdoor, her primary weapon was a twenty-foot-long, pole-like ram sticking straight out of her bow.

She had been owned by a group of businessmen who intended to use her as a privateer, and the ram's conversion had been nearly completed when Hollins and a party of Confederate sailors took her at gunpoint from her civilian crew. Such a choice weapon, Hollins believed, did not belong in the hands of civilians. He could put her to better use fighting the war.

In the predawn hours of October 12, the *Manassas* had driven her ram into the steam sloop *Richmond*, causing little actual damage but so much confusion among the Union ships on the station that they had all gotten under way and fled their blockading post.

Now, six months later, as Farragut's squadron prepared to steam upriver, Hollins and his fleet were far afield at Fort Pillow, Tennessee, despite efforts by New Orleans and Louisiana officials to get the Confederate government in Richmond to send him south. When Hollins learned of the Union fleet's presence below New Orleans, he asked the Confederate Navy Department for permission to return to New Orleans. Not waiting for a reply to his request, Hollins sped downriver, where he thought he could do the most good for the Confederate cause. Major General Lovell then wired the Confederate secretary of war, Brigadier General George W. Randolph, requesting Randolph to ask Secretary of the Navy Stephen Mallory to allow Hollins to remain at New Orleans. He also asked that Hollins be given command over all naval forces assembled for the coming battle. Mallory was livid when he discovered the commodore had steamed south before waiting for his reply. He ordered Hollins to leave immediately for Richmond, where he was to serve on a board reviewing midshipmen for possible promotion. Hollins remained ensnared in Richmond's bureaucracy and out of action during the rest of the war. It was a costly loss of an energetic and resourceful officer for the Confederate Navy. Richmond officials remained unconvinced that Farragut's squadron could pass the forts, and were comfortable in their opinion that New Orleans, so vital a city to the South's existence, was in no danger. Hollins, a potentially important figure in the defense of New Orleans, was removed from the scene and the coming battle at the very moment when he might have made a difference.

Meanwhile, nothing had been done about creating a unified command for the defense of New Orleans. The defense organizations of New Orleans and the river forts remained in a chaotic state as they waited for the arrival of the enemy fleet they knew was gathering above the mouth of the river. They didn't have long to wait.

Downriver, Flag Officer Farragut assembled his squadron and prepared for battle. The sides of the Union ships were covered with chains suspended a few feet above the waterline and extending to several feet below, to serve as armor against enemy shells. Engine rooms were heaped with sacks of sand to protect the engines, and devices were rigged for the lowering of wounded men down hatchways to the decks below, where the surgeons worked. Netting was rigged above the main decks to protect crews from falling sections of mast. All rigging not required for the coming battle was removed from every ship and stowed at Pilot Town. When Farragut gave the order to steam upriver, the Union fleet was stripped for action.

The fleet was separated into three divisions, exclusive of the mortar boats. The first, commanded by Captain Theodorus Bailey, captain of the *Colorado*, which had been left at Ship Island, consisted of eight vessels. These were the sloop *Pensacola*, the side-wheeler *Mississippi*, the corvettes *Oneida* and *Varuna*, and four gunboats, *Wissahickon*, *Kineo*, *Katahdin*, and *Cayuga*. The last served as his flagship. The second division, commanded by Farragut himself, contained three sloops, *Hartford*, *Brooklyn*, and *Richmond*. The third division, under Fleet Captain Henry H. Bell, was comprised of the corvette *Iroquois* and five gunboats, *Scotia*, *Kennebec*, *Pinola*, *Itasca*, and *Winona*. Following the third division were the gunboats of Porter's mortar fleet and, in last position, the sailing sloop *Portsmouth*.

Farragut instructed Bailey to attempt to get as many of his first-division gunboats past the forts as quickly as possible and to maneuver them into position to support a troop landing above the forts, should that become feasible.

On April 14, 1862, the Union squadron began moving up the river. Several of the larger ships, struggling against the powerful and constant flow of the Mississippi, had to be towed.

On April 15, Porter had three of his mortar schooners towed up the river to a point about three hundred yards south of Fort Jackson, to test the range of their guns. During the next hour they fired a series of mortar shells into the fort, until Porter was satisfied that he had selected the most advantageous position for the boats. Return fire from the fort was both slight and ineffectual.

The following day the entire mortar-boat fleet was moved into place just south of the river obstruction, and out of range of the forts' guns. Weeks earlier, both banks had been infested with rebel snipers, but now that danger had abated. A heavy rain had raised the river level high enough to force the snipers to withdraw farther inland.

A few minutes before ten o'clock on the morning of April 18, Good Friday, the mortar boats, locked securely along the west bank of the river, opened fire. They were hidden from view of both forts by a dense stand of large trees. To camouflage them further, tree branches had been tied to their masts. Their primary target was Fort Jackson, at which they fired most of their mortars, lobbing an occasional shell into Fort St. Philip. Throughout the day, the mortar boats fired into the fort, the shells making a spectacular sight as they arced across the sky. Each boat sent a mortar shell racing toward the target at the rate of about one shell every ten minutes. Some exploded prematurely, high above the fort, the result of poor fuses. Others waited until they plunged into the thick mud to explode, causing a muffled roar and little else. But most did find their target and exploded at the appropriate time.

The mortar boats had been provided with extremely precise charts of the forts and surrounding territory, which helps explain their high degree of accuracy—a precision achieved by men who, because of their own invisibility, could not see their target. The charts had been prepared by members of the Coast Survey, who, under heavy fire from the forts and the snipers along the banks, had worked for days in the river, charting every aspect of the locale.

While the mortar boats remained hidden from view of the fort's gunners, several lucky shots from Fort Jackson found their mark, but did little damage to the fragile mortar boats. Several gunboats requested and obtained Farragut's permission to steam upriver in order to draw enemy fire away from the mortar boats. This proved to be a successful tactic, providing additional safety for the mortar crews.

As mortar shells continued to rain down on them, the men in the fort struggled to fight back. Fortunately for the garrison, the damage was minimal despite the earth-shaking roar of the mortars. Wooden structures inside Fort Jackson, especially the barracks, were set ablaze by shells, and one or two guns were driven off their mounts, but that was the extent of the damage. The guns were remounted, and the fires either extinguished or allowed to burn out if they did not threaten the magazine. Unfortunately, most of the clothing and bedding belonging to the garrison was destroyed. This, coupled with the water constantly seeping into the fort from the risen river, made life inside Fort Jackson difficult.

On that first day, more than 1,400 mortar shells and an unknown quantity of shells from the gunboats were fired at Fort Jackson. But it was obvious to the captains of the Union squadron that little real damage had been done, for the fort's gunners kept up an almost steady reply from their own guns. Although he never acknowledged it, it is probable that Farragut was not the least surprised by the result of this first day's bombardment. He had not really believed in Porter's theory that mortars could reduce these well-built forts. Had his opinion been requested before the decisions were made, he would have told Welles and Fox to leave the mortar boats out of the squadron. His own study of naval history told him that the best plan for success was to rush past the forts instead of trying to conquer them with such a head-on assault as mortar boats. He knew from army reports that both forts relied on New Orleans, the object of their protection, for their supplies and communications. Capture New Orleans, he had said often during the past few weeks, and the forts would collapse from their own need. But Welles and Fox had already decided on the plan of action before his appointment, so he had no option but to accept Porter's mortar boats and allow them to do their best against the forts.

The second day began much as the first had, with mortar boats opening up against Fort Jackson shortly after dawn. By late afternoon Porter realized that his pledge to reduce the forts within forty-eight hours was not to be fulfilled. He instructed his captains to keep firing during the night at the rate of one shell every half hour per boat. Still, it was obvious that little real physical damage was being done by the constant bombardment. But, while it was true that Fort Jackson was not suffering any real or lasting physical damage, the constant bombardment was having an effect on the garrison. The men were getting little if any sleep. That, plus the fact that most of them were not ardent supporters of the Confederate cause, made for a restive feeling among the garrison that held the potential for open rebellion against the officers. Apparently the discontent was not strong enough, nor were the men organized enough, to carry out any plan they might have developed. The fort remained in rebel hands, and the men inside did the best they could to protect themselves from the mortars.

On Easter morning, April 20, Farragut summoned the captains of his ships and boats to a meeting on the *Hartford*. At the meeting, Commander James Alden of the *Richmond* read a memorandum from Porter, who was unable to attend. In it, Porter urged the continuation of the bombardment, and stated his belief that the fleet could not possibly pass the forts while they remained in Confederate hands.

Farragut was unmoved by Porter's arguments, or by those of the other captains, most of whom apparently also thought it impossible to get their ships beyond the forts while they both remained standing. He explained to the captains that the ships, especially the mortar boats, were using ammunition at an incredible rate, and would run out of shells long before the forts were destroyed or forced to surrender. The forts could be passed, he believed, and once that was done, army troops could be landed above them. This would isolate the forts and they could eventually be starved into submission.

Farragut knew his own inclination to force his way beyond the forts and continue on to New Orleans was not popular in most quarters. Many of his own squadron officers thought it couldn't be done, and Washington considered it an almost impossible task, one that ran too many risks, even if it were somehow successful. Farragut stood virtually alone in his opinion that his ships could ignore the forts and attack New Orleans successfully.

Two months earlier, Secretary Welles had sent Farragut a memorandum concerning the forts, prepared by Brigadier General John Gross Barnard, chief engineer of the Army of the Potomac. The former superintendent of West Point, from which he graduated in 1833 as second in a class of forty-three, was a highly respected expert who had spent several years teaching military engineering at the academy. He had also served, years earlier, as engineer during the strengthening of both forts. General Barnard was therefore considered not only an engineering expert, but also extremely knowledgeable about both forts. Consequently, Welles expected Farragut to heed Barnard's advice.

General Barnard regarded an attempt to pass the forts without first reducing them to be "not a trifling undertaking." In the memorandum he had detailed why he thought it would be so difficult to pass the forts, even if the enemy were not able to maintain an obstruction across the river.

"From a point in the river 1 and 1/2 miles from the lowest battery of Fort Jackson to another 1 and 1/2 miles above the nearest upward-bearing batteries (of Fort St. Philip) we shall find a distance of 3 miles to be traversed, 2 miles of which under the fire of 100 to 125 guns and the other mile under 50 to 100." He then estimated that taking into consideration the strength of the Mississippi River's current, and the power of the naval steam engines, the majority of Farragut's squadron would take twenty-five to thirty minutes to make this journey "with hot-shot" pouring down on them.

General Barnard then suggested that if there were no alternative but to attempt to pass the forts, it should be attempted at night, because daylight passage, when the rebel gunners would have a clear view of the Union ships, was "too hazardous to be undertaken." But, he cautioned, if the Confederates were able to maintain an obstruction across the river that would stop or at the least slow down the ships, "the forcing of a passage would become almost impractical."

Finally he addressed the issue of what the result might be if the squadron was successful in passing the forts relatively intact. "Would it be prudent, however, supposing these works [the forts] to be all formidably armed, to force a passage, leaving them behind intact, while the fleet advanced on New Orleans? I think not." Unless a large land force was used to support the fleet, something the general described as too difficult to accomplish, "a fleet can not maintain itself long above those works unless the city of New Orleans is captured and held by us." Stranded between the forts and the city, and unable to be resupplied, the squadron "would have to pass the gauntlet again in retiring and our loss become very great."

Despite all opposition, Farragut held fast to his belief that success would only be achieved if the fleet ran the forts, and did so soon. Time was not on his side. He had already written to Secretary Welles complaining that he was "not half supplied with anything." Perhaps preparing Welles for what he now believed was the inevitable change in plans—passing the forts without first reducing them—Farragut told the secretary, "My shells, fuzes, cylinder cloth and yarn to make cylinders are all out. I asked for the shells I wanted and other ordnance stores and am told my demand is out of the question. I have not a solid shot on my ship and none in the squadron except a few on board the *Richmond*. We have only a few grape canister; the fuzes of sufficient length were fired away the first day."

Even Porter's mortar fleet was not faring well. Hidden from enemy gunners, only one had actually been sunk by fire from the forts, but the ceaseless concussions of the firing of their own mortar guns were taking a severe toll on them. Several of the schooners were taking water from leaks caused by the strain and shaking. The crews, unable to sleep because of the noise, and suffering from short rations, were tiring.

Time was on the side of the enemy. As long as the supply line to New Orleans remained open, the forts would continue to receive supplies for the men and the guns. Sooner or later the Confederate government would awaken to the danger posed by the Union fleet, and come to the rescue of the forts. Farragut, in the meantime, would remain without replenishment of existing supplies. He decided the time had come to set aside the orders from Washington, and take matters into his own hands.

Following the Easter Sunday meeting, Farragut issued a general order to all vessels in his squadron. He opened with the following words: "The Flag-Officer, having heard all the opinions expressed by the different commanders, is of the opinion that whatever is to be done will have to be done quickly, or we shall be again reduced to a blockading squadron, without the means of carrying on the bombardment, as we have nearly expended all the shells and fuses and material for making cartridges." He had made his decision: the squadron would run past the forts as soon as the barrier across the river had been opened and the winds, which had been blowing from the north, had changed. He knew his ships would have a difficult time with the flow of the river, and was willing to wait until the wind changed so as to reduce that hindrance to their movement. Once north of the forts, army troops could be landed by way of the various bayous, and the campaign against New Orleans could be conducted as a joint army-and-navy operation. He would, Farragut told the ships' crews, "abide the result—conquer, or be conquered."

The first matter to be dealt with was the barrier. It was made up of mostly old schooners with their masts removed. They were chained together, with their bows anchored facing upriver to reduce the drag caused by the flow of the river. While the entire obstacle could not be removed, it had to be breached enough for the largest Union ships to get through. For this task, Farragut selected his fleet captain, Henry Bell. It was just 10:00 P.M. on the night of the twentieth, when Bell took two gunboats, the *Pinola* and the *Itasca*, and quietly steamed up to the obstruction. A good omen for their mission was the fact that both gunboats were almost invisible to the enemy. The night was wrapped in almost total darkness, and the noise of their engines was silenced by a driving rain and an almost gale-force wind blowing down the river.

The plan called for the two gunboats to plant explosives aboard one of the schooners, which they did. At about that time they were spotted by lookouts from Fort Jackson, and they came under heavy but ineffectual fire from the water batteries below the fort. Porter then ordered his mortar boats to step up their pace of bombardment in an effort to force the enemy gunners to desert their guns and seek safety.

As the firing continued around them, the crew secured the *Pinola* to one of the schooners and, under the direction of explosives expert Julius Kroehl, unloaded and placed five 180-pound charges of powder aboard the schooner. Kroehl then connected a device of his own invention to the charges, and ran insulated wire from the charges to the *Pinola*. Unfortunately, the strength of the current and the wind combined to push the gunboat away from the schooner, causing Kroehl's wires to break before he could ignite the charge.

In the meantime, the *Itasca* had pulled alongside another schooner. Using hammers and chisels, crew members freed the schooner from her restraints and she began to drift downriver. Unfortunately, the *Itasca* became entangled with the schooner's lines and was pushed onto the river's east bank, where she became stuck. Only after great effort, and with the assistance of the *Pinola*, was she finally freed. Once free, she steamed upriver through the opening she had made in the obstacle. When she had gotten almost to the position of Fort St. Philip, the *Itasca* turned her back to the wind and faced downriver. The gunboat was swept along by wind, current, and her own engine. With a great crash, she hit the chain that held several schooners together. Her bow rose up out of the water as the chain rubbed along her keel. Almost the entire forward half of the boat was out of the water when the chain finally gave way, and the gunboat crashed back to the surface. The chain-and-schooner obstruction was opened wide enough for the Union fleet to make its way through.

While this dramatic event was taking place, few aboard the Union ships could sleep, including the flag officer. Everyone understood the importance of the mission Bell had been sent on, and also the danger the two gunboats faced as they struggled with the chain and the schooners almost directly under the guns of Fort Jackson. In a letter written the following day, Farragut told his wife, "I never felt such anxiety in my life as I did until his return. I was as glad to see Bell on his return as if he had been my boy. I was up all night, and could not sleep until he got back to the ship."

The following day, the twenty-first, the breach in the obstruction was ignored by both sides as weather conditions made it impractical for the Union fleet to pass through it, or for the rebels to attempt to repair it. The mortar boats continued their bombardment. As the weather continued cold and windy, the Union boats again kept up their routine on the twenty-second. Despite the heavy bombardment, little real damage had been done to the fort. Inside Fort Jackson, General Duncan kept his men busy remounting guns that had been driven off their mounts, making other repairs, and occasionally firing back at the enemy's ships in the river.

On the morning of April 23, a clear, cloudless, and warm day, General Lovell visited Fort Jackson to inspect the damage and confer with General Duncan. Lovell was surprised to find that the fort had suffered only four casualties, and only slight structural damage. Then, suddenly, at noon, the mortars ceased their incessant firing, and all was calm. Inside the fort, those soldiers not engaged in repairs watched the river anxiously, expecting at any moment to see the Union fleet steaming before them.

Downriver, Flag Officer Farragut spent the afternoon visiting the ships and boats of his squadron, inspecting them and giving encouragement to their crews. His order of the day was to watch the *Hartford* during the night: the signal to begin the passing of the forts would be two red lights hoisted to the top of her mainmast. The men of the squadron were as anxious as the men waiting for them inside the two forts and in their surrounding batteries.

At about eight o'clock that evening, Lieutenant Charles H. Caldwell, commander of the *Itasca*, took a ten-oar boat upriver of the obstruction to test the actual size of the breach. Trailing a long lead, the boat drifted back downriver. He returned and did the same thing again. Each time the lead remained free, failing to catch on anything that might damage a large ship. At eleven o'clock he signaled the *Hartford* that the opening offered no impediment to the passage of the ships.

Meanwhile, the vessels of the squadron were being maneuvered into the positions they had been assigned by Farragut for the run upriver. It was the flag officer's intention to lead the fleet himself, but he was dissuaded from doing so by his captains. They argued that his own passage ahead of the fleet might result in his losing control of the rest of the squadron, especially should any of them get caught in the obstruction.

The Union fleet spent the evening preparing for the coming battle. Hammocks were stowed, and the chain cables that had been hung along the sides of the larger ships were checked. In an effort to reduce their visibility, hulls were smeared with the yellow mud of the Mississippi. Decks were whitewashed to help crews see the darker pieces of equipment during what promised to be a completely dark night.

Inside the forts and the water batteries, men made what preparations they could, but for the most part all they could do was to wait and watch the darkness. Upriver from the forts, the Confederate naval force also sat waiting. The quiet night, unusual since the arrival of the Porter's mortar boats, foretold that the time of battle was quickly drawing near. The River Defense Fleet looked impressive, but would prove of little or no value when the battle began. The only real threat afloat to the Union squadron was the *Louisiana*. Although her engines, defective since she was built, remained silent, there were a large number of mechanics aboard trying to make them work. The huge ironclad remained anchored a half mile north of Fort St. Philip, where she served as a floating battery.

Many people in New Orleans looked on the *Louisiana* as the city's strongest defense, after the forts. Along with her sister ship, the *Mississippi*, the 1,400-ton *Louisiana* represented the Confederacy's greatest naval shipbuilding venture. The keels for both vessels had been laid in December 1861 in shipyards at Jefferson City, Louisiana, a short distance upriver from New Orleans—the *Louisiana* at the yard of E. C. Murray, and the *Mississippi* at the yard of the Tift Brothers. Supply shortages had slowed construction to a crawl, and both remained incomplete when Flag Officer Farragut's squadron entered the Mississippi River. E. C. Murray had been building boats for over twenty years, and had established an enviable record of constructing nearly 120 steamboats, but the *Louisiana* was to be the most unusual craft he had ever undertaken to build. Her superstructure was topped by a flat deck through which protruded her single large smokestack. Belowdecks were four powerful steam engines that had been removed from the former river steamer *Ingomar*. Two were designed to drive two covered paddle wheels located slightly aft of midships, and two were to power more traditional screw propellers. Despite the best efforts of a large number of mechanics and engineers, the transplanted engines never ran. When finally launched on February 6, 1862, the *Louisiana* carried a crew of 250 men, and boasted sixteen six- and seven-inch rifled guns, but she could not move under her own power.

When the *Louisiana* was finally dropped into the river, Confederate Navy Secretary Mallory ordered that she be sent north, where, he believed, lay the strongest threat to New Orleans. Military and civilian officials in New Orleans tried to persuade him to allow the powerful ironclad to remain near the Crescent City, but he refused. The issue was moot, of course, since the ship was unable to steam anywhere, so it was by default that she remained at New Orleans. As the Union fleet prepared to run past the forts, the *Louisiana* remained tied to the riverbank north of Fort St. Philip. Had she been able to gather a head of steam, it is unlikely that she would have played a larger role in the coming battle than she did as a floating battery. The ironclad's own design made her, in the words of her chief engineer, Wilson Youngblood, "unmanageable in the Mississippi River."

During the afternoon of the twenty-third, General Lovell met with Commodore William Whittle, Confederate naval commander for the New Orleans area. Lovell begged Whittle to order Captain Mitchell, commander of the Confederate naval forces on the river, to move the *Louisiana* farther downriver, and anchor her between the forts, where she might serve the more useful purpose of joining the guns in the forts in preventing the Union ships from passing the now breached obstruction. The two men argued over the advisability of endangering the *Louisiana* until she was able to move under her own power, but Whittle finally agreed to telegraph Mitchell with Lovell's request. Lovell's efforts were fruitless. Mitchell refused to move the vessel. He claimed that to move her within range of the Union mortar boats was too risky, for a single mortar shell dropping onto her thinly plated flat decks would pass directly through her, and she would sink.

As darkness settled around the Union fleet, and the ships and boats found their assigned positions as quietly as they could, Farragut paced the quarterdeck of the *Hartford*. Joining him was his clerk, B. S. Osbon, who was also a correspondent for the *New York Herald*. Farragut asked Osbon his opinion of the number of casualties the fleet would suffer in the coming fight with the forts and the rebel vessels. Osbon replied that he believed "we will lose a hundred" of the four thousand men in the squadron. Farragut was surprised at the extremely low estimate. "No more than that?" he asked. "How do you calculate so small a number?" Osbon then explained that he thought the dark night, the dense smoke that would be produced by the guns, and the fact that most ships in the fleet sat low in the water would all contribute to reducing the number of men who would be killed in the action. Farragut's expression was sad as he stared at Osbon, perhaps hoping to find in his clerk's face evidence that his estimate was correct. After a few moments he reflected, "I wish I could think so. I wish I could be as sure of it as you are." Farragut then turned and walked away, alone with his own thoughts of the number of his men who would die or be permanently crippled during the early-morning hours ahead of them.

Aboard Farragut's ships, crews were told that they could sleep until midnight, when they would be awakened in silence, and begin last-minute preparations for passing the forts. Officers retired to their quarters to write what many suspected might be a last few lines to a loved one or close friend. There was no jubilant feeling about the task ahead; most sailors and officers on the Union vessels anticipated that the morning would bring death and destruction on them and their ships.

Inside Fort Jackson, General Duncan, expecting the enemy fleet to move at any time now that the mortar bombardment had ceased, made a final appeal to Captain Mitchell to bring the *Louisiana* farther downriver so she could aid the forts in halting the Union advance. Mitchell replied that he could have the ironclad ready to move by the following evening. Duncan knew that by then the battle would have been decided, and it would be too late. Bringing the floating battery between the forts would permit it to fire directly at the mortar boats, and into the enemy fleet as it steamed upriver. His reply to Mitchell was that "there would be no tomorrow" if he did not move the *Louisiana* into the requested position immediately. The ironclad remained where she was, upriver of Fort St. Philip.

At two o'clock on the morning of April 24, 1862, the darkness surrounding the Union squadron anchored in the Mississippi River revealed two red lanterns as they slowly rose up the mizzenmast of the flagship *Hartford*. Quickly, and as quietly as possible, anchors were weighed. Their chains rattled a signal of their movement to the waiting enemy. On board the ships of both fleets, and inside the forts and the water batteries, men's hearts pumped faster as a mixture of excitement and fear swept all those waiting for the fight to begin.

On the second anniversary of the passing of the forts, Farragut wrote of that night to his son, describing it as "the most anxious night of my life."

Farragut had originally intended to pass the forts in two columns, but the width of the opening in the river obstruction altered his plan. Dangerous as it was, he was forced to order his ships to pass the forts in single file. As was his custom, he spent long hours reviewing every detail and preparing for every possibility.

The lead division, under Captain Bailey, who was aboard the gunboat *Cayuga*, which served as his flag, had some difficulty in weighing all anchors, so it was not until almost 3:00 A.M. that the fleet began to move. Behind the *Cayuga* came the sloop *Pensacola*, the side-wheeler *Mississippi*, then, in order, the *Oneida*, the *Varuna*, the *Katahdin*, the *Kineo*, and finally, the *Wissahickon*. At three-thirty the *Cayuga* was the first to pass through the obstacle. Ten minutes later both forts opened fire with every gun they could train on the enemy ships. Almost simultaneously, the Union mortar boats opened fire, driving many of the rebel gunners away from their guns and into safety.

Within minutes the river was covered in smoke and a constant deafening roar, as both forts, their batteries, the mortar boats, and the approaching divisions of the squadron fired every available gun.

Hundreds of guns were now firing at the same time. Farragut had issued orders to his captains to control their gunners to prevent the accidental firing of their own ships, and at this they were successful.

Piloting the *Cayuga,* as she passed between the schooner hulks chained in the river, was Lieutenant George H. Perkins. Describing the scene, Perkins later wrote, "the air was filled with shells and explosives which almost blinded me as I stood on the forecastle trying to see my way." The gunboat was struck forty-two times by rebel shells, but little actual damage was done to her hull.

After successfully maneuvering through the obstruction, Perkins looked back to see how the second ship, the *Pensacola,* and those that followed her were faring. "My heart jumped up into my mouth when I found I could not see a single one."

As it happened, the *Pensacola* was experiencing some engine trouble as she passed the hulks. Because she had been slowed by this difficulty, Captain Morris had stopped in mid-crossing and fired a complete broadside into Fort Jackson in a successful effort to drive even more rebel crews away from their guns. Once through the obstruction, he stopped again and loosed another deadly broadside. Continuing on, Morris was surprised to discover the infamous ram *Manassas* suddenly speeding out of the darkness toward him. With the skillful maneuvering of her pilot, Lieutenant Francis A. Roe, the sloop was able to avoid being struck by the ram's long nose, and was able to assault the metal turtle with her eleven-gun starboard broadside. The *Manassas* suffered seriously from this attack, but remained at her station in the river.

Passing closely behind the *Pensacola* was the side-wheeler *Mississippi,* Lieutenant George Dewey controlling her helm. Because Captain Melancthon Smith suffered from poor eyesight, especially at night, he instructed his young executive officer to take command with the words, "I cannot see at night. I am going to leave that to you, Dewey." Smith went below to the gun deck to take personal control of the firing from the ship's batteries. After returning the fire from Fort Jackson, the *Mississippi* followed her predecessors under the guns of Fort St. Philip, only to become the second ship to face the potentially fatal encounter with the ram *Manassas.*

Aboard the *Mississippi* was Alfred Waud, an artist and correspondent for *Harper's Weekly.* From his vantage point on the foretop, Waud was the first to spot what he called "a queer-looking customer" approaching the *Mississippi*'s port bow. He pointed it out to Dewey. The future admiral and hero of Manila Bay peered into the darkness and, as he later recalled, "saw what appeared like the back of an enormous turtle painted lead color, which I identified as the ram *Manassas*." Seeking to take advantage of his ship's great weight in comparison to the ram, Dewey turned the side-wheeler directly at *Manassas*. Unfortunately, the ram's commander, Captain Alexander F. Warley, had served on a round-the-world cruise aboard the *Mississippi*, and knew the ship suffered from a lack of maneuverability. By quickly turning his boat aside, Warley was able to both avoid the intended collision and swing around for a counterattack. *Manassas* hit *Mississippi* a glancing blow just behind the ship's port paddle wheel. Although the attack did open up a large hole in her side, the powerfully built Federal warship resumed her progress upriver. The *Manassas* turned and headed for other prey among the enemy fleet.

Farther upriver, Bailey's little flagship, the *Cayuga*, was encountering a new enemy, the Confederate and Louisiana gunboats. Mostly converted river steamers, they had been lined up along the eastern bank of the river behind the *Louisiana* and the *Manassas*. Eleven of the enemy boats attempted to surround the *Cayuga*, but Captain Bailey raked them all with a continuous firing of his guns. Fortunately for the *Cayuga*, the rebel attack was disorganized, owing partly to the split command structure and the absence of the River Defense Fleet, which for the most part had turned and run upriver when the Union gunboats approached. Many of the boats of the River Defense Fleet, which was part of the Confederate Army and not answerable to local Confederate Navy authorities, were destroyed by Union fire as they fled. Few, if any, returned that fire. Hampered by the fact that their boats had not been designed for warfare, three of the rebel navy captains tried to compensate by closing on the *Cayuga* with the intention of boarding her. Morris successfully drove all three off, setting one ablaze. The latter limped away and grounded on the riverbank, where its crew abandoned it to the flames.

The fight among the gunboats increased as the *Oneida* and the *Varuna* soon joined the *Cayuga*. As additional Federal boats appeared, and the odds increased rapidly in the enemy's favor, the rebel commanders became more desperate and reckless in their efforts to halt the Union fleet. A victim of that desperation was the Union gunboat *Varuna*. She had attacked and set ablaze the rebel gunboat *General Quitman*, which drifted to the bank, where she remained, burning to the water line. Then it was the *Varuna*'s turn, as the Louisiana State gunboat *Governor Moore*, commanded by the able and talented Captain Beverly Kennon, closed on her, forcing the Union boat toward the shore. Unable to bring his bow gun to bear on the enemy, Kennon, whose ship was already badly damaged by enemy shells, fired the big gun through his own bow and into the *Varuna* below her waterline. He then rammed her into the bank. As the *Governor Moore* attempted to back away from her victim, the Union sloop *Pensacola* passed behind and fired a broadside into her, wrecking the gunboat and driving her onto the shore. Kennon set what remained of his boat aflame and surrendered to a party from the *Pensacola*. The sloop also lowered a boat to rescue the remaining crewmen of the *Varuna*.

With the first division, minus the gunboat *Varuna*, safely through the obstacle, the second division, comprising the *Hartford*, the *Brooklyn*, and the *Richmond*, began their passage. Farragut was unable to see clearly because of the dark and the increasingly thick smoke from the numerous guns firing continuously. He was concerned that one of his ships might be damaged by a broadside from his own. To prevent this, he climbed up into the *Hartford*'s mizzen rigging, from where he yelled orders down to the gun crews. The noise of the guns and exploding shells was so great that his shouted instructions had to be relayed to the gun crews. Farragut remained where he was until Mr. Osbon, his clerk, finally persuaded him to return to the deck. It was evidently none too soon, for a few minutes later an enemy shell exploded near the point where he had been perched.

As the three sloops of the second division approached the obstacle, they fired devastating broadsides at Fort Jackson. While the captains knew their shells would cause little physical damage, they sought to keep the rebel gunners away from their stations as long as possible. For the most part they succeeded, although many of the fort's gun crews worked their weapons with skill under horrendous conditions.

The *Hartford* made it through the obstacle, but the *Brooklyn* lost sight of her in the dark and smoke, and drifted off course, becoming entangled in the hulks and logs that made up the obstacle. As Captain Craven struggled to free his ship, it swung around and her bow scraped the eastern riverbank, leaving her in a vulnerable position. Gunners on Fort St. Philip caught sight of her, stopped at the obstacle, and opened a terrible fire on the ship. Finally able to free herself, the *Brooklyn* steamed upriver, but not before suffering an attack from the ram *Manassas*, which, however, did little damage. Coming within a hundred yards of the second fort, she exacted revenge for the pounding she had taken by firing broadsides of grapeshot and canister into the fort. The *Richmond* was luckier, following her lead ship through the breach in the obstruction safely, with only minor damage.

Once above the forts, the *Brooklyn* again became the center of enemy attention. Gunners aboard the *Louisiana* found their range and put a shell into her bow above the waterline, but it failed to explode. The Union sloop returned fire to the stationary ironclad in vain. Meanwhile, the *Manassas* made another attempt at ramming her, but accomplished nothing except to create a loud noise when she came in contact with the chain hanging over the sloop's side as armor against just such an attack. The ram slid away and once again looked elsewhere for a victim.

Aboard the *Hartford*, Farragut caught sight of the *Manassas* prowling the river. He told his signalman to "signal the *Mississippi* to sink that damned thing." The steam frigate responded to the flag officer's order by steaming toward the ram and firing so many shells into her that her commander, Captain Warley, said she was "shot through as though she had been made of thin plank." Unable to continue the fight, Warley ran his boat up on the riverbank to allow his crew to get off, then permitted her to fill with water and slowly slip into the brown river and disappear from view. Warley and his crew vanished into the nearby swamps. Before the ram went down, Captain Smith of the *Mississippi* sent a boat to board her and report on her condition with the hope of saving her. But the officer in charge of the boarding party returned with news that the ram was too far gone to rescue. He did, however, manage to recover Warley's diary and signal book.

A short time later the ram rose to the surface, with part of her bow sticking out of the water, and was carried downriver about one mile, where she mysteriously exploded and vanished for good.

In the midst of this activity, the one element missing was the large number of fire boats that had been prepared by the Confederate forces. Loaded with dry wood and tar, they were the ultimate weapon for use against an enemy fleet on a river. Released, with their cargoes ablaze, and allowed to drift downriver with the current, they could at the least create panic and chaos among crews of wooden ships. At their worst, they could quickly set a large warship afire, requiring her crew to fight the blaze to save their own lives. For some reason, control of these rafts had been passed from the Confederate Navy to the Confederate Army's River Defense Fleet, and then back again. The resulting confusion over who controlled these rafts meant that only a few were actually used. The first, released soon after the Union fleet began to move, had created enough chaos to cause several of Farragut's vessels to collide, but only minor damage had resulted.

Suddenly, while the *Mississippi* was engaged with the *Manassas*, a large burning raft was swept downstream, carried by the river current with the help of a tiny unarmed tugboat, the *Mosher*. The *Hartford* attempted to maneuver out of the raft's way, but moved too close to the shore and became grounded. The courageous little tug pushed the inferno right up against the flagship, setting it on fire. Flames leaped up her side and halfway up her mainmast. Only the efforts of her well-trained and drilled fire crews saved her from even worse damage. While these crews extinguished the flames, other crewmen trained their guns on the little tug, blowing her apart and sending her crew to the bottom of the river. As the *Hartford*'s crew fought the flames, Mr. Osbon, the flag officer's clerk, came up with a novel method for pushing the raft away from the ship, the usual methods having failed. He rolled three twenty-pound shells across the deck toward the flames. The heat was so intense that Osbon covered his head with his coat while he knelt to remove the caps from each shell. Seeing him kneeling there, Farragut called out, "Come, Mr. Osbon, this is no time for prayer." Osbon replied that the flag officer was about to witness the quickest answer to prayers he had ever seen. He then rolled the shells off the side into the burning raft. The resulting explosion blew a large hole in the raft. The river rushed through the hole, reducing the danger from the flames until the raft was completely covered by water and its fire put out.

As daylight began to edge over the horizon, the third and final division of the squadron fought its way up the river. The *Scotia*, flying the flag of Fleet Captain Bell, led the way through the obstruction

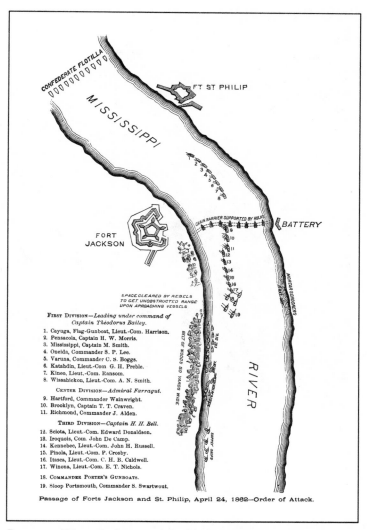

FT ST PHILIP

MISSISSIPPI

CONFEDERATE FLOTILLA

CHAIN BARRIER SUPPORTED BY HULKS

BATTERY

FORT JACKSON

MORTAR SCHOONERS

RIVER

SPACE CLEARED BY REBELS TO GET UNOBSTRUCTED RANGE UPON APPROACHING VESSELS

First Division—*Leading under command of Captain Theodorus Bailey.*

1. Cayuga, Flag-Gunboat, Lieut.-Com. Harrison.
2. Pensacola, Captain H. W. Morris.
3. Mississippi, Captain M. Smith.
4. Oneida, Commander S. P. Lee.
5. Varuna, Commander C. S. Boggs.
6. Katahdin, Lieut.-Com G. H. Preble.
7. Kineo, Lieut.-Com. Ransom.
8. Wissahickon, Lieut.-Com. A. N. Smith.

Center Division—*Admiral Farragut.*

9. Hartford, Commander Wainwright.
10. Brooklyn, Captain T. T. Craven.
11. Richmond, Commander J. Alden.

Third Division—*Captain H. H. Bell.*

12. Sciota, Lieut.-Com. Edward Donaldson.
13. Iroquois, Com. John De Camp.
14. Kennebec, Lieut.-Com. John H. Russell.
15. Pinola, Lieut.-Com. P. Crosby.
16. Itasca, Lieut.-Com. C. H. B. Caldwell.
17. Winona, Lieut.-Com. E. T. Nichols.

18. Commander Porter's Gunboats.
19. Sloop Portsmouth, Commander S. Swartwout.

Passage of Forts Jackson and St. Philip, April 24, 1862—Order of Attack.

Passage of Forts Jackson and St. Philip, April 24, 1862—Order of Attack. *Source:* Loyall Farragut, *The Life of David Glasgow Farragut* (New York: D. Appleton and Co., 1879).

and the forts. After passing Fort St. Philip, she encountered two rebel gunboats, but made short order of them. Enemy gunners were now better able to see the Union vessels, and the other boats in the third division took a heavy pounding as they made the passage. Three ships in the final division failed to make the run. The *Itasca*, the same

Captain David Porter, whose bomb vessels backed the fleet.
Courtesy of Anne S. K. Brown Military Collection, Brown
University Library.

gunboat that had opened the breach in the obstruction, had her engine disabled by a forty-two-pound shot and was forced to float downstream and out of range of the rebel guns. The *Kennebec* and the
Winona, both attempting to race past Fort Jackson in the morning
light, became entangled in the chains, logs, and schooners of the obstacle, and their captains prudently decided to steam back downriver
rather than make the attempt in full view of enemy gunners.

    While the third division was attempting to pass the forts, Captain
Bailey's *Cayuga* took part in one of the most extraordinary incidents
of the campaign. Shortly before 5:00 A.M., as the first light of dawn

rose over the river, the speedy gunboat was pushing upriver far ahead of her cohorts, when the lookouts spotted an encampment of Confederate soldiers on the eastern bank. The gunboat pulled close to shore as the soldiers rose from their places and stared in wonder at the approaching enemy vessel. Bailey fired several rounds of canister at the startled troops, killing and wounding about thirty of the seven hundred men camped there. Dropping anchor when he realized the soldiers were not returning his fire, Bailey ordered Lieutenant Perkins to call to the Confederate officers to surrender or face further assault. Perkins invited the regiment's commanding officer and his staff aboard the *Cayuga* to deliver their swords.

The men on the shore were foreigners, mostly Germans. They had been coerced into the Confederate service, and had little heart for fighting the Yankees. Their commander, Colonel Ignatius Szymanski, readily came aboard the gunboat with several other officers and surrendered. Perkins wrote later how odd it was to see "a regiment on shore surrendering to a ship." Colonel Szymanski later said he had little choice, since there was no possibility his troops could escape the murderous guns of the *Cayuga*, and he could not return the fire with any effect. "I thought it my duty to surrender." Later in the day, Farragut paroled the colonel and most of the regiment's troops, allowing them to return to New Orleans.

At 7:00 A.M., just five hours after the signal to begin running past the forts had been given, the vessels that had succeeded in this task were anchored at Quarantine Point, seven miles upriver from Fort St. Philip. All but one vessel, the *Varuna*, had survived the battle. Thirteen of the seventeen ships that had set out to run the forts dropped anchor at the point. The three other missing gunboats, *Kennebec*, *Itasca*, and *Winona*, which the flag officer at first thought had been lost, had been forced to turn back. As ships reported their condition to the *Hartford*, it was discovered that Mr. Osbon's prediction concerning casualties was actually an overestimate. The final figure was stunningly low, considering the number of guns fired during the battle and the confined area in which it took place. Of the roughly four thousand men aboard Farragut's ships, thirty-seven were killed and 146 wounded. With his squadron around him, cheering his great feat, Flag Officer David Farragut began immediately to plan for his conquest of New Orleans.

4

The Capture of New Orleans

THE UNION FLEET ANCHORED off Quarantine Point for the remainder of the day. Hundreds of flags and banners flew from every ship in celebration of the victory, and cheers welcomed the flag officer each time he appeared on the *Hartford*'s deck. Details of sailors were formed for the somber duty of taking the dead ashore and burying them. Blood-spattered decks were washed, and minor repairs were made to the ships and gunboats. Farragut, following his custom, visited his ships, congratulating the officers and men. On each vessel were echoed the heartfelt cheers of his squadron for having successfully brought them through an engagement that most had believed would result in their own deaths.

Of the big ships, the *Hartford* had been hit eighteen times by enemy shells, but had suffered little lasting damage other than the disabling of two of her guns. The *Pensacola* had been struck nine times, the *Mississippi* eleven, the *Richmond* thirteen, and the *Brooklyn* sixteen. But because none of the shots had struck below the waterline, the ships were in no danger of sinking.

Downriver, the Confederate forts had also suffered only light casualties. Fort Jackson had thirty-three wounded and nine killed, and Fort St. Philip lost two killed and had four wounded. The rebel riverboats suffered more, with about seventy-five dead and thirty-five wounded. Considering the number of shells fired and the close proximity of the opposing forces, the loss of so few men is amazing. It is even more surprising when we read Farragut's description of the battle scene in a letter he wrote home several days later: "It was one of the most awful sights and events I ever saw or experienced. The smoke was so dense that it was only now and then you could see anything but the flash of the cannon."

One Confederate loss that affected Farragut personally was the fatal wounding of the commander of the *Louisiana*, Commander Charles F. McIntosh. The two had become close friends years earlier while serving at Norfolk. The ironclad's executive officer, John Wilkinson, had also served with Farragut years before, and later wrote that the Confederate naval officers stationed below New Orleans expected from the beginning that "Farragut would dare" to make a run past the forts to attack New Orleans.

Having watched the battle from below the forts, General Butler sent a message of congratulations to Farragut: "Allow me to congratulate you and your command upon the bold, daring, brilliant and successful passage of the forts by the fleet this morning." Butler was anxious to get his forces into action, for fear the glory that would come with the now imminent capture of New Orleans would fall entirely to the navy.

Satisfied that his fleet was functioning in proper order, Farragut proceeded with his plans to capture New Orleans. He sent Captain Boggs, formerly of the *Varuna,* in an open boat through the bayous, circling around the rear of Fort St. Philip with communiqués for both Porter and Butler. To Porter, whom he thanked for the support provided by the mortar boats, he explained that he planned to continue upriver "and push for New Orleans and then come down and attend to the forts; so you hold them in status quo until I get back." He suggested that Porter demand the surrender of the forts, explaining that he had cut the telegraph wires leading to the city, leaving them without communications.

Farragut suggested through his emissary, Boggs, that General Butler load his troops into small boats and move them around the back of Fort St. Philip and proceed to Quarantine Point. From there he could use several of Farragut's gunboats to move some of his men across the river, and sequester the forts more effectively from New Orleans, their source of intelligence and supplies. Surrounded by Union troops, and facing additional mortar attacks, he reasoned that the garrisons of the forts might then be convinced to surrender.

Porter, whose position below the forts with his mortar and gunboat fleet precluded him from participating in the capture of New Orleans, was greatly displeased by Farragut's decision to proceed upriver without first capturing the forts. He was also upset about being left behind. Butler, too, was disturbed about Farragut's leaving the forts in enemy hands. Neither appeared to agree with the flag officer's assessment that the forts were of little real value to the enemy once isolated from New Orleans. To Farragut, the target was New Orleans, and such peripheral objectives as the river forts could more easily be dealt with once New Orleans was in Federal hands. General Butler felt that Farragut had left him with the "most troublesome, annoying and anxious business of the campaign." Like Porter, he was also displeased at being left behind while the fleet moved north to New Orleans without him or his troops.

Borrowing one of Porter's gunboats, the *Miami,* Butler returned downriver to his waiting transports. He took the troops of the Twenty-sixth Massachusetts back out through Pass à L'Outre and up the coast to a place east of Fort St. Philip, where they entered Maunels Canal, a large bayou that led toward the rear of the fort. Butler was intent on attacking and capturing the fort. When the waterway became too shallow, the soldiers were transferred to light-draft boats, then eventually were forced to march nearly two miles through the swampy countryside. The soldiers found the going rough as they struggled through what at times was almost waist-deep mud and water. Meanwhile, Farragut had weighed anchor and steamed north, leaving behind the gunboats *Kineo* and *Wissahickon* to support Butler's force. When General Butler and his troops finally arrived at Quarantine Point, he followed Farragut's suggestion, and used the two gunboats to transport units of his command across the river to effectively isolate Fort Jackson as well as Fort St. Philip.

The Federal fleet started north shortly after dawn on the morning of April 25, 1862. Upriver, the city of New Orleans was in a panic. The sailors and marines aboard Farragut's ships witnessed the result of that panic, as dozens of cotton-laden burning vessels, including large ships, swept past them, carried along by the river's current. Mobs at the city's wharfs had torched the cotton and pushed the ships into the stream, hoping to halt the progress of the enemy fleet.

Until the forts had been passed, the mood in New Orleans had been one of subdued confidence. The people had been assured that Fort Jackson and Fort St. Philip could prevent the enemy fleet from reaching the city. Their confidence had been shaken during Porter's mortar assaults on the forts, when on clear nights they could hear the explosions of the Union shells. Despite this, New Orleans's population remained cautiously optimistic that the Union fleet would be defeated. This optimism was buoyed by the local newspapers, especially the *Crescent* and the *Daily True Delta,* both early and vigorous supporters of secession.

The *Crescent* had proclaimed that neither the forts nor the city could be captured. The very morning that the fleet was passing the forts, the *Daily True Delta* had published a portion of a dispatch from General Duncan to General Lovell, in which he boasted, "We can stand it [the bombardment], with God's blessing, as long as they can." While this may have cheered the hearts of early-morning readers, rumors that Federal gunboats were north of the forts changed the mood of people quickly. The rumors had been confirmed by the pealing of church bells at nine-thirty on the morning of the twenty-fourth. Throughout the city, people stopped to count the number of tolls from each church steeple. By the time they reached twelve rings, the alarm signal instructing all soldiers and militiamen to report to their armories immediately, everyone knew the rumors must be true.

By the morning of the twenty-fifth, as Farragut's ships steamed north of Quarantine Point, the citizens of New Orleans knew their city was doomed to be captured by the enemy. Louisiana Governor Thomas O. Moore, a powerful secessionist leader, realized the imminent surrender of New Orleans meant that the capital, Baton Rouge, would inevitably fall into Union hands. He issued orders that morning that all cotton stores within the area facing Federal occupation be either removed or destroyed. Those planters with the transportation to do so hauled their cotton into the interior, as far from the danger as possible. Those unable to remove their cotton, which for most represented the basis of their wealth, ordered their slaves to split open the thousands of bales stacked on the city's wharves and splash them with whiskey, which was also to be kept from the enemy's hands. The slaves then pushed the bales off the docks into the river, and used burning pine knots to set the cotton ablaze. Thousands of bales of flaming cotton drifted downriver. Most were caught in the eddies along the riverbanks and drifted harmlessly against the shore, where they burned themselves out. Those succeeding in gaining the center of the stream were destroyed by their own flames before they reached the Federal ships.

At New Orleans, the destruction of valuable equipment and supplies being carried out by state officials at the governor's order cracked the thin veneer of hope that the city would be saved from capture. Crowds broke into warehouses and boarded ships, carrying away bacon, rice, sugar, corn, and any other foodstuffs they could find. Cotton bales stacked on the wharves were set ablaze by enraged mobs who took out their frustrations on anything they could find. The mobs turned even more violent as word spread that General Lovell had decided not to defend New Orleans against the Federal ships that were even then steaming toward the city.

General Lovell recognized that the city could not be defended, and that any attempt to do so would subject New Orleans to the devastating fire of the enemy's warships. The river had risen to such a level that when the Union ships came alongside the wharves, their guns would be so high that they would easily dominate the entire city. Lovell had hoped to be able to put up a staunch defense against a land invasion by Butler, but his men were poorly armed, most having nothing but old shotguns or obsolete muskets. These were not the proper weapons to use against oceangoing warships or well-armed infantry and cavalry. Lovell met with New Orleans mayor John T. Monroe and other city officials and told them of the hopelessness of resistance against Farragut's fleet. For years afterward, Lovell suffered abuse for his decision not to defend New Orleans, even after military experts from both sides found it to have been a reasonable decision that, in fact, probably saved the city from destruction.

Lovell sent detachments of troops into the commercial section of the city along the wharves to try to stop the violence and restore order. However, by then the wholesale pillaging had become so widespread and involved so many people, especially those from the poorer neighborhoods, that he gave up the attempt. Instead, the military commander of New Orleans concentrated on extracting military supplies from Confederate government warehouses. All Confederate troops and state militia, except for some foreign units, were ordered to march to the Jackson railroad station. At the station, every available freight and passenger rail car was pushed into service. The few working locomotives were brought out and hitched to the cars and waited with their engines running for the order to pull out of the station.

The area around the station was one of almost complete bedlam, except for the soldiers, who for the most part marched in silence to their appointed places on the trains. Civilians fought for the few places not already occupied by troops. Confederate soldiers were jammed inside the coaches and boxcars. Latecomers were ordered to stand on the vestibules at the ends of the cars, or sent to sit atop them. Quickly the roofs of the cars were packed with soldiers. The men on top grumbled and complained about their treatment, especially after a heavy rain began pouring down on them, leaving them soaked to the skin. Supplies and equipment rescued from the rampaging mobs were loaded into the box cars, many already crowded with troops seeking a dry place in which to stand or sit if lucky enough. The crowd of civilians milling around the station in hopes of finding an escape route grew each minute as a steady, apparently endless stream, mostly of women and children, arrived.

Upriver at Jefferson City the scenes of chaos and fleeing crowds were repeated. At the Tift Brothers' boatyard the partially completed giant ironclad *Mississippi* stood in silence, abandoned by the men who had been working on her. It was on the *Mississippi* and her sister ship, the *Louisiana,* still tied to the riverbank north of Fort St. Philip, that the Confederate government had pinned its hopes for the defense of New Orleans. Until the forts had been passed by Farragut's ships, Commodore William Whittle, Confederate naval commander of the New Orleans region, had hesitated to take jurisdiction of the ironclad from the Tifts. She had not yet been commissioned into the Confederate Navy, and Whittle believed he lacked the authority to do so, even though several fellow officers had urged that action on him. But now, with Federal ships steaming toward New Orleans, he feared the potentially powerful vessel might fall into enemy hands and be used against the Confederacy, and so he acted.

Without waiting for approval from Richmond, Whittle summoned Commander Arthur Sinclair, who was waiting to take command of the vessel when she was completed. He instructed Sinclair to prepare the *Mississippi* for a run upriver, out of harm's way. But this was not her fate, since the ironclad was not yet able to move under her own power. Whittle then obtained the assistance of two river steamers, the *Peytona* and the *St. Charles*. The two spent the next few hours attempting to pull and push the mighty but helpless ironclad against the river's powerful southbound current, but failed to gain any headway. In great frustration, Sinclair tied her to a nearby dock, and took the *Peytona* downriver to New Orleans in a fruitless search for more steamers.

Meanwhile, the victorious Union squadron steamed upriver. From the various sugar plantations lining the riverbanks, black slaves dropped their tools and converged on the banks, shouting and waving at the ships, welcoming their liberators.

The lead ships of the Federal fleet approached English Turn, about five miles below New Orleans, at ten-thirty in the morning. Flag Officer Farragut expected to have his squadron anchored at New Orleans before the day was over. It was just above here in 1815 that General Andrew Jackson's riflemen, stationed behind large earthworks, had driven off an attack by seasoned British regulars with such terrible results that the battle and its site became nationally honored. Confederate army units had been assigned to virtually the same positions that Jackson's men had occupied, with the hope of repeating Jackson's glorious defense. The earthenwork forts had been enlarged and strengthened, and the two batteries, the Chalmette on the eastern bank and the McGehee on the western, mounted a total of thirteen thirty-two-pounders.

Captain Bailey and the *Cayuga* were far out in front as the Union ships approached English Turn. Farragut had no intelligence concerning these batteries, and so did not know what to expect. As the Union gunboat approached, the batteries appeared to be deserted, encouraging Bailey to continue upriver toward New Orleans. When the *Cayuga* came within range of their guns, Confederate sharpshooters who had been hidden behind the earthworks rose as a single man and opened fire. A barrage from the guns on both sides of the river followed immediately. In a matter of moments the gunboat was struck by fourteen shots, and Bailey decided it was more prudent to fall back than to attempt to battle his way through. Once out of range of the enemy gunners, he waited for the arrival of the larger members of the fleet. The first to arrive on the scene was the *Hartford*, which, in the words of Flag Officer Farragut, gave the two batteries a fire "as they never dreamed of." The *Pensacola* followed quickly behind the flagship, firing volley after volley at the Chalmette battery. Behind her came the *Brooklyn*, firing her own loads of grape and shell into the McGehee battery.

The two batteries were manned by militia troops under the command of Brigadier General Martin L. Smith. Equipped with only a small supply of ammunition, their defense was more symbolic than actual. Neither Smith nor his men expected to halt the enemy's advance upriver. When they ran out of ammunition, and could do nothing but stay hidden from the terrible firing of the great ships' guns, Smith ordered them to withdraw. The battle lasted less than twenty minutes.

Union sailors and marines cheered as they watched the enemy gunners and riflemen flee their guns and disappear into the nearby woods. The ships of the fleet resumed their positions and continued their voyage up the river.

At New Orleans, thousands of anxious and angry people crowded along the wharves. They listened intently as the battle at English Turn took place. When the guns stopped firing, they knew that the enemy fleet was almost within sight. All eyes were on Slaughter Point, a short distance downriver, where the Mississippi made a sharp turn. It would be there that the Union ships would first appear. Many stood with tears running down their cheeks, caused by both the impending loss of their beloved city and the pall of black smoke that hung over the entire area from the burning cotton and vessels. Suddenly the cry went up, "There they are!"

It was a few minutes after noon when the citizens of New Orleans could make out the tops of the masts of the larger enemy ships above the tree line of Slaughter Point. A great cry of anguish arose as the first of the ships came into view. It was the swift gunboat *Cayuga*, with the Stars and Stripes proudly snapping in the breeze.

From the deck of the *Hartford*, Flag Officer Farragut looked out on a "scene of desolation, ships, steamers, cotton, coal, etc., were all in one common blaze." He later wrote to his wife and son that he had never witnessed such vandalism as the destruction of property he saw at New Orleans. A dark cloud of smoke covered the river and most of the city, undiminished by a drizzling rain that had begun a few minutes earlier.

In a dramatic moment that struck even deeper into the hearts of those watching from the shore, the ironclad *Mississippi*, that great hope of the people and the government for New Orleans's defense, suddenly appeared in the river above the city. She was moving at a rapid pace, and almost drew a cheer from the crowds before they noticed the flames and smoke pouring from her gun ports. The giant ironclad floated harmlessly past the Union ships as they dropped anchor off the city. Unable to move her north to safety, Commander Sinclair had ordered her put to the torch.

As the angry crowds shouted and jeered the ships, some waving rifles stolen from government stores, Farragut issued an order decreeing eleven o'clock the following morning as the hour at which the officers and men of his fleet "would return thanks to Almighty God for His great goodness and mercy in permitting us to pass through the events of the last two days with so little loss of life and blood."

Within an hour of dropping anchor, Farragut sent Captain Bailey, along with Lieutenant Perkins of the *Cayuga*, to demand the surrender of the city. The two were taken ashore in one of the steamer's oar boats, landing at the wharf normally reserved for the river packet that in peaceful times traveled north to Memphis. When the two naval officers disembarked, they were greeted by a jeering, threatening mob. Shouts of "Hang them!" "Hurrah for Jeff Davis!" "Shoot them!" "Kill them!" roared from the crowd, where it appeared every third hand waved a weapon. Large and small Confederate flags were waved in their faces, as were cocked pistols. Bailey asked directions to City Hall, but no one would respond, until one man finally recognized the fruitlessness of keeping the two officers on the wharf, and gave them directions.

As Bailey and Perkins began their fateful walk toward City Hall, "the mob followed us in a very excited state," Perkins later wrote. "They gave three cheers for Jeff Davis and Beauregard, and three groans for Lincoln. Then they began to throw things at us, and shout: 'Hang them! Hang them! Hang them!'"

A young New Orleans citizen, George Washington Cable, later described the scene. "Two officers of the United States Navy were

Admiral Farragut and other officers on the deck of the USS *Hartford*. Courtesy of the Library of Congress.

walking abreast, unguarded and alone, not looking to the right or left, never frowning, never flinching, while the mob screamed in their ears, brandished pistols in their faces, cursed, crowded, and gnashed upon them. So through the gates of death those two men walked to the City Hall to demand the town's surrender. It was one of the bravest deeds I ever saw done."

Finally arriving at City Hall, Bailey and Perkins found Mayor Monroe and a group of New Orleans's most influential and powerful citizens assembled in the Common Council meeting room. On being introduced to the mayor, Bailey informed him, "I have been sent by Captain Farragut, commanding the United States fleet, to demand the surrender of the city, and the elevation of the flag of the United States over the Customs House, Mint, Post Office, and City Hall."

There was some brief quibbling over Bailey's credentials, to which the naval officer responded by listing the fleet's victories as it steamed upriver to the city. Bailey said this string of victories provided all the credentials he required. Monroe was less than satisfied by Bailey's response, but saw that it was all he was going to get. He explained that the city was, and had been for some time, under martial law, and that therefore he did not have the legal authority to surrender the city. Instead he asked the two officers to wait while he sent a messenger to General Lovell, asking him to join them. During the half hour it took for Lovell to arrive, Bailey commented on the destruction he had witnessed after arriving in the city, regretting that it had taken place. Monroe's sullen reply was that it was no one's business other than that of the people of New Orleans.

Outside the building, the mob had grown in both size and ferocity. Some even displayed their anger by kicking at the locked door of the council room itself. Suddenly a loud cheer arose, followed by the clatter of horses' hooves on the pavement, announcing the arrival of General Lovell. The general entered the room and shook hands with Bailey and Perkins. Captain Bailey restated Flag Officer Farragut's demand for the city's surrender. Lovell told Bailey he would not surrender, and went on to explain that he had withdrawn his troops from the city. Then, with a bit more grandiosity than the occasion called for, he declared that if the Union navy wished to shell a city filled with women and children, he could not prevent them. Bailey responded that Farragut had no intention of doing such a thing, that he expected the city to be surrendered peacefully. Lovell stated that he felt the withdrawal of his troops returned control of the city to the civilian officials, leaving him without the authority to surrender it to Farragut. No one, it seemed, wanted to be responsible for the surrender of New Orleans.

Upset over the evasiveness of both the mayor and the general, Captain Bailey realized there was little more he could accomplish. He asked Lovell if he could arrange a safe passage for himself and Lieutenant Perkins, since the mob outside appeared more violent than ever. Lovell, who soon after departed the city himself to catch the last troop train to Jackson, Mississippi, said he would. Two Confederate Army officers who had accompanied General Lovell slipped the Union naval officers out through a rear door, and returned them by closed coach to the wharf where their boat was waiting. Upon arriving at the wharf, the two army officers had to draw their swords to force a way through the throng that had remained to hurl abuse on the Union sailors who were waiting with their boat for Bailey's return. Bailey shook hands with both men and thanked them for their help.

As jeers and threats were flung at them, Bailey and Perkins boarded the small boat and returned to the fleet.

Bailey reported what had happened to Farragut, who sent several of the civilian river steamboats that had escaped the torches of the mobs to Quarantine Point to pick up General Butler and his troops to prepare for the inevitable occupation of New Orleans. Farragut decided to give the city officials some time in which to come to terms with their fate. During the early evening the side-wheeler *Mississippi* moved in close to the city and its band struck up "The Star-Spangled Banner." A group of mostly women and children standing near the wharf waved and cheered as the music filled the still evening air. Suddenly a group of mounted men appeared from behind some warehouses and rode down on them, firing wildly into the crowd of civilians. The *Richmond*, anchored nearby, recorded the incident in its log, stating that the ship's officers had considered firing a volley of grape at the horsemen, but decided against it for fear of the innocent lives it might take.

As night closed in on the fleet, with fires still burning at various places along both shores, Farragut issued orders that each ship's armory be opened, and that every man be given a cutlass and a revolver to fight off anyone attempting to board. The afternoon New Orleans newspapers had carried announcements calling for volunteers to band together and board the enemy ships in the river during the night "to save our homes and families from destruction and the tyrannical rule of the Northern vandals." Because most of the young and strong men of the city were already off somewhere else fighting in the Confederate Army, few responded to the call, and the plan was aborted. There were no recorded attempts to board any of the Union vessels.

Early the next morning a rowboat approached the *Hartford*, with a messenger from Mayor Monroe. The man turned out to be an old friend of Farragut, Marion A. Baker, whom he greeted warmly. Baker brought word that the Common Council would consider his surrender demand at a meeting set for ten o'clock that morning. Secure in the knowledge that he was master of the situation, Farragut agreed to wait for the council meeting. With New Orleans almost completely surrounded by water and virtually impassable swamps, Farragut knew the city was his to take at any time. Lacking enough armed men to secure what he could take, he had little choice but to wait for the city officials to surrender, or for General Butler's troops to arrive to force the capitulation. The city was incapable of holding out against the combined power of the fleet and Butler's army. The destruction caused by the mobs had reduced its food supplies to a few days' worth, and the only nearby potential military threat was rushing away on the railroad line to Jackson, Mississippi. The officials in New Orleans might continue trying to avoid responsibility for the city's surrender, but it was only a matter of a short time before they had no choice but to capitulate. Because he was a patient man who had no desire to destroy New Orleans through a naval bombardment, Farragut would wait.

Farragut's assessment of the situation in the city was correct. No one of any position wanted to be branded forever as the man who had surrendered New Orleans to the enemy. Mayor Monroe asked the Common Council for its advice. He told the council members that in his opinion he lacked the power "to perform a military act such as surrender of the city to a hostile force." His position was that the city was incapable of mounting any resistance to the enemy's occupation and could only yield to the superior strength of the fleet, but that it be made clear to Farragut "that we maintain our allegiance to the Government of the Confederate States."

When Marion Baker departed the *Hartford*, he brought back with him the first of what became a series of communications between Flag Officer Farragut and Mayor Monroe. After briefly recounting the meeting between Bailey and Monroe, Farragut explained his position and his demands: "It must occur to your honor that it is not within the province of a naval officer to assume the duties of a military commandant. I came here to reduce New Orleans to obedience to the laws of, and to vindicate the offended majesty of the Government of, the United States. The rights of persons and property shall be secure. I therefore demand of you, as its representative, the unqualified surrender of the city, and that the emblem of sovereignty of the United States be hoisted over the City Hall, Mint, and Custom House by meridian this day, and that all flags and other emblems of sovereignty other than those of the United States shall be removed from all the public buildings by that hour."

Farragut then placed the onus of responsibility for controlling the populace squarely on the mayor's shoulders. "I particularly request that you shall exercise your authority to quell disturbances, restore order, and call upon all the good people of New Orleans to return at once to their vocations; and I particularly demand that no persons shall be molested in person or property for professing sentiments of loyalty to their Government. I shall speedily and severely punish any person or persons who shall commit such outrages as were witnessed yesterday—armed men firing upon helpless women and children for giving expression to their pleasure at witnessing the old flag."

In this first written communication between the two, Farragut made it clear that as long as his fleet had the power to prevent it, "no flag but that of the United States" would be allowed to fly in its presence. Since doing so could result in bloodshed, he asked Monroe to give this order the widest possible circulation among the population of the city.

Later that morning, just before the scheduled meeting of the Common Council, Farragut sent another message to the city's leaders. This time it was delivered by Lieutenant Albert Kautz and Midshipman John Read. The two were accompanied by a squad of marines. When the party landed, they were greeted by an angry mob similar to the one that had threatened Bailey and Perkins the day before. The presence of the heavily armed marines aroused the rabble that had been hanging around the wharf yelling insults at the Union ships anchored in the river. A member of the City Guard, which the mayor had deputized in an attempt to bring order to his streets, persuaded Kautz to leave all but one marine behind, and proceed to the City Hall under his protection with a flag of truce. The naval officer followed his advice, and delivered Farragut's letter. In it the flag officer restated his demand that all flags be removed from public buildings, and be replaced by the flag of the United States.

Following the Common Council's meeting on the morning of April 26, Mayor Monroe sent Farragut a long, rambling response to his earlier communiqués. In it he told Farragut that General Lovell had returned control of the city to civilian authorities, that the city had no military means to defend itself from the enemy's ships, and that he possessed no authority to either defend or surrender New Orleans. "To surrender such a place (the undefended city) were an idle and unmeaning ceremony," wrote Monroe. "The city is yours by the power of brutal force, and not by any choice or consent of its inhabitants." Monroe must have recognized that without troops in sufficient quantity, Farragut was unable to take actual possession of the city. Until those troops arrived, he would continue to be not uncooperative, but certainly less than completely cooperative with the enemy commander.

As to the matter of raising the U.S. flag on public buildings, Monroe used less deception to camouflage his position when he wrote, "the man lives not in our midst whose hand and heart would not be palsied at the mere thought of such an act, nor could I find in my entire constituency so wretched and desperate a renegade as would dare to profane with his hand the sacred emblem of our aspirations [i.e., the Confederate flag]."

Farragut was a patient man, and he recognized following the first communication with the city's mayor that local officials were going to take whatever actions they could to delay the Union occupation. For his part, the naval officer could do little other than bombard the city from his ships, something he was loath to do. He did not have enough men, either sailors or marines, to invade and occupy the city; that was a job for thousands of well-armed troops. The Union commander had no reliable intelligence concerning the presence of Confederate or state troops, other than the word of General Lovell that he had withdrawn those under his command. Obviously, from the experience of his envoys, the people—at least those thronging the waterfront and nearby streets each day—were armed and likely to retaliate should he attempt to put numbers of armed men ashore. New Orleans was his, but until the city's officials surrendered and ordered its populace not to engage in any resistance, he could do little but wait for General Butler's troops to arrive.

Unable to take more concerted action against the city and its recalcitrant officials, Farragut decided the time had come for him to let them know that the United States government was now in de facto control of New Orleans, whether they cooperated with him or continued on their unproductive path. He instructed Captain Morris of the *Pensacola* to take two boatloads of his marines into the city, take possession of the U.S. Mint located there, and hoist the United States flag from the building's rooftop flagpole. Ignoring the howling mob, Morris and his well-armed marines accomplished their task with little real difficulty and returned to their ship. Farragut knew that was the easier part of showing that the city now belonged to the national government; it would be much more difficult to keep the flag flying.

Without enough armed men to guard the building and protect its flag, Farragut was forced to leave the emblem of the nation for which he fought to its fate. He did, however, station several sharpshooters and two howitzers in positions aboard the *Pensacola* so they could fire on anyone attempting to lower the flag.

Shortly before noon, as the crews of the Federal fleet took part in the prayerful services decreed by Farragut, they were suddenly jolted by the firing of one of those howitzers. A party of men had made its way to the roof of the mint building, and were lowering the U.S. flag from its staff. The guard fired the gun at them with a load of grape, but the distance and the speed of the rebels resulted in no one being killed or wounded. The flag was brought into the street, where the frenzied mob tore it to shreds. The leader of the party was a local gambler and rabble-rouser named William Mumford. Following the occupation of the city by Union forces, General Butler would order Mumford arrested for his crime. In June he was executed as an example to others who continued to voice their Confederate sentiments. To ensure that no one failed to understand what Mumford's crime was, Butler ordered him hanged from a window of the same mint building from which he had torn down the United States flag. Thousands watched in helpless frustration as the execution took place. It was one of several incidents that led to Butler being called "the Beast of New Orleans."

His patience running out, Farragut decided to take additional action to further weaken the Confederacy's hold on New Orleans and the Mississippi River. He was getting bored waiting either for the city to capitulate, or the army troops to arrive to allow him to silence the arrogant Mayor Monroe. He was anxious to return civility to the streets of the city in which he had spent his own childhood. Fortunately, the situation in the city was improving. Monroe had turned to the European Brigade, composed of New Orleans residents who were citizens of France, Spain, Germany, Italy, and Portugal, for help. He requested its commanding officer, Brigadier General Paul Juge Jr., to order the brigade to patrol the city's streets in an effort to reduce the lawlessness that had been running rampant. A 9:00 P.M. curfew was put into effect, and strictly enforced by Juge's gaudily uniformed soldiers.

Late that afternoon, April 26, Farragut sailed up the river with intentions to attack and destroy the Confederate batteries at Carrollton, located about eight miles north of New Orleans. Accompanying the *Hartford* were the *Richmond*, the *Pensacola*, the *Brooklyn*, and the *Oneida*. Arriving there prepared for battle, the flag officer found the long line of earthworks deserted, and the battery's cannons spiked by the withdrawing Confederate soldiers, who lacked transport sufficient to take their guns with them.

Farragut returned to New Orleans the following morning, just before the Confederate gunboat *McRae*, which had performed so bravely against the Union fleet, arrived flying a flag of truce. She was escorted by one of the gunboats Farragut had left at Quarantine Point. On the *McRae* were the seriously wounded soldiers that had been evacuated from Forts Jackson and St. Philip during a truce arranged by General Duncan and Commander Porter.

While Farragut was conducting the frustrating negotiations with Mayor Monroe, General Duncan continued his efforts to get the *Louisiana* moved to a position between the two forts in order to work more closely with the batteries of both forts, should additional enemy vessels attempt to force their way through the river obstruction. The floating battery could also serve to protect the forts, most of whose guns faced downriver, from attack by the Union ships and gunboats located upstream. Commander Mitchell agreed to move the ironclad, but was unable to do so since she lacked the ability to move under her own steam, and there were not enough Confederate gunboats left afloat after the earlier fight against Farragut's fleet to accomplish the task. The last great hope of New Orleans remained where she was, unable to do anything to protect the city or the forts.

Later, in a report concerning the status of the forts at the time, General Duncan wrote, "At daylight [of April 27] the steamer which had been observed the day before working her way up in the back bays was in view, immediately in the rear of Fort St. Philip, and near the mouth of Fort Bayou. A frigate and five other vessels were also in sight towards Bird Island, one of which was seen working her way up the bay. From ten to thirteen launches were visible near the bayou back of Fort St. Philip, by means of which troops were being landed at the Quarantine above us."

At noon that same day Commander Porter sent one of his gunboats, under a flag of truce, to the forts. For the second time he demanded their surrender. Once again the demand was refused, but this time the soldiers of the garrisons were aware that their situation had taken a dramatic change for the worse. Enemy vessels controlled the river north and south of the forts, enemy troops had landed behind one fort and quite possibly also behind the other, and no word had been received concerning the fate of New Orleans. Several couriers sent to the city had never returned. As rumors that the city had been taken by the enemy spread among the soldiers, their mood became one of subdued obedience to their officers. Gone was the "cheerful, confident, and courageous" enthusiasm Duncan had noted in earlier reports.

At midnight a large number of the garrison of Fort Jackson revolted. Officers and soldiers who remained loyal were disarmed and the fort's guns were spiked, except for those protecting the gates, which were reversed to face the fort's interior. Seeing no way of regaining the loyalty of the men who had joined the revolt, many of whom had demonstrated their personal bravery during the mortar bombardment, Duncan decided it was best to allow those who wished to leave the fort to do so peacefully. More than 250 men, roughly half the garrison, departed with their firearms. Many made their way to the Federal pickets stationed around Quarantine Point, where they surrendered themselves. Every company save one, the St. Mary's Cannoneers, lost men to the mutiny.

When the mutineers had left, Duncan quickly saw "that there was no further fight in the men remaining behind; that they were completely demoralized, and that no faith or reliance would be placed in the broken detachments of companies left in the fort." He prepared himself for the inevitable surrender.

General Duncan's position was untenable, as he later described in his report. "With the enemy above and below us, it will be apparent at once to any one at all familiar with the surrounding country that there was no chance of destroying the public property, blowing up the forts, and escaping with the remaining troops. Under all these humiliating circumstances there seemed to be but one course open to us": surrender. Following a hurried meeting with officers from Fort St. Philip, where no mutiny had yet taken place, but where the garrison had also fallen into a state of gloom and despair, it was decided to send word to the enemy gunboats below the forts with a written acceptance of the terms of surrender that had been offered on the twenty-sixth.

Once terms had been accepted, it would have been illegal for any officer to destroy weapons or equipment. Commander Mitchell was determined that the *Louisiana* not fall into enemy hands; therefore the surrender was made on behalf of the army forces occupying the forts and the water batteries, not the remnants of the naval forces gathered around the big ironclad. The document sent by Duncan to Porter stated specifically that the officer accepting the terms of surrender offered by Porter has "no control over the vessels afloat." Since the ironclad was immobile, Mitchell saw that his only course of action was to destroy her. He met with the officers of the *Louisiana,* and they all concurred that no alternative was available to them except to set her ablaze. They immediately began preparations to do so.

When Porter received the message from Duncan, he steamed upriver in his flagship, *Harriet Lane,* to accept the surrender of the forts. He was accompanied by the gunboats *Westfield, Kennebec,* and *Winona,* all flying the white flag of truce. On the morning of the twenty-eighth, Duncan, accompanied by Lieutenant Colonel Edward Higgins, who was actual commander of Fort Jackson under the overall command of General Duncan, boarded the *Harriet Lane* to formalize the surrender. During the solemn ceremony, Porter asked Duncan where the naval commander was. Duncan reminded Porter of his comment in the surrender acceptance that he did not command the naval forces, and therefore could not surrender on their behalf. As the hands of the clock on the wall of the cabin in which this discussion was taking place approached 11:00 A.M., an officer entered the cabin and informed Porter that the *Louisiana* was ablaze, that the ropes holding her to the shore had burned, and she was drifting downriver. Porter asked Duncan if the ironclad's guns were loaded and her magazine full, to which Duncan responded that he assumed so, but had no direct knowledge concerning the vessel.

The surrender negotiations continued as the huge, burning floating battery picked up speed in her downriver rush. The *Louisiana*'s guns fired in all directions at once as they became overheated by the inferno. Suddenly, as she came abreast of Fort St. Philip, her magazine exploded, sending shells and shrapnel high into the air. The deadly missiles rained down on the fort, where one Confederate officer was killed and several others wounded. The loss of the iron-clad, which he had hoped to capture, enraged Porter, who railed against Mitchell and the other Confederate naval officers. Porter later came under criticism for wording the surrender document so it read that the forts had surrendered to his mortar flotilla, and not to Farragut's squadron, of which the mortar flotilla was a part.

At 4:00 P.M., General Duncan and the other officers and men remaining in Fort Jackson were loaded into two Federal gunboats and taken to New Orleans, where they arrived the following day under parole. They were allowed to keep their sidearms, and the Confederate flag was not removed from the fort and replaced by the United States flag until they were out of sight. The following day, the officers and men of Fort St. Philip were likewise sent upriver to New Orleans.

Early on the morning of the twenty-ninth, before word of the surrender of the forts reached him, Farragut sent a final message to Mayor Monroe, giving him forty-eight hours in which to remove all Confederate and state flags or "the fire of this fleet may be drawn down upon the city at any moment." In those forty-eight hours, all women, children, and other noncombatants, including employees of the various foreign consulates, were to be evacuated from the city. Farragut backed up his demand by sending Captain Bell ashore with detachments of sailors and marines, all armed, along with two howitzers, to remove the Confederate flags from the mint, the post office, and the customs house, and replace them with the flag of the United States. Bell was also told to remove the Louisiana flag from City Hall, but not to replace it, because it was not the property of the Federal government. Bell carried out his assignment with no interference from the mobs, in part because the loaded howitzers remained aimed at them during the exchange of the flags.

When the captured Confederate officers and men formerly of Fort Jackson arrived, a great cheer arose from the sailors and marines on the decks of the anchored warships. In contrast, a sullen silence fell over the citizens who watched as the men came ashore. General Duncan quickly made his way to City Hall to inform the authorities that the forts had fallen, and could no longer be counted on to prevent additional enemy ships from coming upriver to resupply Farragut's fleet.

David G. Farragut shortly after his promotion to rear admiral, July 1862. This photo was taken by E. Jacobs of New Orleans. Courtesy of the Nimitz Library, U.S. Naval Academy.

On May 1, General Butler arrived aboard the *Mississippi*, which Farragut had sent to Quarantine Point to fetch him. His troops landed in the city, and formal occupation of New Orleans was established.

The fall of New Orleans was a devastating blow to the Confederacy. It not only denied this important center of commerce to the rebel government, but struck a blow at Southern morale from which the people of the South never recovered. In her much-quoted diary, Mary Boykin Chesnut noted, "New Orleans is gone, and with it the

Confederacy!" Her reaction was universal throughout not only the Confederacy, but also, and perhaps more important, in Europe, where Napoleon III was threatening to break the blockade of the Gulf ports if the Confederacy would support his claims on Mexico, and in England, where the loss of New Orleans was seen as the beginning of the end, even by the Confederacy's most ardent supporters in Parliament and at Queen Victoria's court. Because of the fall of New Orleans, Europeans now viewed the Confederate cause as lost.

Farragut's success proved he had been correct about the forts. Mortars could not reduce them, as inspections by army engineers proved following their capitulation. General Butler said both forts were "substantially as defensible as before the bombardment began." Lieutenant Godfrey Weitzel of the Engineer Corps found both forts as strong after the thousands of mortars had fallen on them as they had been before the first shell was fired. Despite protests from Porter, who attempted to claim the victory for himself, the forts had fallen because the powerful Union fleet had passed them and isolated them from the rest of the Confederacy, especially New Orleans. This isolation had made both forts irrelevant, and spelled their doom as no mortar shells could have done. David Farragut alone, among almost all navy and army officers and government officials, had recognized the effect his running the forts would have on them and on New Orleans.

For some inexplicable reason, most of the first Northern newspaper reports of the passing of the forts and the capture of New Orleans failed to mention Flag Officer Farragut. Those few that did include his name did so only in passing. The credit for the success at the forts was at first given to Commander David Porter, while the fall of New Orleans was ascribed to General Butler. It took several days, and a reading of news reports in Southern newspapers, before the population of the United States learned that David Farragut had led the triumphant charge of his fleet up the Mississippi River past the mighty forts and conquered New Orleans. A national hero, his name quickly became a household word throughout the country.

5

Running the
Vicksburg Batteries

Flag officer farragut was greatly relieved to turn New Orleans over to General Butler. Butler was by vocation a politician, and, as such, could better deal with the obstructionist tactics of the city's politicians. Besides, Butler had an army of nearly eighteen thousand troops to persuade the rebellious Mayor Monroe and his cohorts to his point of view.

Over one hundred miles of the lower Mississippi River, from its mouth to New Orleans, was now controlled by the Union navy. But that control was tenuous. Rebel soldiers, some in organized bands, others operating independently, regularly fired at Federal vessels from well-concealed points along the shore. They especially favored sharp bends in the river, or rapids, where boats and ships were forced to slow their speed. The smaller Union gunboats were kept busy patrolling the river and returning the fire of the elusive, hidden enemy.

With New Orleans under the control of Butler's army of occupation, Farragut made preparations to move even farther up the Mississippi. A joyful Farragut wrote home, "I am now going up the river to meet Foote—where, I know not—and then I shall resume my duties on the coast, keep moving, and keep up the stampede I have upon them. I have so much to say to my dear wife and boy that it will be the occupation of my declining years, I hope, by the bright fireside of our happy home."

In a more melancholy vein, he told Virginia, "It is a strange thought, that I am here among my relatives, and yet not one has dared to say 'I am happy to see you.'"

Farragut was undecided about his next course of action. His orders from Secretary Welles, dated January 20, 1862, appeared to be explicit enough. They said that if the Union naval expedition led by Flag Officer Andrew Hull Foote, which was moving downriver from Cairo, Illinois, "shall not have descended the river, you will take advantage of the panic to push a strong force up the river to take their defenses [meaning Vicksburg, Mississippi] in the rear. You will also reduce the fortifications which defend Mobile Bay and turn them over to the army to hold."

Welles made it all seem so easy. He appeared to believe that the river approaching Vicksburg from the south would not be strongly defended, and that the Confederate forts overlooking the channel entrance to Mobile Bay would fall at the mere sight of Farragut's damaged fleet and exhausted crews. Farragut's own inclination was to return to the Gulf and sail to Mobile, where he would "put it to them." His uncertainty is revealed in his correspondence, including letters to Welles. In one letter to the navy secretary he wrote that he would be heading upriver to attempt to link up with Foote. Four days later he told Welles he was preparing to sail to Mobile. The second letter caused much consternation in Washington. Welles and Navy Undersecretary Fox felt Mobile could be taken at any time, but that the opportunity of gaining complete control of the Mississippi River was too important for Farragut to withdraw. The confusion over the flag officer's plans was compounded when Captain Bailey arrived in Washington bearing Farragut's report on the passing of the forts and the capture of New Orleans. Bailey also presented Welles with Confederate battle flags taken during these actions.

Anxious for news that the squadron had moved upriver, Fox and Welles asked Bailey how many ships Farragut had sent north. When Bailey replied that none had been sent, which was the case when he left the fleet, Fox became alarmed at this "terrible mistake." But he soon calmed down when word reached him that Farragut had indeed moved upriver. Welles and Fox were impatient to get complete control of the river, because Grant, following his success at Shiloh, was driving Beauregard's Confederate forces westward out of Tennessee. Union control of the river to Memphis would prevent the rebel army from escaping to the relative safety of Arkansas, across the river. There the Confederates would have the time and opportunity to rest and reorganize for a future attack back across the river. As it turned out, Beauregard decided to move his army southward, toward Corinth, Mississippi, so Farragut's move north was not as vital as the Washington navy establishment expected.

On May 1, 1862, the same day that Butler landed his men in New Orleans, Farragut ordered Porter to return to Ship Island with his mortar flotilla. He was to wait there pending instructions to proceed to the Alabama coast to take part in actions against the forts guarding Mobile Bay. Farragut warned him not to undertake any operations against the fortifications himself until the large ships of the squadron arrived. Reports were reaching New Orleans that the Confederate Navy had stationed two large, heavily armed ironclads in Mobile Bay. He feared they could easily destroy Porter's small ships.

Having decided to proceed upriver, Farragut first sent the *Brooklyn* north in company with several gunboats. She was still commanded by Captain Craven, whose personal notes revealed a disdain for Farragut, whom he constantly referred to as "the little man." Craven was instructed to sail to Vicksburg, where he was to shell and attempt to destroy the large railroad center there. Steaming north, the *Brooklyn* passed Baton Rouge without incident, but ran into trouble before reaching its destination. Two of its accompanying gunboats, the *Itasca* and the *Sciota*, suffered engine trouble. Fearful of grounding his ship, which regularly scraped the bottom of the river at various points, Craven decided to turn back. Nearing Baton Rouge again, Craven met Commander S. Philip Lee, aboard the gunboat *Oneida*. He was accompanied by two other gunboats, the *Pinola* and the *Kennebec*. Lee carried new orders for Craven from Farragut. The flag officer had learned that the river above Baton Rouge had reached its highest level and would soon begin to drop, making passage of a large ship dangerous. Concerned that the *Brooklyn* would be grounded and subject to enemy attack, Farragut instructed Craven to go no farther north than Baton Rouge.

Soon afterward, the *Iroquois* arrived with additional orders. The gunboat's commander, James S. Palmer, was instructed by Farragut to capture Baton Rouge, while Lee was ordered to continue north and capture Natchez. Craven was to wait at his anchorage at Tunica Island, north of Baton Rouge, until the flag officer arrived with additional ships.

On the evening of May 7, the *Iroquois* dropped anchor off Baton Rouge harbor, and sent word to the city's officials demanding their surrender. When no satisfactory answer had been received by the following morning, Lee sent an armed party ashore with orders to take possession of the Federal arsenal located in the town. This was done with no resistance from the local inhabitants, who numbered about seven thousand. The flag of the United States was raised on the arsenal, and this sight greeted Farragut when he arrived the following day.

Commander Lee took his own gunboat, the *Oneida*, along with the *Pinola* and the *Kennebec*, to Natchez, sixty miles north of Baton Rouge. On May 13 he captured that town with no resistance. While Baton Rouge and Natchez offered no opposition, the officials at both took the same tack as Mayor Monroe of New Orleans, refusing to surrender formally.

When Farragut, aboard the *Hartford*, arrived off Baton Rouge on May 9, he was pleased to see the United States flag flying from the flagpole atop the arsenal building. Farragut brought with him 1,500 of Butler's troops, under the command of Brigadier General Thomas Williams. In the early morning of May 14, the two steamers that served as army transports, the *Ceres* and the *Burton*, were sent north to Natchez. They were protected by the sloop *Richmond*. The *Brooklyn* and several gunboats had arrived at Natchez a few hours after the city was taken by Lee's small flotilla. With the arrival of the *Brooklyn*, Lee took his gunboats and the two army transports farther upriver to test the mettle of the Confederate forces at Vicksburg. Intelligence concerning that city's defenses was lacking, and no one knew what Lee could expect to confront there.

A few hours after the army transports left Baton Rouge, the *Hartford*, which had been having engine trouble, steamed away from the city and headed north to Natchez. Farragut planned on assembling as many ships as possible for an assault on Vicksburg. A few miles north of Baton Rouge, the *Hartford* ran aground. The crew worked frantically to free her, but the mighty warship remained stuck fast in the mud. Reversing her engines proved fruitless, as did rocking her from side to side, which was accomplished by having the crew run first to one side, then to the other. The failed efforts frustrated Farragut, who knew that the level of the river could drop rapidly at any time. If this happened, his ship might be stuck indefinitely in the river, a standing target for every Confederate soldier and cannoneer along the riverbanks.

The gunboat *Itasca* arrived and added her efforts to those of the *Hartford*, and still the ship refused to move. Farragut sent the gunboat to the nearby river town of St. Francisville, where a ferry and a lighter were docked. The entire day of May 14 was spent transferring the *Hartford*'s coal, guns, and shot to the *Itasca* and the ferry and lighter. It wasn't until ten-thirty the following morning that the *Itasca* was able to pull the *Hartford* free, to the grateful cheers of the sloop's sailors and marines.

While Farragut struggled to free his ship from the Mississippi mud, fifteen hundred miles away in Washington, President Lincoln sent a request to Congress that Farragut be given a vote of thanks for his capture of New Orleans. The vote was not taken for two months, but was the first step leading to Farragut's selection as the first rear admiral in the United States Navy.

In midafternoon of Sunday, May 18, Farragut finally arrived at Natchez, accompanied by the *Itasca*. Awaiting him were the *Brooklyn*, the *Richmond*, and the *Iroquois*. They were all anticipating news from Lee concerning the situation at Vicksburg. When word arrived by way of the gunboat *Kennebec*, which Lee had sent downriver, it was not good. On Sunday afternoon Lee had anchored in the river and sent a small boat toward the city with his demand that Vicksburg be surrendered. The boat was met by a rebel gunboat, which took the communiqué on board and promised to deliver it to the proper authorities.

Unlike New Orleans, Natchez, and Baton Rouge, Vicksburg was a strongly defended city that would not fall easily to the Federal fleet. After retiring from New Orleans to Jackson, General Lovell had sent four thousand veteran Confederate troops to Vicksburg well in advance of the Union progress upriver. The arrival of these men, who were the best Lovell had available, strengthened the determination of the local militia and state forces in the city not to surrender without a fight.

On May 12, Lovell assigned overall command of the defense of Vicksburg to a distinguished and accomplished army engineer, Brigadier General Martin Luther Smith. A graduate of the West Point class of 1842, Smith had overseen the improvements of the fortifications guarding the entrance to New Orleans that had so successfully withstood Porter's mortar bombardment. Smith immediately set about establishing a series of seven batteries along the river south of Vicksburg. Those batteries were manned by experienced artillerymen and boasted twenty-six cannon, and were mounted along a three-mile stretch of bluffs overlooking the river. The bluffs, ranging in height from 150 to over two hundred feet, gave the Confederate guns, which included a variety of rifled and smoothbore cannon, complete command of the river. Their height prevented most naval guns from reaching them, since the latter could not be elevated enough to fire up the bluffs. Ships traveling the river would be subjected to a plunging fire in which shells could pass directly down through a vessel, causing her to sink rapidly.

While he waited for a reply, Lee surveyed the situation around him. He quickly concluded that the guns mounted on the high bluffs, combined with the speed of the river's current, made passing Vicksburg extremely difficult if not impossible. The river was running at about three knots, while the ships could make no more than eight knots. Above the city, the river makes a sharp U-turn before turning again and continuing north. Ships approaching this turn would be forced to slow down, especially the larger sloops, which would make them nearly stable targets for the rebel gunners. While the ships struggled against the current, enemy guns would be raining shells down on them from relative safety. Lee was not at all enthusiastic about attempting to pass the Vicksburg batteries with anything approaching the luck the fleet had below New Orleans.

By the time the sun set along the western shore, Lee had received three replies to his surrender demand. Vicksburg's mayor, Laz Lindsay, asserted that the city's residents would never permit him to surrender. Brigadier General Smith, who commanded most of the troops defending Vicksburg, wrote simply, "Having been ordered to hold these defenses, it is my intention to do so." The most flamboyant reply came from Colonel James L. Autrey, military governor of the district. "Mississippians don't know, and refuse to learn how to surrender," Autrey wrote. "If Commodore Farragut or Brigadier General Butler can teach them, let them come and try."

Lee knew he was outgunned, but decided to test the resolve of Vicksburg's defenders anyway. He sent Mayor Lindsay a message in which he said his gunboats would shell the city if it did not surrender within twenty-four hours. He warned Lindsay to evacuate the city's women and children to a place of safety. Lee received no reply to his threat. Indeed, the twenty-four hours came and went without any guns firing. The citizens of Vicksburg waited patiently, most of them taking refuge in their basements, but the roar of cannons did not disturb the peace.

His bluff having been called, Lee waited for reinforcements from downriver. On May 20, Farragut arrived aboard the gunboat *Kennebec* for a personal inspection of the situation. The remainder of his fleet was ordered to assemble at Grand Gulf, fifty miles south of Vicksburg. Farragut quickly recognized the futility of trying to run the Vicksburg batteries as he had the New Orleans forts. With batteries positioned both south and north of the city, and taking the current into consideration, he estimated it would take a ship about fifty-five minutes to travel from below the southernmost battery to a point beyond the range of the northernmost battery. And most of this time it would be subject to fierce bombardment from the shore batteries, including several at the level of the river and those on the bluffs high above.

Farragut asked Brigadier General Williams if he thought his detachment of 1,500 men could successfully assault the city or any of its fortifications. Williams had received erroneous intelligence that the city was garrisoned by eight thousand soldiers, and that another ten thousand were near enough to be rushed to support them, should a Union landing be attempted. He told Farragut he could do nothing in the face of such odds. The position Williams took was totally defensible, even if he had had the correct figures concerning the city's defenders, who numbered well in excess of four thousand men. The odds against a successful landing were overwhelming, and once ashore, his men would be badly outnumbered by an enemy infinitely more knowledgeable about the terrain.

Farragut, who was at Vicksburg against his own better judgment, decided there was little he could do against this rebel stronghold at the time. His ships were in dire need of repair, his guns could not reach the batteries on the bluffs, he did not have enough army troops to attempt a landing, and he was running dangerously low of supplies, including coal to fuel his steam engines. He was now four hundred miles north of New Orleans, the closest place that could serve as a repair and refueling depot. In addition to these difficulties, the river was beginning its annual decline, having earlier been at its highest point in years. He decided to return to New Orleans, and await the outcome of the approaching battle at Corinth, Mississippi. Having withdrawn from Tennessee, General Beauregard had selected this small town near the Tennessee/Mississippi border as the place he would take a stand against the invading Union army commanded by General Henry Halleck. The result of this battle could decide whether additional rebel troops would be available to reinforce those defending Vicksburg, or whether Union troops could be sent to attack it.

War news from the east was mixed. The Army of the Potomac was only eight miles from Richmond, but seemed unable to capture the rebel capital. A dark cloud, in the form of a sixteen-thousand-man Confederate army led by Generals Thomas J. "Stonewall" Jackson and Richard S. Ewell, began a long, successful sweep up the Luray Valley area of the Shenandoah, leading toward a victorious battle at Front Royal, Virginia, on May 23 against forces commanded by General Nathaniel Banks.

On May 23, Farragut joined the *Hartford* and the other ships of his fleet at Grand Gulf. He left six boats behind at Vicksburg to conduct a blockade of the river south of the city. Remaining at Vicksburg were the corvettes *Oneida* and *Iroquois* and the gunboats *Sciota*, *Winona*, *Katahdin*, and *Wissahickon*.

Within a few hours of returning to his fleet, Farragut decided that he should make at least one attempt to force Vicksburg to submit before returning to New Orleans. At four o'clock the following afternoon, May 24, the fleet dropped anchor four miles south of the first Vicksburg batteries. After several reconnaissances during the next two days, Farragut, who had fallen ill with one of the many river-related fevers that were plaguing his crews, ordered a limited shelling of the town. The Union commanders were surprised when the batteries on the bluffs failed to return fire. Actually, the Confederate artillery commanders were waiting for an attempted landing before beginning their devastating fire. The landing never took place, and the fleet, its commanders satisfied that they could accomplish nothing without a strong army to attack the city and the batteries from the rear, withdrew downriver.

At Grand Gulf the ships were attacked by several light batteries hidden along the riverbanks on both sides. The troop transport *Laurel Hill* suffered heavy shelling, and several of the shells damaged her boilers, disabling them. Unable to maintain power, she drifted helplessly down with the current. On board, dozens of soldiers had been killed or badly wounded. Captain Craven, aboard the *Brooklyn*, returned the fire, aided by several gunboats. The town itself was shelled, at a cost of much damage and several lives.

When the fleet reached Baton Rouge, Farragut was annoyed to see that the United States flag that had been flying over the city's arsenal had been removed. After dropping anchor, the *Hartford*'s chief engineer, James B. Kimball, went ashore with several sailors in search of a laundress to do his laundry. Before the boat could land, a group of mounted men arrived and opened fire from the shore. Kimball and two other sailors were wounded in the attack. In retaliation, Farragut ordered the *Hartford* and the *Kennebec* to shell the town. The firing did considerable damage, and continued until a group of citizens appeared in a rowboat, waving a white flag. They told Farragut that the shooting had not been the work of local people, but of guerrillas over whom local officials had no control. The city's mayor pleaded with Farragut, who was in a towering rage over the wounding of his men. He claimed no resistance would be offered by Baton Rouge if the flag officer would only halt the shelling. Farragut, by now disgusted with the chicanery of Southern mayors, roared at the cowering officials that if another attack against his ships or men occurred, he would order his entire fleet to level the city, town, or plantation from which the offending shots were fired. Before continuing down the river to New Orleans, Farragut put General Williams's troops ashore to occupy the town, and left two gunboats behind in support.

Upon arriving back at New Orleans on May 30, Farragut found messages from Welles and Fox waiting for him. He was surprised by their contents. Following congratulations on taking the forts and New Orleans were rebuffs for not doing the same at Vicksburg and for not continuing upriver to Memphis, where he could link with the Western Flotilla, commanded by Flag Officer Charles H. Davis. Davis had replaced Foote, who was suffering from the effects of a wound that refused to heal. The flotilla was comprised mostly of ironclad gunboats that had acquitted themselves well as they fought down the river, finally destroying a large Confederate gunboat force and capturing Memphis.

Farragut was irritated by the way in which Welles and Fox assumed that his fleet of mostly oceangoing ships could steam up the Mississippi River with such ease. He wrote both the secretary and the undersecretary of his need for additional ships, the extensive repairs required on the ships he had with him, his concern over neglect of the ships remaining in the Gulf on blockade duty, his constant shortage of supplies, and the fact that the enlistments of half his crews had expired and the men were clamoring to go home. His greatest concern, however, was the falling level of the river. He told Welles he feared that if he returned upriver, especially if he went as far as Memphis, which is four hundred miles north of Vicksburg, his ships would not be able to descend the river until the following spring, "if at all." He pleaded with Fox for an ironclad of the *Monitor* type, which, he wrote, was "worth all the gunboats in the river."

Farragut was also concerned for the safety of the gunboats he had left on duty near Vicksburg. Although they were out of range of the enemy's guns along the bluffs, and could hold their own against rebel gunboats, he feared something far more dangerous. Hidden away in the Yazoo River, near Vicksburg, was a new Confederate ironclad ram, CSS *Arkansas*. One hundred sixty-five feet long and thirty-five feet wide, the twin-screw gunboat was still in the final stages of construction, but rumors about her had reached the Union fleets on both ends of the river. She was known to have ten guns and a crew of two hundred men. No one in the Union camp knew when she might suddenly appear, but all eyes were on the alert for what was expected to be a dreadful vessel, and all ears listened for the cry "The *Arkansas* is coming!" Farragut knew his gunboats would be no match for the rebel ironclad, and wanted to order them to join him at New Orleans.

Washington would have none of what some saw as Farragut's timidity. Notwithstanding the condition of his ships, or his supply problems, he was to return to Vicksburg and close the river to enemy traffic.

To his wife, Virginia, he wrote, "They will keep us in this river until the vessels break down and all the little reputation we have made is evaporated. They expect me to navigate the Mississippi nine hundred miles in the face of batteries, ironclad rams, etc. They expect impossibilities." He failed to see any real value in the Navy Department requiring that he endanger his ships and men on a foolish venture. His own opinion was that Mobile was the next most important target for his energies. Welles and Fox, apparently standing by an earlier plan for the linking of the two river fleets regardless of the conditions in the river, disagreed. A reluctant Farragut made preparations to return upriver to Vicksburg.

In the predawn hours of June 8, Flag Officer Farragut once again got his fleet under way, steaming upriver instead of down, as he would have liked. Along with the flagship *Hartford*, the fleet included the *Brooklyn*, the *Richmond*, the gunboat *Pinola*, several army transports, and sixteen mortar boats along with their accompanying gunboats. Porter, anxious not to be left out this time when a large city was captured, used the gunboat *Octorara* as his flagship. General Butler, probably seeing there was no glory to be gained at Vicksburg, decided to stay in New Orleans. Instead he sent three thousand troops along to join the command of General Williams, who was to leave a strong garrison at Baton Rouge and take command of the troops to be used against Vicksburg.

Along the way the larger ships had the usual problems of groundings, including the *Hartford*, which was stuck in the mud for nearly twenty-four hours. "It is a sad thing to think of having your ship in a mud bank," wrote the obviously despondent Farragut, "five hundred miles from the natural element of a sailor." The flag officer had much to be despondent about. He had already been to Vicksburg, and although he considered that he might be able to run the batteries surrounding the city, he would then be stuck upriver. The Vicksburg batteries would be between him and his line of supplies. Unlike the forts in the lower Mississippi, these batteries would not be isolated and forced to surrender until a powerful Union army attacked and captured Vicksburg. He saw this voyage as a futile and costly exercise. His fleet had lost more anchors and he had seen more vessels damaged than he had witnessed in his many decades at sea. Fighting in this river was much more difficult than the bureaucrats in Washington imagined. "The elements of destruction in this river are beyond anything I ever encountered," he wrote Welles, but to no avail.

Finally, after a long and tedious journey, struggling against the current and the declining water level, the Union fleet anchored near Warrenton, Mississippi, seven miles below Vicksburg. All ships were at the anchorage by late morning of June 25. When he arrived, Farragut had hoped to receive word that Davis's fleet was at anchor north of Vicksburg. He was disappointed to learn that no Union vessels could be seen upriver. This meant he would have to attempt to pass the batteries without the additional firepower of the Western Flotilla.

It was at this point that a courageous and irrepressible United States Army officer named Lieutenant Colonel Alfred Ellet entered the scene. Alfred was the younger brother of Colonel Charles Ellet. Charles was a highly talented engineer who had been responsible for the construction of numerous bridges, including the 1,010-foot bridge spanning the Wheeling and Ohio rivers, the longest suspension bridge in the world at the time. Charles Ellet had developed the concept of using steam-driven vessels as rams against large ships, but failed to find support for idea. During the Crimean War he traveled to Sebastopol and attempted to convince the Russian navy that steam-powered rams could break the Allied blockade of that city. The Russians turned him away, as did a series of American secretaries of war, until the Confederate ironclad ram *Virginia* sailed into Hampton Roads, Virginia, on March 8, 1862, and successfully attacked and sank two Federal warships by ramming them.

After witnessing the great potential of the steam-powered ram, the War Department commissioned Ellet to build a fleet of them for use against Confederate gunboats operating in the western rivers. Alfred Ellet, who was then a captain in the Fifty-ninth Illinois Infantry, was promoted to lieutenant colonel and assigned as second-in-command of the nine old steamboats that Charles had converted to improvised rams. These boats carried no guns, relying on their speed and rams as their only weapons. They became known as the Ellet Ram Fleet. Alfred brought three officers and fifty men from the Fifty-ninth to serve as crews aboard the rams.

The rams had proved their worth in the battle against the Confederate River Defense Fleet protecting Memphis, and were an important part of Flag Officer Davis's victory there on June 6, 1862. In fact, much to Davis's dismay, it was a party of soldiers from one of the rams that actually landed in Memphis and ran the United States flag up over the city's post office during the battle. Davis, like most naval officers, disliked the idea of having army boats manned by soldiers integrated into his command. In a stroke of tragic irony, the only casualty suffered by the Ellet Ram Fleet during the battle for Memphis was its creator, Colonel Charles Ellet. With his brother's death, Alfred Ellet was promoted to commander of the little fleet.

Instead of sailing south from Memphis for Vicksburg, Davis permitted himself to be distracted by a campaign up the White River in Arkansas. Under instructions from Welles, Davis had sent a fleet of gunboats and army transports to aid the beleaguered army of Major General Samuel Curtis. Ellet refused a request from Davis that his rams be put under naval command, so they were left behind. Although the White River campaign had ended in victory, it was a hollow one that cost many lives and left the crews of the navy gunboats demoralized.

On June 18, tired of waiting for Davis to gather himself together and continue the advance downriver, Ellet informed the flag officer he was leaving Memphis and heading for Vicksburg. When he arrived north of the city, he learned that Farragut's fleet was at anchor below, waiting for Davis to join the fight. Ellet knew the cautious Davis would not be arriving for at least several more days, so he sent a small party of soldiers, which included his son Edward and his nephew Charles Rivers Ellet, to make contact with Farragut. The soldiers slogged their way through the swamps on the bank opposite Vicksburg until they were below the city. There they commandeered a small rowboat and quietly approached the *Hartford* while she lay at anchor in midstream. They brought news that Davis was moving south slowly, but that the Ram Fleet was just north of the city and prepared to cooperate with Farragut in any way he wished.

It was with mixed emotions that Farragut received the news that Federal boats were above Vicksburg. He was glad someone was there, but would have been happier if it had been a regular naval fleet instead of the unarmed rams. He sent word back to Ellet, requesting that his boats keep watch along the stretch of the Mississippi from Vicksburg to the mouth of the Yazoo River. He also asked the colonel to send word to Davis that Farragut was waiting for him at Vicksburg. He told Davis he planned to attack Vicksburg in the next forty-eight hours, and the presence of his flotilla "would add greatly to the chances of success." Having eyes to see for him above Vicksburg was extremely vital, especially since rumors persisted that the *Arkansas* might be coming down the Yazoo any day.

Impatient with the notoriously cautious Davis, Farragut decided to attempt to run the Vicksburg batteries without his help. His plan called for the fleet to pass Vicksburg on the morning of June 27. Starting the day before, Porter's mortar boats were to try their best to reach the bluffs and put as many of the enemy guns out of commission as possible. The passage would be made in two parallel columns. The sloops were to form the starboard or eastern column, closest to the batteries. The *Richmond* was first, followed by the *Hartford,* then the *Brooklyn.* This would mean the larger ships could fire their broadsides at the enemy without fear of hitting other Union vessels. The port or western column would include the corvettes *Oneida* and *Iroquois,* and the gunboats *Wissahickon, Sciota, Winona, Pinola, Kennebec,* and the *Katahdin.* The corvettes were to precede the *Richmond,* while the gaps between the sloops would be used for firing by two gunboats each. The *Kennebec* and *Katahdin* were to follow behind the *Brooklyn,* being the last to pass the batteries. Farragut ordered the sloops to maintain a wide gap between themselves so the gunboats could have a clear field to fire at the enemy shore without being forced to fire over the larger ships. He recommended the extensive use of shrapnel against gun crews.

This was to be an organized steaming past the batteries, not the mad dash the fleet had engaged in passing Forts Jackson and St. Philip. The flag officer wanted as much damage done to the defenses of Vicksburg as possible, since whatever survived the attack would still be there when the fleet headed south again. There were other differences between running the Vicksburg batteries and the earlier run past the New Orleans forts. Farragut mentioned these in a letter to his wife, written before the attack began. "The work is rough. Their batteries are beyond our reach on the heights. It must be done in the daytime as the river is too difficult to navigate by night. I trust that God will smile upon our efforts, as He has done before. I think more should have been left to my discretion; but I hope for the best, and pray God to protect our poor sailors from harm."

The day before the attack was to begin, Porter brought his mortar boats up to within two miles of the city and began a steady bombardment. While there was some heavy damage to buildings in the city, the height of most of the batteries protected them from the mortars, many of which fell short of their targets. Porter's boats put on a

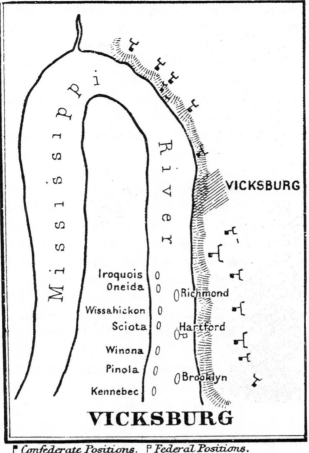

‡ *Confederate Positions.* P *Federal Positions.*
Vicksburg. *Source:* H. W. Wilson, *Ironclads in Action*
(Boston: Little, Brown, 1898). Used with permission.

spectacular light and sound show, but accomplished little damage of
any military value.

The attack was postponed until the early morning of the twenty-
eighth, when the signal to get under way was given. At 2:00 A.M., two
red lights were hoisted at the mizzen aboard the *Hartford*, and the
Federal ships raised their steam and began to move. The mortar boats
kept up their constant barrage as the fleet approached the batteries.

Porter brought his gunboats as close as possible to lend their fire-power, and the ships and boats opened their own fire as they neared enemy targets. Most of the Federal shells that were aimed at the bluffs fell short, and the hillsides below them were lit with the explosions and fires of spent shells.

As Farragut had ordered, the Union ships moved slowly, pouring a raking fire at whatever enemy positions they could reach. The guns on the bluffs, as well as those that had been located along the shore, were briefly silenced by the broadsides, but returned each time the firing sloop moved on. At one point the *Hartford* actually stopped at Farragut's order, to permit the *Brooklyn* and her accompanying gunboats to catch up. As was his habit, when the firing caused dense smoke to cover the river, Farragut climbed to the mizzen rigging for a better view of the battle. This time it almost cost him his life. A few minutes after the officer commanding a nearby gun crew had coaxed him down, the rigging where he stood was carried away by an enemy shell. The same shell cut the lines on his flag, dropping it to half mast and causing the other vessels to think he had been killed.

With shells flying in all directions, every ship moving upriver suffered damage, some more serious than others. By 6:00 A.M. the fleet had dropped anchor four miles north of Vicksburg, out of range of the enemy guns. Missing were the sloop *Brooklyn* and the gunboats *Kennebec* and *Katahdin*. These last three ships in line failed to make the passing, because of a misunderstanding in their orders. Captain Craven of the *Brooklyn* thought Farragut had instructed that no operational batteries be left behind. When he halted to attempt to silence several batteries, the guns on the bluffs concentrated on his ship and the nearby gunboats. The intensity of the shelling caused all three to withdraw back downriver.

Farragut was now above Vicksburg, but to what purpose he could not tell. Surprisingly, he had lost few men, only fifteen killed and thirty wounded. But without a large number of troops he could not subdue Vicksburg, and unless the army attacked the city's defenses, they would be there waiting for him when he returned, as he must, to the south before the level of the river fell so low that he could no longer move his ships.

Farragut's successful passing of the Vicksburg batteries offered the people of the north only a mild salve for the pain they felt over

Robert E. Lee's campaign to drive Union forces away from Richmond, later called the Seven Days Campaign.

Given command of the Confederate forces defending Richmond on June 1, Lee quickly began to build a reputation that resulted in his becoming the most famous soldier of the war, on either side. By the end of June, the Army of the Potomac, under Major General George B. McClellan, which had earlier appeared to be poised to capture the Confederate capital, was in full retreat, and Lee continued to take the offensive against the invading force.

6

"Above Vicksburg"

OUT OF SIGHT OF THE VICKSBURG BATTERIES, around the sharp bend in the river, the captains of the Union vessels rushed to a meeting aboard the flagship as quickly as each could drop his ship's anchor. An anxious Farragut took stock of his fleet and realized that three vessels had not made the run past the batteries. He sent word to Captain Craven of the *Brooklyn* via an overland messenger. Fearing that the sloop and two gunboats had been severely damaged and forced to turn back, he wrote, "I hope your ship has not been disabled and that your casualties have not been great, but I am prepared to hear the worst."

While he waited for Craven's reply, Farragut sent the *Wissahickon* to the mouth of the Yazoo River to watch for the *Arkansas*. He did not want to get his ships caught between the Vicksburg batteries and the giant ram without some warning. Following breakfast with his captains, Farragut did the only thing he could do, now that he was above Vicksburg: search for forces that would enable him to capture the city or, at the very least, permanently disable its defenses. Using the services offered by Lieutenant Colonel Ellet of the Ram Fleet, Farragut sent communiqués to General Halleck and Flag Officer Davis, as well as an official announcement to the naval authorities at Memphis that the Vicksburg batteries had been passed. This message was to be forwarded to Washington.

To the Navy Department he wrote, "The Department will perceive from [my] report, that the forts can be passed, and we have done it, and can do it again as often as may be required of us. It will not, however, be an easy matter for us to do more than silence the batteries for a time, as long as the enemy has a large force behind the hills to prevent our landing and holding the place." It was a cold report that transmitted the author's feelings about being required to move so far upriver for so little gain. "I am satisfied," he wrote, "it is not possible to take Vicksburg without an army of 12,000 or 15,000 men. General Van Dorn's [Confederate] division is here, and lies safely behind the hills. The water is too low for me to go over twelve or fifteen miles above Vicksburg."

Farragut's report provided his superiors in Washington with a detailed description of the passing of the Vicksburg batteries. He singled out several officers and men of his command for special mention, as he usually did when it had been earned by meritorious valor or hard work. To them he added the names of General Williams, Colonel Ellet, "and the army officers of this division generally," for doing "everything in their power to assist us."

Although General Williams had brought three thousand men with him, his force was still too small to do anything of value against the Vicksburg batteries. Frustrated by his inability to assault the town, he managed to place his own light batteries on the shore opposite Vicksburg. From there he added to the firepower of the fleet and was able to distract some of the city's guns.

Farragut's communications to Flag Officer Davis and General Halleck repeated his opinion that Vicksburg could not be taken without a large army. Major General Ulysses Grant would realize the truth in this statement when he undertook several unsuccessful assaults on Vicksburg during the next eighteen months. While Davis could offer no troops, since he had none with him, he did rush his flotilla of ironclad gunboats south to aid Farragut. General Halleck, who commanded a large army, replied that the "scattered and weakened condition of my forces renders it impossible for me at the present to detach my troops to cooperate with you on Vicksburg." This was a curious reply from Halleck, whose troops had taken and occupied Corinth, Mississippi, and were now virtually inactive. The general claimed he might be able to send an army within a few weeks, but Farragut knew he had little time left as he watched the level of the Mississippi River continue to recede.

Meanwhile, Captain Craven's reply to Farragut's inquiry arrived on the flagship. Craven laid much of the blame for the failure of the *Brooklyn* and her two accompanying gunboats to follow the main body of the fleet north of Vicksburg on Porter's mortar boats and gunboats. He claimed that as his ship had passed across the front of the southern batteries, Porter's boats had ceased firing, so that "all the batteries which had previously been partially silenced, immediately renewed the action, hailing a cross fire on this ship and the two gunboats." He then went on to fault Farragut for giving him what he termed unclear instructions concerning whether the *Brooklyn* should attempt to silence all the Confederate batteries before proceeding upriver. Craven claimed he had asked Farragut before the run began, "was it your wish or desire for me to leave any batteries behind me that had not been silenced, you answered, 'No, sir; not on any account.'" The interpretation of Farragut's reply to Craven's question lay at the heart of Craven's failure to follow the flagship north of Vicksburg. Farragut believed his reply meant that Craven should not "on any account" expose his ship to enemy fire any longer than necessary. Craven understood it to mean he must stand before the batteries as long as necessary, until he had silenced them all. This actually would have been impossible for him to do, because the guns on the higher bluffs were beyond reach of all but a handful of the Federal guns participating in the engagement.

Farragut was furious over Craven's misinterpretation of his orders. What made matters worse was the latter's report concerning the condition of his ship, which the flag officer expected had been heavily damaged. "We were hulled but twice," Craven reported, "one shot taking effect below water, on our starboard bow; and we received some damage to our rigging. We have no casualties on board." This made Farragut even angrier, since his own ship had received more damage running the batteries than had the *Brooklyn*, yet she had succeeded in her mission. He wrote back to Craven explaining that the captain had failed to quote the entirety of his instructions, which hinged on the words "When the vessels reach the bend in the river." All ships and boats were to advance north beyond the reach of the batteries, because that, rather than an attempt to silence all the enemy batteries, was the objective of the passing. Furious over what he considered insulting treatment by Farragut, Captain Craven immediately asked to be relieved of his command. Uncharacteristically, Farragut agreed, replacing him with Captain Henry Bell, who had been serving as fleet captain. It was a shame that this misunderstanding led to the squadron's loss of an able and talented captain. Perhaps the root cause was Craven's obvious dislike for Farragut, something that might not have escaped the flag officer's observations.

In any event, Bell was not very happy with his assignment. Like everyone else in the fleet, including Farragut, he wanted most of all to get out of the river before the water level dropped too far, and they were forced to remain there during the notoriously insect-infested summer. "This is a heavy blow to me and interferes with my calculations for getting free of the river," he wrote.

Free of the river! As the days grew hotter, the swarms of insects thicker, and the water shallower, everyone wanted to get free of the river—everyone, that is, except the officials in Washington, who appeared to believe that by simply running past the Vicksburg batteries and linking with Davis's fleet, Farragut could gain control of the Mississippi River. How wrong they were would soon become obvious.

The importance the Federal government placed on Farragut's joining with Davis and gaining control of the river can be seen in a letter from Navy Secretary Welles to Farragut. Although the letter is dated May 22, 1862, communications between Farragut's fleet and Washington was a slow process that could take several weeks. The flag officer probably received this dispatch sometime around the end of June.

"Sir: The Department learns with much pleasure that you have gone up the Mississippi. The opening of that river is the first object to be attained since the fall of New Orleans. The ironclads of the enemy have made an attack upon our flotilla in the west, and have been repulsed. They are mostly fitted up as rams, but are not equal to those you have already so gloriously extinguished."

Welles then suggested that Porter's mortar boats and gunboats should attack Fort Morgan, one of the forts guarding the entrance to Mobile Bay. He offered to send the *Susquehanna*, a side-wheel steamer similar to the *Mississippi* in Farragut's fleet, to work with the mortar boats once they were able to enter the bay.

Farragut was annoyed and dismayed by Welles's cavalier attitude toward the defenses of Mobile Bay, and his lack of understanding of what could be accomplished by the fragile mortar vessels and their small gunboat escorts. He wrote Welles that he had no doubt the mortar boats had done "great damage" to the Vicksburg batteries, and had helped to distract the enemy gunners while the fleet ran past, but he believed they would be easy prey for the ironclad rams the Confederate Navy had stationed in Mobile Bay. As for the *Susquehanna*, she would be operating alone as the only large ship, and would have difficulty fighting off the large number of small gunboats in the bay, as well as the ironclads, without the assistance of other warships. Mobile would have to wait until a genuine fleet of warships supported by mortar boats, ironclads, and other vessels could be organized and sent there. Meanwhile, the flag officer responsible for much of the Gulf Coast of the Confederacy was stuck up the Mississippi River, and none too happy about it.

In a letter to Welles dated June 30, 1862, and marked "Above Vicksburg," Farragut reminded the secretary that his presence on the river did not necessarily mean the stream was under Union control. The riverbanks for hundreds of miles were infested with Confederate army units, some equipped with light artillery pieces. These rebels would lie in wait for Union vessels to approach, then attack them in hit-and-run raids that often did considerable damage. Without large numbers of Federal troops to keep the riverbanks clear of the enemy, the river was little more than a gauntlet to be run by Farragut's ships and boats. Any attempt by unarmed merchant ships to travel the river would be disastrous. Even the army transports required gunboat escorts when they moved about in what many in Washington considered an occupied and controlled river.

Vicksburg remained an enemy stronghold. Below it on the river, Porter's mortar boats kept up a steady barrage against the batteries they could reach. He placed over a dozen howitzers behind a line of earthworks he had his crews throw up along the riverbank to protect against a surprise attack from rebel troops. The timed firing of the mighty mortar guns echoed up the river, reminding the Union sailors above the city and the rebel soldiers in it that they were under siege from a powerful enemy.

Meanwhile, Farragut's position continued to deteriorate. The river kept dropping, and he was now isolated from his own supplies. If he had not received word from Davis that he intended to leave Memphis and rush to Vicksburg "at the earliest possible moment," Farragut would probably have run back past the batteries.

Farragut was anxious for news concerning the *Arkansas*, which was rumored to be in the final stages of construction up the Yazoo River. Since his own vessels drew too much draft to travel that river, Farragut looked to the shallow-draft rams of the Ellet Ram Fleet for help. Alfred Ellet had just received word of his promotion to colonel, and his assignment as commander of the ram fleet, replacing his dead brother. Colonel Ellet suggested he take two rams and reconnoiter up the Yazoo as far as possible, to learn whatever he could about the *Arkansas*. Farragut quickly agreed.

The ram fleet was still very much a family enterprise. The two rams that steamed up the Yazoo were the *Monarch*, under Colonel Ellet's command, and the *Lancaster*, commanded by Alfred's nephew, Charles Rivers Ellet. At Memphis, the nineteen-year-old Charles had led the party ashore that hoisted the flag over the city's post office.

The journey up the Yazoo on June 30 was made with little of the fanfare and élan that usually accompanied an Ellet Ram Fleet expedition. These were the first Union vessels on this river deep in enemy territory, and the soldiers and their officers did not know what to expect. They had heard rumors that the river was spiked with torpedoes, now called mines, and that the banks had been lined with Confederate army batteries to protect the big ironclad from attack. Despite their apprehensions, the trip went without incident and without sighting a rebel sailor or soldier for several miles.

Then, suddenly, as the two rams, their paddle wheels churning the brownish waters as quietly as possible, rounded a gradual bend in the river, they were shocked to find three Confederate gunboats in the river just ahead of them. Anchored in the narrow river were the gunboat-ram *General Van Dorn*, the only survivor of the battle between the Confederate River Defense Fleet and the Ellet Ram Fleet at Memphis, and two wooden gunboats, the *Polk* and the *Livingston*. The latter pair were the remnants of the river fleet formerly commanded by Commodore George Nichols Hollins, who had attempted to support the defenses of New Orleans against Farragut's fleet in spite of his orders from Richmond.

Although the Union rams were armed with only two howitzers each—much less firepower than the three gunboats—their sudden appearance in the river shocked the Confederate troops manning the gunboats. Unable to build a head of steam quickly enough to move their vessels, the rebels decided to set them ablaze so the enemy could not capture them. They then scattered into the nearby countryside. Colonel Ellet watched in disappointment as the three boats burst into flames and burned rapidly to their waterlines. He decided there was little else he could do, since the fleeing soldiers would sound a warning of his presence, making further movement up the river exceedingly dangerous. The *Monarch* and *Lancaster* slowly turned in the river and returned south to the fleet.

The following morning, July 1, 1862, Flag Officer Farragut was having breakfast with several of his officers when the cry "Vessels approaching!" was heard from a lookout. Rushing to the deck, Farragut looked north to see a dense cloud of black smoke drifting above the river. Then gradually into view came a small fleet of vessels known as the Western River Flotilla, commanded by Flag Officer Davis. The saltwater sailors aboard the warships looked in gaping surprise at the approach of the smoke-belching armored gunboats, which hunkered low in the water with a menacing appearance. They looked like a group of dangerous turtles swimming downstream. On board the gunboats, the crews looked back in awe at the first majestic seagoing warships most had ever seen. The men aboard both fleets waved and called to each other until many were hoarse.

The strange little river-war boats of the flotilla, which some referred to as "stinkpots," dropped anchor alongside the sloops and gunboats of the Gulf Squadron. As the junior of the two flag officers, Davis was rowed to the *Hartford* to be welcomed by Farragut. The two had been close friends for many years, and had not seen each other since the early months of the war. The officers and sailors of the *Hartford* watched and cheered as the two men greeted each other with genuine warmth and friendship. Despite their close relationship, Farragut and Davis were completely different as men and as naval commanders. Both attempted to camouflage their baldness by brushing their hair across their pates, but there the similarity ended. Farragut was a clean-shaven, effusive man unafraid to show his emotions, while Davis, who sported a very large mustache, was reserved, quiet, and scholarly. One of the few naval officers who had a formal education, he was a Harvard graduate. Welles referred to him as more a scholar than a sailor. Farragut, as we have seen, was impatient, and hated nothing more than waiting around for the action to begin. Davis was slow to act, weighing all his options before moving. Once he moved, it was at a slow pace that permitted him to continue examining all options as they appeared or changed.

At Farragut's suggestion, Davis moved the few mortar boats he had in his flotilla down the river so they could fire on Vicksburg in cooperation with Porter's mortars. They contributed to the din and destruction to which the citizens of Vicksburg were growing accustomed.

The following day a force of two thousand Confederate soldiers armed with light artillery batteries launched an attack on Porter's mortar boats. The earthwork defense line Porter had constructed held, and the howitzers behind it cut the charging infantry down. Within minutes every available mortar and gunboat south of Vicksburg opened a deadly fire on the attackers. Abandoning their guns, the men fell back in chaos under the heavy fire. Counterattacking Union sailors captured dozens of rebel soldiers who had become stuck in the mud and were unable to escape.

The combined fleet honored Independence Day with an abundance of flags flying from all vessels, and twenty-one-gun salutes roaring up and down the river. In Vicksburg and her defending batteries there was no mistaking that the Federals were celebrating. Farragut accepted an invitation from Davis to join him on his flagship, the *Jessie Benton*, for a trip downriver for a look at the enemy's batteries above the city.

It was a cautiously reluctant old deep-sea sailor who climbed into Davis's boat for his first trip aboard an ironclad. The *Benton* was one of the largest and most powerful ironclads in the United States Navy, but this gave little comfort to Farragut, who dearly loved the open decks of the mighty warships on which he had served. Built in St. Louis the year before by the noted ironclad contractor James B. Eads, the *Benton* was two hundred feet long, with a beam of forty-five feet. Her casements were covered with nearly four inches of iron, and slanted down and outward so that shells hitting her would slide off into the water. She was armed with nine rifled guns, seven seven-inchers, and two nine-inchers, as well as seven thirty-two-pounders.

Unfortunately for the men aboard *Benton*, a new rifled battery had been added to Vicksburg's defenses, which offered Confederate gunners a better opportunity to target the ironclads. When she came within range of this battery, it opened a devastating fire. As the *Benton*'s gunners tried to get the range of the battery, a shell pierced her armor close to the spot where Farragut was standing. The explosion killed several men who had been near the flag officer. An excited Farragut told Davis, "Everybody to his taste. I am going on deck; I feel safer outside."

To occupy their time, the vessels of both fleets engaged in periodic shelling of enemy positions, and patrolled the riverbanks for Confederate infantry units attempting to lift the siege of Vicksburg. Boredom and the heat, however, were the worst enemies the sailors and marines had to deal with. The monotony was broken by an occasional false rumor that the *Arkansas* had left her dock at Yazoo City and was steaming down the Yazoo River toward the Mississippi. The Union fleets were anchored just below the place where the Yazoo emptied into the Mississippi, so these rumors helped to create heightened levels of anxiety.

The heat was unrelenting, and helped produce swarms of insects that attacked any exposed flesh. Of the heat, Davis wrote, "I never can describe to you the heat, the succession of still and breathless days—long, long, weary, red-hot, gasping days."

Frustrated by the inability to use his three thousand troops to help Farragut capture Vicksburg, General Williams hit on an idea that he thought might make the city and its batteries superfluous. Just above Vicksburg the river made a complete U-turn, forming a long finger of land opposite the city. This peninsula was called DeSoto Point. It was here that Williams had placed his batteries when Farragut's ships ran past Vicksburg. Looking over a map of this stretch of the river, Williams decided that if he could dig a canal across the peninsula below the Vicksburg batteries, Union ships could avoid passing Vicksburg. This would leave the rebel batteries without any targets, and make for a safe passage.

The canal would be fifty feet wide, and one and one-half miles long. Ships entering the canal three and one-half miles below Vicksburg would leave it six miles upriver of the city, and vice versa. Williams hoped to dig a cut through the peninsula five feet wide and four feet deep. Once opened to the powerful river current, he expected the rush of water through the cut to widen and deepen it sufficiently to allow the ships to pass through. The idea definitely had

merit; the main obstacle was manpower. The list of soldiers and officers down with illnesses related to the heat and insects grew every
day. To supplement his own force, Williams sent groups of soldiers
into the surrounding countryside to "liberate" slaves from nearby
plantations. The slaves were promised their freedom in return for
working on the canal. Within days, more than two thousand slaves
joined the work. Used to the heat, they were better able to maintain
a steady schedule, while the soldiers, many of whom were from northern climates, continued to fall ill.

The cut reached the far side of the peninsula on July 11. But just
a few hours before the final earth was to be removed and the river allowed to enter, disaster struck. The cut had reached a depth of thirteen feet, some eighteen inches below the level of the river, and eighteen feet wide. Everyone was hopeful of the results when the water
smashed its way through. Suddenly the banks of the cut began slip-
ping into the hole, and large sections caved in completely. Work crews
rushed to repair the damage, but the river, which was rapidly dropping, fell to a level below the cut before they could finish their work.
After three weeks of backbreaking toil, the cut was completed, but
the river had dropped so low that only a trickle of water found its way
into the deep trench.

The days of boredom ended during the night of July 14, when
two Confederates claiming to be deserters hailed the *Essex*, a former
ferryboat that had been converted into one of Davis's ironclads. They
told a story of the *Arkansas* being readied for a trip downriver to attack the Union fleets. Both flag officers doubted the truthfulness of
the report, but decided to send several boats up the Yazoo the next
morning to investigate.

The history of the ironclad ram *Arkansas* is one of high hopes and
deep disappointment. Her construction was begun at Memphis in
October 1861. Before she was completed, the city came under attack
by the Ellet Ram Fleet, and she was moved to the safety of Yazoo
City for completion. Construction, which had been proceeding slowly,
speeded up when she was assigned a new commander, Lieutenant
Isaac N. Brown. A twenty-eight-year veteran of the U.S. Navy, the
Kentucky-born Brown was a man of great energy and determination
who swept obstacles aside with zest. A shortage of materials and
craftsmen hindered his work, as did the falling river. Brown used his

most persuasive arguments to obtain the services of slaves from nearby plantations, and two hundred soldiers from a local military camp. Work on the boat went on twenty-four hours a day, and when blacksmiths and mechanics were required, he sent troops into the countryside to locate and press into service those he needed. Railroad rails were used as armor where regular boiler plate could not be properly fitted, and shell and shot were obtained far and wide for her ten guns.

On July 12, 1862, the *Arkansas*, not yet completed, but forced to move because of the rapidly dropping river, steamed out of Yazoo City and headed south for the Mississippi. Overall command of the vessel had been given to General Earl Van Dorn, as part of the Vicksburg defenses. Van Dorn instructed Brown to bring the boat out of the Yazoo and to Vicksburg as quickly as construction would permit. The plan was for the *Arkansas* to sweep into the Mississippi, surprising the enemy fleet at anchor, do as much damage to it as possible, and proceed to Vicksburg. There she would take on coal and then attack the mortar boats below the city. After that she was to steam downriver to attack the enemy vessels at New Orleans. Following that, she was to force her way through the mouth of the river into the Gulf, destroying as many blockade ships as she could. Once in the Gulf, she was to run to Mobile, bolstering the Confederate defenses of that port.

In the early morning hours of July 15, as the mighty ram steamed slowly downriver, the clearing morning mist revealed three enemy vessels approaching from downstream. The three were the wooden gunboat *A. O. Tyler*, a converted side-wheeler from Davis's flotilla, followed by the Ellet ram *Queen of the West*, and the ironclad gunboat *Carondelet*, also from Davis's flotilla.

At the same moment the *Arkansas* spotted the Union boats, lookouts aboard the *Tyler* roused her commander, Lieutenant William Gwin, from his breakfast. Knowing that his little wooden gunboat was no match for the ironclad, Gwin turned her around and headed back downriver with her stern gun firing for all she was worth. The ram *Queen of the West*, unarmed except for two howitzers tied to her deck, made as quick a turn as she could and sped south ahead of the *Tyler*. The only Union ironclad at the scene, the *Carondelet*, tried to maneuver into position to both fire at the enemy and turn around, something the bulky craft required room to accomplish. When the *Arkansas* opened fire, the *Carondelet*'s commander, Henry Walke, realized he would be "a simpleton to 'take the bull by the horn' " and risk the fatal ramming, "which the enemy desired." She also fled downstream.

The Confederate ram raced after the Union ironclad and, after nearly an hour, succeeded in pulling alongside her. The river was not wide enough to allow the *Arkansas* to ram the *Carondelet*, so instead Brown lowered his guns as far as they would go and fired a broadside into the *Carondelet* that crippled her steering gear. The power of the volley pushed the Union boat against the riverbank, where she became entangled in the reeds and stuck in the mud. The *Arkansas* then turned her attention to the two other boats. The little *Tyler* raced south as fast as she could, but to Lieutenant Gwin's great credit, he kept his single stern-mounted thirty-two-pounder firing at the huge ironclad. Good fortune smiled on the Union that day, for the *Tyler* was able to maintain enough distance from the *Arkansas* to prevent the ironclad from ramming her. In an incredible feat of bravery, the *Tyler*'s gun crew found the range and began doing serious damage to this hope of the Confederacy. As the two sped down the narrow river, one shot knocked Brown off his feet, temporarily rendering him unconscious. Another hit the pilot house, killing the river pilot, while another caused several steam leaks. The brave little wooden gunboat soon drew even farther ahead, as the steam pressure in the *Arkansas*'s boilers quickly dropped, slowing her considerably.

Gwin was everywhere on the *Tyler* at once, shouting for more steam and calling for the gunners to keep firing as the two forward guns of the rebel ironclad sent shells overhead or splashing in the water to either side. Belowdecks, the engineers flung every flammable liquid they could find into the boiler to raise the pressure a few pounds more. They watched the pressure gauge as it lingered at the spot where the red line began, the signal that the pressure was dangerously high.

Aboard the *Arkansas*, the situation was even worse. The temperature in her engine room reached 130 degrees, and the gun crews were required to spell the exhausted engineers for brief periods so they would not be felled by the heat. Meanwhile, the boiler pressure continued to drop. At the beginning of the battle it had reached 160 pounds, but as the ironclad reached the Mississippi, it was down to twenty pounds, and she was moving no faster than three miles per hour.

Aboard the Federal ships anchored along both shores of the river, sailors and officers listened to the gunfire. Most assumed the three vessels sent up the Yazoo had encountered army batteries stationed along the shores of the river. But not all. Aboard Davis's flagship, the *Benton*, the ship's captain asked the flag officer for permission to get steam up. On Farragut's flagship, several gun crews began preparing their guns for action, apparently without having been given orders to do so. Other than these, the firing in the distance raised little concern. Of the thirty ships in the combined Union fleets, only one had a full head of steam, the army ram *General Bragg*, but she did nothing while she awaited orders to attack the enemy ram. The rest of the vessels had banked their boilers in order to conserve fuel.

At 7:15 A.M. the *Queen of the West* suddenly appeared in the river with a full blast of smoke sweeping from her funnels. Following closely behind was the *Tyler*, also belching black smoke. At first some sailors thought the *Tyler* had a prize vessel in tow, but they quickly recognized that the third vessel was a huge ironclad, and her guns were firing. The *Tyler* and the *Queen* swept down into the midst of the fleet and sought sanctuary.

As the *Arkansas* slipped into the Mississippi, her crew gazed in awe out her gun ports at the enemy ships. Masts and funnels filled the scene ahead of them, and more than one wondered if he would survive the gauntlet. Brown had little choice but to continue downriver. He did not have enough steam to turn back, so he allowed the river's current to aid his crippled boiler and increase his speed.

With surprising ease the rebel ironclad slipped past the army rams and the ironclads of Davis's flotilla. As she moved, all her guns fired, belching smoke ahead, astern, and to each side. Aboard the Union ships, thousands of men scrambled into action. The first round of firing aroused Farragut, who, to the amusement of his crew, appeared on deck wearing only his nightgown.

The first Federal ship to take action against the rebel ram was the army ram *Lancaster*. As she began to move in an attempt to ram the approaching enemy, the *Arkansas* put a shot right into her boiler, sending steam and scalding water splashing over her crew, most of whom died instantly or were lost when they jumped overboard.

For the next thirty minutes the roar of cannons filled the air for miles around, as every Union boat fired every gun that could be brought to bear on the Confederate vessel. Most of the shots, including terrifying broadsides from the large sloops, did little damage, although a few succeeded in either penetrating the armor at a weak spot or were lucky enough to enter through a gun port. Brown later described the experience with these words: "As we advanced, the line of fire seemed to grow into a circle constantly closing." He also remarked about being able to see old "valued friends" on the decks of the enemy ships as he passed. The last Union vessel in line was Davis's flagship, the *Benton*. After exchanging a broadside with the *Arkansas*, she managed to get up enough steam to give chase, but withdrew when she came within range of Vicksburg's northern batteries.

At Vicksburg, thousands of people had gathered along the river to watch for the approach of the *Arkansas*. They cheered wildly as she came into view. It was not until the boat was secured to a wharf that soldiers and civilians understood the price the crew of the ironclad had paid for their minor victory. An officer on General Van Dorn's staff remarked that "it was the most frightful scene of war" he had ever witnessed. There was so much blood about that soldiers who acted as stretcher bearers attempting to remove the wounded and dead were forced to spread ashes on the decks and stairs in order to keep their footing.

The scene had such a lasting impact on those who saw it, that when Brown attempted to locate replacements for his dead and wounded crewmen before he continued downriver, he could find none.

Upriver, Farragut was mortified by the ease with which the Confederate vessel had run past his ships. It was without a doubt the most embarrassing incident of his long career, and he was determined to seek immediate revenge. Boarding the *Benton*, he told Davis he intended to get under way immediately and attack the *Arkansas* with every ship in his fleet. Davis, also embarrassed by the incident, but less volatile than Farragut, urged restraint. He later told his wife that Farragut "treated my reason as very cold and repulsive," although he did so in a "perfectly friendly" way.

Davis succeeded in persuading Farragut not to attack immediately, something the latter would soon regret. Orders from the flag officer to the ships of his fleet called for every gun to seek out the *Arkansas* as its target. "No one will do wrong," Farragut told the captains of his fleet, "who lays his vessel alongside of the enemy or tackles the ram. The ram must be destroyed." One delay piled up on another, and it was not until seven o'clock that night that Farragut's ships got under way. Davis placed his boats just upriver of the city in order to engage the northern batteries while Farragut's ships swept in close to the city side of the shore. Once again the river was filled with the roar of cannon fire, but seek as they might, the Union gunners could not find a trace of the *Arkansas* in the twilight. One of Farragut's gunboats, the *Winona*, was badly damaged during the battle and had to be run aground to prevent her from sinking.

Farragut continued to feel humiliated by the ironclad ram's persistent survival, as if it personally sought to destroy his reputation. Aside from that, the ram endangered every Union vessel on the Mississippi. The mortar boats were quickly sent south, and the supply ships were told to be prepared to flee at a moment's notice should the *Arkansas* suddenly appear in the river. No one in the Union fleet realized how much damage had been done to the ram, and that her career as a warship was, for all practical purposes, ended. The best she could do was defend herself against attack. In the meantime she remained hidden behind another vessel at the wharf.

Farragut was all for steaming upriver once again in search of the ram, but was dissuaded from doing so by Captain Bell and the other senior officers. He continued to rage against the ram, however, swearing that he would trade his commission "for a crack at her." During the following week, communications sped between the two flag officers. Farragut wanted to launch a two-pronged attack against the Vicksburg wharfs, he coming from below and Davis from above. The cautious Davis refused to participate, in part out of fear that his flotilla would be stranded below Vicksburg, unable to reach its own supplies. Finally, Colonel Ellet suggested that he lead his ram fleet against the *Arkansas*, while Davis's gunboats engaged the batteries from upriver, and Farragut's ships did the same from below the city. They agreed.

The attack, launched on July 22, was a dismal failure. The *Arkansas* put up a gallant defense against the rams, and Ellet's boats were badly damaged by the shore batteries. Despite the best efforts of everyone involved, the ironclad remained in service. From Welles came news that both the Navy Department and the country found the escape of the *Arkansas* cause for "serious mortification."

The failure to sink the *Arkansas* was the last straw for Farragut. If he hadn't been stuck in this muddy river, he would not have had to suffer such a humiliation. Orders arrived that he should withdraw downriver at his own discretion. Following a conference with Davis, the two parted on friendly terms. Davis wrote of Farragut to his wife, "You must not think Farragut and I differ unkindly," he wrote. "Nothing can exceed his kindness, candor, and liberality; our old ties have been strengthened by our present intercourse. He is a man who unites with a bold and impetuous spirit an affectionate temper, and a generous and candid nature."

Every man in Farragut's fleet and General Williams's detachment was relieved to be away from Vicksburg. They left in the predawn hours of July 24. Leaving the ram *Arkansas* still afloat was something that would haunt Farragut for a long time. Williams and his troops were dropped at Baton Rouge, and Farragut continued on to New Orleans, arriving there on July 28. Davis withdrew his flotilla on July 31, and returned to Memphis. Once again the center section of the Mississippi River was under the control of the Confederate government.

From Vicksburg, General Van Dorn wrote to President Jefferson Davis, "The whole of the lower fleet and all the troops have disappeared downriver." Thinking of it as a victory, Van Dorn soon began dreaming of moving south, with the help of the *Arkansas*, and recapturing Baton Rouge and New Orleans.

7

Free of the River

NEW ORLEANS OFFERED LITTLE COMFORT from the ravages of the mosquitoes and the torrid summer heat. Farragut and the salt-water sailors of his fleet were anxious to be free of the river and back on the open sea. His only hesitation was that the fate of the ram *Arkansas* remained undecided. He could imagine the ram steaming down the river, wreaking havoc on the gunboats he left to guard Baton Rouge, and then repeating the destruction at New Orleans. The *Arkansas,* and the potential danger she posed to the Union position on the river, kept him from returning to the Gulf. Fortunately, that issue would soon be resolved. In the meantime, the strength of Farragut's forces declined steadily as the fleet's sick list grew each day, as did the roll of those who died from the effects of the climate.

While Farragut's fleet had been steaming downriver from Vicksburg, David Porter and most of his mortar flotilla had been detached from Farragut's command and transferred to Hampton Roads. Farragut expressed disappointment at losing Porter from his fleet. He did not know, or refused to believe it if he did, that he was rid of an obstacle to the success of his own missions. Even before the first of Farragut's large ships had entered the Mississippi, Porter had used his direct link to Welles and Fox to attack Farragut and the older captains of his fleet with innuendo and false statements. Fortunately for the outcome of the campaigns on the river, Fox was not completely taken in by Porter. In a letter written to Welles in 1871, Fox said of Porter, "He came back disparaging the old hero, who, when the fire of battle came near, towered head and shoulders above such men, and this

Porter could not forgive. He felt he should have been the naval hero of the war." Porter was a disruptive element in the fleet, constantly undermining the older captains and trying to win favor with the younger officers. Farragut was better off without him.

Farragut's first order of business at New Orleans was to arrange for the repairs of his badly damaged ships. Most of the work could be performed by carpenters brought to New Orleans for that purpose, but the *Richmond* required such extensive repairs that he sent her to the navy yard at Pensacola. The few mortar boats Porter had left to the fleet were literally coming apart from the pounding of their own big guns, so Farragut had them towed to Pensacola for repairs also. He did not anticipate needing their assistance in the Gulf until he was ready to attack Mobile Bay.

A great shock descended on the Union army and naval commanders at New Orleans on August 1 and 2, when communiqués from General Thomas Williams informed both Farragut and General Benjamin Butler that a Confederate army was advancing on Baton Rouge. Williams also reported that the *Arkansas* had left her berth at Vicksburg and begun steaming downriver to aid the forthcoming attack on Baton Rouge.

The assault on Baton Rouge was the brainchild of Confederate general Earl Van Dorn, commander of the defenses of Vicksburg. Van Dorn's main objective was to build an impenetrable position at Port Hudson, a small village upriver from Baton Rouge. Located on bluffs overlooking the river, Port Hudson would provide the Confederates a good place from which they could close the river to enemy traffic up to Vicksburg. This was of strategic importance because the Red River, the lifeline of supplies from western Louisiana and Texas to the heart of the Confederacy, empties into the Mississippi between Port Hudson and Vicksburg. Supply boats traveled down that river loaded with beef cattle, sheep, corn, and war materials imported from Europe for the Confederate armies. If Van Dorn could keep that lifeline open, the fall of the northern and southern sections of the Mississippi River would be acceptable losses to the Confederacy.

By launching an attack on Baton Rouge, Van Dorn hoped to either recapture the Louisiana capital itself or, at the least, buy enough time to fortify Port Hudson by bottling up the Federal garrison there. The *Arkansas* was an indispensable part of Van Dorn's plan, since Farragut had placed gunboats on station at Baton Rouge. Left unmolested in the river, these boats would contribute considerably toward defending the city by bombarding the Confederate attackers. They could also do great harm to the planned construction of the Port Hudson fortifications before they were completed.

Van Dorn sent four thousand men from the Vicksburg garrison, under the command of Major General John C. Breckinridge, to assault Baton Rouge. Breckinridge had been Vice President of the United States under James Buchanan, and had run for the presidency in the 1860 election. Breckinridge left Vicksburg on July 27, and arrived at Camp Moore, Louisiana, sixty miles northeast of Baton Rouge, the following evening. More than two thousand soldiers were felled by fever during the overcrowded train ride or soon after arriving at Camp Moore. Breckinridge was able to add the one thousand troops at Camp Moore to his force, but this was little consolation for the effects the insect-infested camp had on the men. Baton Rouge was still a strenuous two-day march away. When the rebels left Camp Moore on August 2, they had deteriorated into a ragtag army of poorly clothed men suffering from the insidious heat and a chronic shortage of drinking water. Nearly a third of them had no shoes. During the forced march, men, either individually or in small clusters, dropped out. Some suffered from either the fever that was ravaging the ranks, or from a terrible thirst that drove many to drink from brackish ponds, while others were unable to continue walking because the sandy soil had rubbed the skin from the bottoms of their feet.

At eleven o'clock on August 4, this miserable little force of Confederates attacked the Union positions on the outskirts of the city. Baton Rouge's defenders were not much better off, and had only a slight advantage over the attackers.

The day before, General Williams, commander of the Baton Rouge garrison, had received reports from scouting parties of the approach of the large Confederate force. He had prepared for the expected attack by deploying three regiments along an outer perimeter defense line. Four additional regiments were stationed along an interior line. These were supported by four artillery batteries. Unfortunately, nearly half of Williams's soldiers were afflicted with the same fever that had struck the rebels. Out of a garrison of almost four thousand men, he had about two thousand actual effectives.

Meanwhile, at two o'clock on the morning of August 3, the *Arkansas* silently slipped her lines and, building a head of steam, left the sleeping city of Vicksburg behind. The ram's commanding officer, Isaac Brown, had been promoted to captain as a result of his daring feat in passing the Union fleets. When the vessel left Vicksburg, Brown was ashore, bedridden with the fever. Before leaving his executive officer, Lieutenant Henry K. Stevens, in command of the ironclad, he had instructed him not to sortie the ram until his return. When General Van Dorn ordered the reluctant executive officer to attack the Union gunboats at Baton Rouge in support of Breckinridge's troops, he gave Stevens no option except to obey. As military commander of the Vicksburg area, he easily convinced the district's naval commander, who had no idea of the poor condition of the *Arkansas*'s engines, that she should participate in the attack on Baton Rouge. Mechanics from as far away as Mobile, Alabama, had been brought to Vicksburg to work on the *Arkansas*'s engines. Some of these men were still aboard when the ram left Vicksburg.

Union spies quickly sent word downriver that the *Arkansas* was back in action, and heading south.

Manning Baton Rouge's exterior line of defense were the Twenty-first Indiana, the Fourteenth Maine, and the Sixth Michigan. Opposing them were troops from Alabama, Kentucky, Louisiana, Mississippi, and Tennessee. Breckinridge divided his command into two divisions for the assault. The one on the left was commanded by Brigadier General Daniel Ruggles, the one on the right by Brigadier General Charles Clark. Unit designations on both sides of the battle meant little, since there was not a brigade or a company in either army that was anywhere near its normal strength. Both armies suffered heavily from the fever.

The battle raged for Baton Rouge across the eastern approaches to the city, with the Federals first falling back, then regrouping and advancing. For the first few hours the battle continued to move back and forth, as the fairly equally matched sides put up a strenuous fight. Toward midmorning the Confederates controlled a large portion of the city, when a shot through the heart killed General Williams as he urged his men to counterattack a rebel advance. The leaderless Federal soldiers fell back to the river district, where they sought the safety of the Union gunboats. During the battle, Breckinridge and his staff listened for the guns of the *Arkansas* from the nearby river, but all they heard was the booming of the Union gunboats. Once the Federal sailors found the range, they laid a deadly barrage of fire on the rebel positions. Disappointed that he had not received the help he had been promised, and recognizing he would not be able to hold the city while the Union boats controlled the river, Breckinridge pulled his forces back to the city's outskirts shortly after 10:00 A.M. His men needed a rest.

Meanwhile, upriver, Lieutenant Stevens had been forced to make several stops during his trip from Vicksburg. First one, then the other, of the *Arkansas*'s two engines gave out. Luckily the mechanics on board had been able to restart the ram's power plants after each failure. The last and fatal engine failure occurred just four miles north of Baton Rouge. Stevens tied the vessel to the riverbank and waited while the mechanics tried in vain to restart the engines.

Word that the *Arkansas* was close by drew a large crowd to the river. People cheered when they saw the ram tied to the shore, but the cheering soon changed to dismay as the noise and smoke of approaching Union gunboats filled the air.

Having driven off the Confederate troops of Breckinridge, the Union gunboats had steamed north from Baton Rouge in search of the *Arkansas*. In the lead was the *Essex*, an ironclad that had been converted from a snag boat. Actually a part of Flag Officer Davis's flotilla, the *Essex*, along with the little ram *Sumter*, had steamed past Vicksburg in company with Farragut's ships. Unwilling to run the risk of having the two return above the city without the protection of Farragut's large ships, Davis assigned them the responsibility of patrolling the river from Vicksburg to Baton Rouge. The *Essex* was commanded by Commodore William Porter, the older brother of David Porter. Following her were three gunboats Farragut had left to help defend Baton Rouge, the *Cayuga*, the *Kineo*, and the *Katahdin*. Last in line was the ram *Sumter*.

William Porter was as much a glory hound as his brother. He saw in the approaching Confederate ram his opportunity to lift himself above the ranks of the other gunboat commanders, and he was determined "to go up and destroy her." In truth, the *Arkansas* was a prize that had eluded two flag officers and could bring a great deal of fame and recognition to the man whose boat sank her.

Commander William D. Porter of the *Essex.*
Courtesy of the U.S. Army Military History
Institute.

As the enemy boats neared, Lieutenant Stevens ordered the
Arkansas's engines started. When both roared into life and belched
smoke, her crew cheered. With lines to the shore quickly cut, the
Arkansas slowly swung out toward the center of the river to meet the
oncoming gunboats. Seeing their favorite preparing for action, the
thousands of people lining the eastern shore cheered their support of
her as loudly as they could.

The big ironclad headed straight for the *Essex*, intending to ram her. She gradually picked up speed for nearly three hundred yards, coming within easy pistol shot of the gunboat, when suddenly her starboard engine snapped a connecting rod and stopped dead. The force of the ram's port engine and the power of the river current swung her around and drove her into the thick brush and trees lining the western bank. Now her vulnerable stern faced the enemy boats. Unable to maneuver his vessel so he could fire his guns to any effect, and desiring to keep the ram out of enemy hands, Lieutenant Stevens quickly issued handguns to his crew and ordered them to abandon ship. As the men scrambled across the deck and onto the shore, Stevens and several other officers set lines of gunpowder alight and made their own escape. As the ram caught fire, she somehow broke loose and drifted into the river. Porter fired several shells at her, but did little or no damage. The shelling was not needed, for the flames inside the ironclad raged, consuming everything that would burn. The heat building up inside the iron vessel caused her loaded guns to fire wildly into the river and against the nearby shore. Then the magazine was caught in the blaze, and the once-glorious ram, the last of a short line of giant ironclads on which the Confederate Navy had pinned its hopes, exploded and blew apart. Within minutes, nothing was left of her but pieces of rubble floating on the surface of the river.

In his report of the engagement, William Porter claimed it was the hot fire his boat poured into the *Arkansas* that had caused her demise. Both Farragut and Davis refused to believe his story, because they heard what actually happened from the commanders of the other boats. In General Van Dorn's report of the incident, he went to lengths to discredit Porter's claim that his boat was responsible for destroying the ram, saying, "She was no trophy won by the *Essex*."

Like his brother David, William was quick to write letters to those in Washington who could help further his career. To Welles he wrote an erroneous account of the death of the *Arkansas* in which he gave full and direct credit for the destruction of the ram to the *Essex*. He followed this with an error-filled account of why his vessel had failed to destroy the Confederate ironclad while she was tied up at Vicksburg. The *Essex* had joined the Ellet Rams when they attacked the *Arkansas* on July 22. It was the only gunboat that had any real opportunity of shelling the ram, since the Ellet boats were armed with only two howitzers each, which were virtually useless against the *Arkansas*. Porter placed the blame for that earlier failure to destroy the *Arkansas* not where it belonged, on what Farragut called "the unmanageableness of his vessel," but instead on what he claimed was the lack of cooperation from Flag Officers Farragut and Davis.

From Hampton Roads, David Porter supported his brother's claims, and urged Welles to remove Davis from his command. David Porter was evidently seeking command of the river flotilla for himself. On October 1, 1862, Porter was granted what he had sought with such cunning and duplicity, when Davis was returned to Washington. Porter was promoted to flag officer and given command of the newly reorganized Mississippi Squadron, with responsibility for the river north of Vicksburg. Below Vicksburg the river remained the responsibility of David Farragut.

In response to General Williams's call for help, Farragut hastily organized the crews of several vessels, many of whom were ashore on leave. He rushed upriver with the *Hartford*, the *Brooklyn*, and four gunboats. The flag officer was determined not to leave the ram operational in the river before he was himself forced to take his large ships back to sea. Farragut arrived at Baton Rouge at noon on August 7. By then Breckinridge had learned of the fate of the *Arkansas* and had withdrawn entirely. Two days later Farragut steamed downriver toward New Orleans, leaving the four gunboats *Essex, Oneida, Kineo,* and *Katahdin,* and the small ram *Sumter,* behind to guard the river around Baton Rouge from further attack.

On the return trip down the river, Farragut halted briefly at the town of Donaldsonville, Louisiana. For several months this small river town had been used by rebel guerrillas to attack Union boats steaming up and down the river. Town officials had been warned several times that the fleet would destroy the town if the shooting at Union vessels was not stopped. On the trip to Baton Rouge, the *Brooklyn* was fired on by riflemen hidden along the town's wharves. Return cannon fire drove them off, but they later came back to harass an army transport. Farragut had sent word earlier to Donaldsonville that all women and children should be evacuated because he planned on shelling the town on his voyage downriver.

In front of Donaldsonville, the *Hartford* and the *Brooklyn* fired into the town for a brief period. The shelling set fire to several warehouses along the wharves, and drove out the Confederate riflemen who had attempted to pick off gun crews on the sloops. Small boats landed several parties of marines and sailors, who quickly swept through the town in search of the home of the local guerrilla leader, Captain Phillippe Landry. Finding Landry gone, the men set his home ablaze. Fires were also set at the town's two hotels.

Upon arriving back at New Orleans, Farragut was delighted to learn that he had been commissioned the first rear admiral in the United States Navy. General Butler honored him with a fifteen-gun salute, which the *Hartford* joyously returned. That night an army band serenaded the new rear admiral. Along with the commission came a vote of thanks from the Congress to the men and officers of the fleet for their "successful operations on the lower Mississippi River, and for their gallantry displayed in the capture of Forts Jackson and St. Philip and the city of New Orleans, and in the destruction of the enemy's gunboats and armed flotilla."

Farragut attempted to assuage the feelings of General Butler, whose role in the engagements had been belittled by David Porter. Porter's report gave the impression that he, not Butler, had sent the troops around the rear of the forts. Writing to Butler, Farragut expressed his desire to share with the army the honor of taking Mobile next.

To Virginia and Loyall he wrote, "Yesterday I hoisted my [admiral's] flag at the main, and the whole fleet cheered, which I returned with a most dignified salute. I called all hands, and read an Act of Congress complimentary of their achievements." Farragut then began preparing his fleet for the trip downriver and into the Gulf. The ships were to steam to Pensacola for badly needed repairs.

Meanwhile, far up the Mississippi, General Van Dorn was carrying out his plans to fortify Port Hudson. General Daniel Ruggles's force was detached from General Breckinridge and sent to Port Hudson to begin the work. Port Hudson stands on a commanding height nearly eighty feet above the river, near a hairpin turn that forces vessels to reduce their speed. Along those bluffs Captain James Nocquet, a talented Confederate Army engineer, built battery positions for the guns Van Dorn shipped down from Vicksburg. When Nocquet was finished with his work, the Confederate army had constructed a bastion stronger even than Vicksburg. Now three hundred miles of the Mississippi River, from Port Hudson to Vicksburg, and including the intersection with the vital Red River, were solidly in Confederate hands.

On August 14 the Federal ram *Sumter* lost power while patrolling the river above Port Hudson and was run aground. Fearing an attack from Confederate troops in the area, the sailors abandoned her and fled the scene aboard a small steamer. While a group of rebels attempted to remove her two thirty-two-pounders, another Union gunboat came on the scene. Rather than lose their prize, the rebels set her ablaze. When the enemy had passed, they returned and managed to rescue the two cannons from the river. These were added to the batteries at Port Hudson.

The following week, amid accusations of rape and looting by the Baton Rouge garrison, and anxious over a rumored Confederate attack against New Orleans, General Butler withdrew all Federal army troops from the Louisiana capital. The only Union presence remaining at Baton Rouge was provided by the four gunboats and one ram left by Farragut to guard the city's port facilities. The naval officers, unable to prevent Confederate troops from occupying the city in the usual manner, threatened Baton Rouge officials that if such an occupation took place, they would destroy the entire town through a naval bombardment.

At New Orleans, Farragut had once again to look after the needs of his fleet. Nearly every ship under his command required repairs, some extensive. In addition to the toll taken by enemy guns, the receding water level left many hulls with bottom damage from scraping the riverbed. The narrowness of the river in many places caused numerous collisions that left the sides of numerous ships and boats damaged.

Back in Gulf waters, Farragut was once again able to resume active command of the ships he had left to conduct the blockade of Confederate ports. The blockade had not been especially successful, due in part to the fact that the best fighting ships of Farragut's squadron had joined him in the Mississippi River campaign. Of those left on blockade duty during the river campaign, a dozen were old sailing ships that could do little against the steam-powered blockade runners employed by the Confederacy. The powered craft of the blockade squadron included two small screw steamers and three larger side-wheelers. In truth, the squadron maintaining the blockade while Farragut was on the Mississippi was little more than a token Union naval presence in the Gulf.

Matters improved quickly for the blockade and the crews now that the Admiral was free of the river. Farragut's requests for additional ships were answered when newly commissioned vessels arrived from the north for blockade duty. Two ships that had been on duty in the Gulf for a long time, and whose crews suffered from an epidemic of scurvy, were sent home. Blockade duty provided Farragut's crews with the opportunity for badly needed rest from the tensions and anxieties of being up the long river in the heart of the Confederacy.

In other parts of the country, bad news plagued the Union during the second half of 1862 and the first half of 1863. The Union Army of the Potomac faltered in its invasion of Virginia, owing in part to the constant change in its commanding general. Frustrated by the army's lack of aggressiveness, President Lincoln replaced General George McClellan with General Ambrose Burnside in November 1862. In January 1863, Burnside was himself replaced by General Joseph Hooker. "Fighting Joe" Hooker lasted until that June, when General George B. Meade was given command. In mid-December 1862, the Army of the Potomac sent more than 106,000 men against Confederate positions guarding Fredericksburg, Virginia. The daylong assault failed to dislodge a Confederate force of 72,000 commanded by Lieutenant Generals Thomas "Stonewall" Jackson and James Longstreet, in what became known as the First Battle of Fredericksburg. The Federal army suffered 12,700 killed or wounded at Fredericksburg in what one Union soldier described as "a great slaughter pen." In its first Vicksburg campaign, a Union army under the command of Major General Ulysses S. Grant failed to secure the city in part because a Confederate force under General Van Dorn managed to get behind Union lines and capture or destroy $1.5 million in supplies.

Farragut's squadron was not immune to the Union's run of bad luck. Two places along the coast gave the new rear admiral the most difficulty. One was the great port of Mobile, Alabama. The port was inside Mobile Bay, the entrance to which was protected by several forts, including the powerful Fort Morgan. Rebel and European ships slipped in and out of Mobile Bay almost at will. One infamous incident at Mobile Bay resulted in an injustice that permanently damaged the career of the grandson of Commodore Edward Preble, hero

of the naval war against the Barbary pirates. Commander George H.
Preble of the gunboat *Oneida* was on station off Mobile Bay when, at
5:00 P.M. on September 4, 1862, what appeared to be a British warship
approached. The vessel was actually the Confederate cruiser *Florida*.
Built in Liverpool, she was an exact copy of a British warship. Because of this, and the fact she was flying the English ensign, Preble
approached her with caution. All ships' commanders on blockade
duty had been warned to deal delicately with vessels of foreign
powers.

The *Florida* steamed as straight as an arrow toward the entrance
to Mobile Bay. This contributed to the deception, since a blockade
runner would normally have attempted to avoid coming too close to
a Union warship. The *Oneida* steamed toward the intruder, and Preble hailed her several times, but received no response. Preble then
fired several shots across her bow. When she failed to stop, he followed with a broadside that did considerably more damage than was
visible to him. Preble kept up his firing until both ships came within
range of Fort Morgan's guns, at which time he returned to his station.

Preble brought much of his trouble on himself by filing an incomplete report of the incident with Farragut, his commanding officer. In it he made it sound as if he had failed to fire on the enemy
ship until it was well past his position, and that he had done it little
damage. The *Florida*'s skipper, Captain James N. Maffit, later described the damage inflicted on his ship by the *Oneida* as making her
"a perfect wreck." It took nearly four months to make the *Florida*
seaworthy again.

With few facts concerning the incident in his hands, Secretary
Welles decided to make Preble an example to other ships' commanders who might be "timid" in the performance of their duties. After
twenty-seven years of service, Preble's name was struck from the rolls
of the navy without so much as a hearing. Public pressure forced President Lincoln to reinstate him in February 1863, but Welles assigned
him to command a sailing ship in European waters, where he remained for the rest of the war. In 1872, following years of campaign-
ing, Preble received the court-martial hearing he wanted. Among
those who testified was Captain Maffit. The court found that Preble
"did all that a loyal, brave, and efficient officer could do to capture or
destroy" the rebel cruiser.

While the *Florida* affair embarrassed Rear Admiral Farragut, he knew Preble to be a competent and brave officer. Once the complete facts of the incident were known to him, he wrote Welles expressing his belief that Preble had hesitated firing on the cruiser because she appeared to be a British warship. It was, Farragut wrote, Preble's desire to "avoid giving offense to foreign nations in enforcing our blockade."

Captain Maffit again succeeded in embarrassing the United States Navy in January 1863, when he ran his vessel through a Union blockade that had been established around Mobile Bay especially to prevent the *Florida* from reaching the open seas. One of the blockading vessels, the gunboat *Cuyler*, under Commander George F. Emmons, unsuccessfully chased her for nearly three months. The Confederate cruiser went on to an illustrious career as a commerce raider. By the time bad health forced Maffit to relinquish command of the cruiser in August 1863, she had taken fifty-five prizes.

Although it provided much-needed rest, blockade duty could be a dismal service for sailors of the Federal navy. Days and sometimes weeks of tedious, routine work left the crews in less than top condition when their boring duty was suddenly broken by the approach of a blockade runner or an enemy cruiser. Hours of practice drills and firing their guns at targets did little to relieve the feeling that they were no longer a part of the great war. Sailors often wrote home of the hardships they endured while lying off the coast, waiting for something to happen. The ships were subject to the ravages of powerful tropical hurricanes and winter gales. Many had to seek temporary relief in Pensacola to repair damages caused by the weather. The crews in several sections, especially those along the Texas coast, were often struck down with yellow fever or scurvy. Although the blockade has received considerably less attention than the more exciting great land battles of the war, most historians agree that it was the strangling effect of the blockade, the largest ever imposed until that time, which brought the Confederacy down, not the Union army's force of arms. During the term of the blockade, from April 1861 until the close of the war, 1,504 ships were captured by the blockading squadrons, with a value exceeding $30 million.

The Southern attitude concerning the impact of the blockade is evident from the amount of money spent and the effort exerted by the Confederate government in attempting to break it. The development of ironclad gunboats, submarines, and rams was the direct result of the struggle against the blockade. The Richmond government, which spent millions of dollars on vessels designed to break the blockade, would much rather have used the money to build ocean-going ships. These could have taken cotton from Southern ports to Europe and returned with supplies needed for the war effort.

Equally troublesome to Farragut as Mobile Bay was the Texas coast from the Sabine River to the Rio Grande. This low, sandy shore provided numerous locations for small rebel boats to meet incoming supply ships and offload them with virtual immunity. Farragut had only a handful of ships to attempt to control several hundred miles of Texas coast. In October 1862 he ordered a force of five Union vessels into Galveston Bay to capture the city of Galveston. Under the command of Commander William Renshaw of the gunboat *Westfield*, the expedition included three other gunboats, the *Harriet Lane*, the *Clifton*, and the *Owasco*, as well as the mortar schooner *Henry James*. They accomplished their mission with little resistance. Holding the city proved to be a far greater problem, since Commander Renshaw had too few troops to conduct an effective occupation.

During the next few months the Federal naval forces controlled Galveston by day, but withdrew to the waterfront district while Confederate cavalrymen freely roamed the city at night. In an effort to help Renshaw hold the city around the clock, Farragut had two gunboats transferred to Galveston, the *Corypheus* and the *Sachem*. From New Orleans the army sent three companies of the Forty-second Massachusetts Infantry. The newly combined army/navy command was now large enough to control most of the city during the night, but not of sufficient size to defend it against a concerted attack by regular Confederate forces massing nearby. The Massachusetts troops were stationed along Galveston's waterfront, where they could be aided by the firepower of the gunboats if attacked by a substantial enemy force.

This situation continued until the early morning hours of January 1, 1863, when a group of rebel boats used the moonless night to attack the Union gunboats standing off the coast. Two "cottonclad" gunboats, the *Bayou City* and the *Neptune*, accompanied by their tenders, the *John F. Carr* and the *Lucy Gwin*, steamed into the bay as part of a combined land/sea attack to recapture the city. Aboard each gunboat were one hundred dismounted Texas cavalrymen commanded by Colonel Thomas Green. Both gunboats, formerly river steamers, were armed with field artillery pieces, including a thirty-two-pounder on the *Bayou City*. On their decks were stacked bales of cotton to absorb the shells of enemy guns, and also as protection for sharpshooters stationed behind them—hence the term "cottonclad." The bales were very effective—more so than one might imagine—at serving as a sort of armor plating. The overall attack was planned and directed by Major General John Bankhead Magruder. When Magruder took command of all Confederate forces in Texas at the end of November 1862, he made the recapture of Galveston his number-one priority.

When the Union troops stationed in the city came under attack, Renshaw took his gunboat, the *Westfield*, closer to land in order to fire his guns at the attackers. The gunboat grounded on a sandbar from which it could not be refloated. The *Clifton* came to the aid of the grounded boat, but failed to pull her free. Meanwhile, the battle along Galveston's waterfront intensified, and the rebel gunboats drew closer. On board the cottonclads, the Texas cavalrymen fired their rifles at anyone who moved on the decks of the Union boats.

With shells and rifle fire pouring across his decks, Union commander Jonathan M. Wainwright drove his *Harriet Lane* into the *Bayou City* in an attempt to sink her. Both vessels suffered only slight damage. The riflemen aboard the cottonclad were briefly stunned by the collision, which reduced their firing for a time. Turning away from the *Bayou City*, the *Harriet Lane* was herself rammed by the second cottonclad, *Neptune*. The Union gunboat again suffered only minor damage. The *Neptune* received the worst of the ramming and pulled back from her enemy as she began to sink, costing the lives of many of those aboard her. Turning again, the *Harriet Lane* was rammed by the *Bayou City*. This time the two vessels were locked together. With the two boats unable to pull apart, the cavalrymen on the *Bayou City* immediately began boarding the Union gunboat. The badly outnumbered sailors put up a gallant struggle, but after a few minutes were forced to surrender. Among those killed in the action were Commander Wainwright, whose grandson would command troops at Bataan nearly eighty years later. The Confederate flag was run up the *Harriet Lane*'s mast by the cheering rebels as Union sailors and soldiers looked on from other vessels and the shore. Loss of the side-wheeler to the enemy proved to be a lasting embarrassment to Farragut and the entire United States Navy. For the remainder of the war the navy searched in vain for her. Built in 1857 and named for the niece who served as White House hostess during James Buchanan's presidency, she was the first steam-powered revenue cutter in U.S. service.

While the *Harriet Lane* was being captured, Commander Renshaw continued his efforts to free the *Westfield* from her grounding. The remaining Union vessels began withdrawing from the harbor at Renshaw's command. After refusing an offer of truce that would have permitted him and his crew to withdraw but leave the boat behind, Renshaw transferred most of his crew to the *Clifton*. Determined not to allow his gunboat to fall into rebel hands, he set her ablaze. Unfortunately, before he and the few men with him could get away from her, the gunboat's magazine exploded prematurely. Renshaw and those with him were all killed in the explosion.

Lieutenant Commander Richard Law of the *Clifton* led the four remaining Union vessels to safety outside the harbor. Left behind were the three companies of the Forty-second Massachusetts who were forced to surrender. Galveston remained under Confederate control for the rest of the war. Her value as a port for arriving war materials for the Confederate Army endured until the Union navy finally closed the Mississippi River to traffic from the Red River.

Farragut was back at New Orleans when word of the Galveston disaster reached him. True to the impulsive nature that had earned him the nickname "Daring Dave," the admiral's first thought was to steam to Galveston immediately with his warships, recapture the port, and destroy the enemy's vessels. He was talked out of doing this by Commodore Henry Bell, who had been promoted to this rank in August as reward for his service with Farragut on the Mississippi. Bell volunteered to take an expedition to the Texas coast to see what could be done about reestablishing the blockade of Galveston. This seemed to satisfy Farragut, who had the highest regard for his friend's ability.

Even Commodore Bell's efforts were not without embarrassing moments, however. On the afternoon of January 11, 1863, one of his ships, the gunboat *Hatteras*, had a running battle with the famous rebel cruiser *Alabama*, under the equally well known Captain Raphael

Semmes. The two ships steamed along together in almost parallel lines, firing broadsides into each other. Finally, after a quarter hour, Lieutenant Commander Homer Blake was forced to break off the engagement and surrender. The *Hatteras* was burning beyond control at two locations, and she had taken several hits below the waterline. Blake asked for help in removing his crew before the ship sank, and Semmes responded by sending his boats to rescue sailors from the sinking *Hatteras* and the sea around her.

Twenty-eight miles away, Bell heard the firing and rushed his flagship, the *Brooklyn*, to the scene. Arriving too late, all he found was the flotsam that remained of the *Hatteras*, and a few sailors clinging to the debris. The *Alabama* and her prisoners were long gone.

The blockade of the Texas coast continued to go badly, in part because of Magruder's determined efforts to break it. Magruder widened his campaign to open Texas ports by sending two cotton-clads armed with field artillery pieces and loaded with Texas infantry to attack the Union sailing ships off Sabine Pass. The attack was launched on January 21, and proved completely successful. The Union ships were nearly becalmed and unable to maneuver as the rebel steamers could. Both Federal ships on the Sabine Pass station, the *Morning Light* and the *Velocity*, were captured after a brief fight.

Commodore Bell spent some time shelling Galveston, but was unable to launch an attack on the city because he had too few troops for such an encounter. Besides, Magruder had bolstered Galveston's defenses by moving a large number of infantry and several heavy guns into the city. Nothing could be done but stand offshore and conduct as effective a blockade as possible. General Magruder infuriated the Federal navy by issuing a proclamation that the Texas coast was "open to trade" with all nations. Bell responded by declaring that any merchant vessel caught entering or exiting any Texas port would "be captured . . . and sent into an open port of the United States for adjudication."

Rear Admiral Farragut reluctantly left Pensacola for New Orleans on November 7, 1862, after receiving reports that the Confederate Army was building strong fortifications at Port Hudson. Sailing with him was his son, Loyall, who had traveled to Pensacola on a navy warship for an extended visit. Loyall accepted his father's offer to serve as his secretary, and so became a part of the *Hartford*'s company.

Several powerful batteries had already been put in place at Port Hudson, and Farragut knew his place was back in the river to deal with this new threat to Union control of the Mississippi River. Moreover, he had given up all hope of launching a combined sea/land attack on Fort Morgan and the other Mobile Bay fortifications in the near future. The army had suffered a series of disastrous setbacks near Richmond, Confederate forces had invaded Maryland, and troops could not be made available for Farragut's project. General Butler had earlier commmitted troops from his command for a campaign against Mobile Bay, so Farragut had a second reason to revisit New Orleans.

The *Hartford*, along with the *Richmond* and a group of gunboats, arrived at New Orleans shortly after noon on November 9. To Farragut's dismay, Butler explained that his command was engaged in a series of campaigns throughout the region, and he could not spare any troops for Farragut's use until those campaigns were completed. Instead, Butler urged Farragut to consider attacking Port Hudson until he could supply the manpower required for assaulting Mobile Bay.

But, in a reversal of the previous year, the Navy Department urged Farragut not to go upriver until it had risen well beyond the minimum required by his ships. Farragut remained anxious to deal with Port Hudson, hoping perhaps that a victorious land/sea operation there would help him put together the expedition he needed for Mobile Bay.

In response to Butler's urging, Farragut sent four gunboats, under the command of Lieutenant Commander George M. Ransom, upriver to reconnoiter the fortifications at Port Hudson. On his return to New Orleans, Ransom reported that the Port Hudson fortifications had been completed and were situated in such a way as to be "capable of resisting more effectually than Vicksburg the passage of any vessel or fleet." Within days of Ransom's return, Butler changed his mind about attacking Port Hudson. Behind this change was a report from Brigadier General Godfrey Weitzel, Butler's chief engineer, that Port Hudson was garrisoned by at least twelve thousand Confederate soldiers. Weitzel offered the opinion that the fortifications could not be taken by a force of any fewer than that number.

The situation in New Orleans, and the outlook for some action for Farragut's fleet, changed on December 16, with the arrival of six large troop transports. On board was Butler's replacement as commanding officer of the Department of the Gulf, General Nathaniel P. Banks, and twenty thousand additional Union soldiers. Banks brought with him instructions from the President to take whatever actions were necessary to open the Mississippi River to Union traffic and close it to Confederate use. A former governor of Massachusetts and a self-made businessman, Banks was one of a long list of politicians who received military commissions from a grateful President Lincoln when the war began. His wartime career had been rather uninspiring and would probably have been ended before he was assigned to New Orleans except for the personal intervention of Lincoln. The single feature of importance that Banks had over Butler was the force of twenty thousand soldiers he brought with him. In them Farragut saw the troops he needed to capture both Port Hudson and Mobile Bay.

As the year 1862 came to a close, Rear Admiral Farragut began planning for his attack on Port Hudson. First he had to persuade General Banks to reoccupy Baton Rouge so it could be used as a base against Port Hudson, and then commit the number of troops required to launch a combined attack on the dangerous fortifications themselves. Farragut's hope of winning Banks's support was a letter from President Lincoln introducing Banks to Farragut and requesting the admiral's cooperation with Banks in opening the river. Banks also brought a photograph of the President inscribed to Farragut, who was flattered by the gift. He wrote Virginia that he and Banks were "likely to get along well." Farragut's relations with General Butler had always been good, with the latter cooperating in every way he could. But Butler had been constantly short of the manpower required to guard the city and engage enemy forces in the region. Because of this, Butler could offer only limited assistance, as he had at Baton Rouge and Vicksburg. Farragut hoped this condition was now corrected.

On December 19, Farragut wrote Welles, "Sir: I have the honor to inform the Department that on the arrival of General Banks with his troops I recommended to him the occupation of Baton Rouge. He approved of the move, and ordered his transports to proceed directly to that city. I ordered Commander James Alden, in the *Richmond*, with two gunboats, to accompany them and cover their landing. Baton Rouge is only twelve or fifteen miles from Port Hudson, and is therefore a fine base of operations. I am ready to attack the latter place and support General Banks the moment he desires to move against it."

8

Under the Guns
of Port Hudson

THE DEFENSES OF PORT HUDSON were similar to those at Vicksburg in several ways. Both were located on the eastern bank of the
Mississippi River. Both sites dominated the river from high bluffs that
permitted defenders to fire down on enemy ships while they remained relatively safe from most naval guns. Ships approaching either
location could not raise many of their guns enough to fire up the
bluffs with any accuracy or achieve satisfactory height. The river
above both series of bluffs made sharp left turns that forced north-
bound ships to reduce speed in order to negotiate the bend. The
south-flowing current of the river was fast, usually about nine knots
at Port Hudson. Now each of these Confederate strongholds was occupied by nearly sixteen thousand rebel soldiers. General Van Dorn
considered Port Hudson as vital a stronghold as Vicksburg for the continued existence of the Confederacy.

Opposite Port Hudson, on the western bank, was a flat, sandy
plain that stretched back from the river and gradually rose to form a
low plateau. Numerous small streams flowed from the plateau into
the river. Although none of these was powerful individually, their
combined strength as they emptied into the river had the effect of
gently pushing ships toward the eastern bank. Under normal conditions, river pilots easily compensated for this, but in wartime, with the
enemy high up on the bluffs, these streams pushed ships directly under the fire of powerful guns.

Downriver at New Orleans, Farragut waited for Banks to decide
when he would attack Port Hudson. Having his son with him, and

169

time on his hands, gave him reason to accept invitations to the few social events in the occupied city. One of these was an opera sponsored by a ladies' society to raise money for the poor. Farragut, doing what he considered his humanitarian duty, purchased a box for himself, Loyall, and several of his officers—even though he knew he was "giving my money to those who would not give me a Christian burial if they could help it." Time dragged while Farragut's active brain planned his campaigns against Port Hudson and Mobile Bay.

On December 17, Baton Rouge had been reoccupied by Brigadier General Cuvier Grover with eight thousand men. The river alongside the city was controlled by vessels of Farragut's fleet under Commander James Alden of the *Richmond*. The capital of Louisiana was little more than a ruined shell of its former self, having suffered from the earlier naval bombardment and land battle. Grover did his best to maintain order among his troops, but there were frequent reports of looting and plundering. Slaves escaping from nearby plantations were attracted to the city in search of the freedom promised them by Federal officials. They were put to work cleaning up the town and rebuilding its defenses against another attack.

Once he learned of the strength of the Confederate forces at Port Hudson, Banks proved as reluctant to move against the fortified town as Butler had been. Unknown to the admiral, Banks had informed the army's general-in-chief, Henry W. Halleck, that his force was too small for a successful campaign against Port Hudson. Banks's Army of the Gulf had fewer than forty thousand men in Louisiana. More than half his troops were nine-month enlistees with little or no combat experience. In detriment to their relationship, Banks attempted to shift some of the blame for his reluctance to attack Port Hudson onto Farragut, and told Halleck that the available naval forces were not strong enough for such a campaign.

Farragut learned of these remarks from a New York newspaper. Infuriated by this backbiting, he wrote Welles explaining that his river squadron was "ready for action at all times." On Farragut's letter, Welles penned his own feelings that he "never doubted the readiness of Admiral Farragut to act."

In a letter to his wife, Virginia, Farragut wrote, "You will no doubt hear more of 'Why don't Farragut's fleet move up the river?' Tell them, because the army is not ready. Farragut waits upon Banks as to when or where he will go."

While some may have been critical of Farragut's inactivity at this time, Navy Secretary Welles never lost confidence in his rear admiral. In a diary entry dated February 10, 1863, concerning a successful attack by two Confederate ironclad rams against blockading ships commanded by Flag Officer Samuel F. du Pont at Charleston harbor, Welles commented that it "was not what we expected of him; [du Pont] is not like the firm and impetuous but sagacious and resolute Farragut."

That Farragut was anxious to get upriver and wrest control of the section of the Mississippi between Port Hudson and Vicksburg from the Confederates is evident in the following account from Captain Thornton Jenkins. On January 20, Jenkins reported aboard the *Hartford* as Farragut's new flag captain. Following introductions to the other officers in Farragut's cabin, the admiral asked everyone but Jenkins to leave. According to Jenkins, Farragut told him, "I wish to have some confidential talk with you upon a subject which I have had in mind for a long time. . . . I have never hinted it to any one, nor does the Department know anything of my thoughts. The first object to be accomplished, which led me to think seriously about it, is to cripple the southern armies by cutting off their supplies from Texas. Texas at this time is, and must continue to the end of the war to be, their main dependence for beef cattle, sheep, and Indian corn. If we can get a few vessels above Port Hudson the thing will not be an entire failure, and I am pretty confident it can be done."

Jenkins agreed with Farragut's evaluation of the situation. He suggested the need for support by the army, to which Farragut agreed. However, as we have already seen, army participation in an assault against Port Hudson was not forthcoming.

The impetus to strike upriver without the army was given Farragut by his adopted brother, David Porter. Promoted to acting rear admiral in charge of the naval forces in the upper Mississippi following Flag Officer Davis's recall to Washington, Porter was as anxious as Farragut to close the Red River to enemy supply boats. When the rebel steamer *City of Vicksburg* was reported unloading supplies at the Vicksburg wharf after steaming down the Red River, Porter decided he had to take positive action to close the exit of that river to enemy use. He ordered Charles Rivers Ellet to take his dual-side-wheel ram, *Queen of the West,* under the guns of the Vicksburg batteries and ram and sink the steamer. Following that, he was to continue downriver and make every effort to close the Red River to enemy traffic. Charles Rivers Ellet, like all the Ellet clan, was a daring army officer who took naturally to naval river duty. At Memphis he had led a party of his soldiers into the city while the battle was going on, and raised the flag. He had joined his uncle at Vicksburg, and now, at nineteen, was a lieutenant colonel of the Mississippi River Brigade. His uncle Alfred was its commanding general.

The *Queen* set out on her mission at four-thirty on the morning of February 2, 1863. Porter hoped the ram could make the passage before dawn, and thus surprise the men aboard the rebel steamer. Knowing the chivalrous attitude of the Ellets concerning rescuing men from burning enemy boats, and not wanting Ellet to expose himself to danger any more than required, Porter told him, "It will not be part of your duty to save the lives of those aboard [the *City of Vicksburg*]."

Ellet knew from previous experience that when a ram made such a dangerous run, the boat's pilot came in for special attention by enemy gunners and sharpshooters. With this in mind, the vessel's pilot house was moved to a somewhat more protected location. However, when the side-wheeler was under way, the temporary cable leading from the pilot's steering wheel snapped. The *Queen* was forced to stop while the wheel was moved back to its original place. This lost time meant the attack would have to be made shortly after sunrise. Surprise would no longer be on Ellet's side.

As the Union ram came within range, the upper Vicksburg batteries opened fire on her. Unable to return the fire, Ellet concentrated on his mission, to ram the *City of Vicksburg*. Unfortunately, the Southern steamer was tied to a wharf that protected her from direct attack. This forced Ellet to turn his ram at a ninety-degree angle in order to approach her. As he did so, the river current caught the stern of the *Queen* and swung her around with such force that Ellet lost both speed and direction. The *Queen's* bow no longer faced the *Vicksburg*. Shot and shell punctured the boat in numerous places. Two shells almost completely destroyed the pilot house. When several cotton bales used to protect the starboard paddle wheel were set on fire by enemy shelling, Ellet was forced to give up the attack. The ram dropped downriver, out of range of the batteries.

After stopping for repairs, Ellet took his ram on a series of raids against enemy shipping. In quick succession he captured two steamers loaded with supplies for Port Hudson, and a third that had already unloaded her cargo there. Running low on coal, he sent a signal overland to Porter, who floated an unmanned barge loaded with coal past the Vicksburg batteries. Also joining Ellet was a small steam tug, the *De Soto.* Together the two entered the Confederacy's main trans-Mississippi supply highway, the Red River. On February 12, Ellet's lookouts spotted a Confederate Army wagon convoy full of military supplies. The soldiers landed quietly and proceeded to attack and destroy the twelve-wagon convoy. When shots were fired from a nearby plantation, wounding one of his men, Ellet put every building on the plantation to the torch.

Ellet continued his destructive raids until his vessel became grounded on the evening of Saturday, February 14, during a battle with rebel steamers at Fort DeRussy. Enemy fire set the *Queen* ablaze, forcing Ellet and his crew to abandon her. Although a few of Ellet's men were captured, most escaped by floating downriver on cotton bales. The survivors of the battle crowded aboard the *De Soto.* The tug soon had her own problems, as the rebel boats pursuing them closed in. A broken rudder prevented the tug's skipper from managing her properly, but he was able to ride the river's current and make his escape. With the tug unable to be steered properly, Ellet put all his men aboard a captured Confederate steamer, the *Era No. 5,* where he had left a prize crew aboard earlier. The entire party returned to the Mississippi and headed north.

On Sunday afternoon, Ellet was cheered to meet the newly completed Union ironclad *Indianola* south of Natchez. Lashed to the sides of the ironclad were two coal barges with enough fuel to keep both boats at their posts for several weeks. The *Indianola* was commanded by Lieutenant Commander George Brown. Porter had sent the ironclad below the Vicksburg batteries to support Ellet in his campaign against Confederate river traffic. Brown ordered Ellet to turn his boat around and head south with him, his intention being to use both boats to close the mouth of the Red River.

Taking up the *Indianola*'s station blockading the entrance to the Red River, Brown decided to send the overcrowded *Era* north. He expected that when word reached Porter that the *Queen* had been lost, another vessel would be sent to aid him. Porter, however, was away when word of Ellet's mishap reached his fleet. His subordinates failed to take any action pending Porter's return.

Meanwhile, up the Red River, a Confederate expedition was forming for the purpose of dislodging the *Indianola* from her station. The Union ironclad was a powerful vessel, but, unknown to the Confederates, Brown had only enough trained gunners to man two of his heavy guns. He prudently decided not to follow Ellet's example and steam up the Red River in search of Southern vessels; instead, he anchored near the entrance to that river and waited for enemy vessels to fall into his trap. The two coal barges remained tied to the *Indianola*'s sides. Brown knew that when help arrived, both his vessel and those sent to help him would need the coal in order to operate against enemy traffic.

Under the command of Major Joseph L. Brent, the *Queen* was repaired and refloated. Brent was ordered to steam down the Red River with a small flotilla and attack the *Indianola*. Along with the *Queen*, Brent had an ironclad gunboat, the *Webb*, and two cottonclad steamers loaded with Confederate infantry, the *Grand Era* and the *Doctor Beatty*.

In the early hours of February 24, Brown learned from local sources that the Confederate flotilla was steaming downriver to attack him, and that it included the ram *Queen* and at least one ironclad gunboat. The *Indianola* quickly weighed anchor and headed north toward Vicksburg. Brown hoped to meet the support boat or boats he expected Porter to have sent before he was forced to fight a numerically superior enemy. The swift ironclad could have outrun her pursuers if Brown had unleashed the two coal barges. However, he remained ignorant of the fact that no help was coming, and continued to operate under the impression that the coal would be needed when help arrived. The coal barges remained tied to the sides of the *Indianola*, slowing her speed substantially. Because of this, the pursuing Confederate boats caught up with the Union ironclad shortly before nine-thirty that evening.

When vessels were reported approaching from the south at high speed, Brown had his boat rounded in order to meet the flotilla head-on. The Confederate boats steamed straight toward their prey at top speed. At 150 yards, Major Brent gave the order to fire. With all guns blazing, the rebel boats attacked from three directions, limiting Brown's ability to fight all at the same time. When several attempts to ram her failed because of the barges tied to her sides, the ironclad's exposed stern came in for special attention. First the *Queen* rammed the *Indianola*'s stern with such force that she broke through the latter's hull, causing serious damage. Pulling free, the *Queen*'s skipper, Captain James McCloskey, found his newly won vessel listing so badly that one of her huge paddle wheels spun helplessly in the air, completely out of the water. As the *Queen* backed away, the *Webb* moved in and rammed the identical spot, causing even more extensive damage. Meanwhile, the coal barges were hulled by shells fired from the two cottonclads. Both began to sink, pulling the ironclad down with them. Confederate riflemen aboard the *Beatty* and the *Grand Era* prevented Union sailors from reaching the deck and untying the barges. The ramming soon turned the *Indianola* completely around in the water. Her rudder was destroyed, and her ability to fight diminished by the damage the ramming had also caused to her gun positions.

In an attempt to save what he could of his vessel, Brown managed to head it toward the western shore of the river, which was ostensibly under the control of Union troops sent down by General Grant. With his stern now underwater, two enemy boats preparing to ram what was left of his vessel, and another loaded with infantry attempting to grapple and board her, Brown feared his boat would go down with little chance of his crew surviving. His only alternative was to surrender, which he did. The Union sailors were taken aboard one of the cottonclads. Later they were sent to a prison in Jackson.

Pulling the ironclad free of the western bank, where Union cavalry units were known to be operating, Brent had the vessel towed across the river and grounded on the eastern bank. A work party soon arrived and began efforts to repair the extensive damage sustained by the ironclad in the battle. Brent hoped to refloat another Union boat and use it against the enemy, just as he had the *Queen*.

In the meantime, north of Vicksburg, Porter had returned and learned what had happened to the *Queen of the West*. When he heard the gunfire from downriver, he realized that the fate of the *Indianola* was in question as well, but there was nothing he could do. Porter had already sent many of his ironclads off on another mission, and he needed the few he had to guard his position on the river. To order another vessel below Vicksburg alone would invite another disaster, so assistance was not sent to the *Indianola*.

While these events transpired, Porter's staff had been developing a subterfuge that, if successful, would cost the Vicksburg batteries some of their guns. Earlier, when the *Queen* and the *Indianola* had steamed down the river, several enemy guns had burst from the constant firing. Since rebel gunners had sacrificed their guns trying to sink dangerous Union boats, it was hoped that any vessel they thought was a Union gunboat trying to get below the city would elicit the same response. At Porter's direction, the hull of an old barge was used to build an imitation of a large *Monitor*-type ironclad. Tarred pine boards were used to simulate huge paddle-wheel boxes and a large gun turret, and barrels were stacked end-to-end to give the impression of smokestacks. Pots of tar and oakum secured below the stacks produced the required black smoke. Mimicking naval guns, series of logs stuck out of gun ports on both sides as well as from the stern and bow, giving her the appearance of carrying enormous firepower. Union officers christened the three-hundred-foot-long mock ironclad the *Black Terror*. She was towed into the center of the river, where it was hoped the current would carry her past the enemy batteries. The *Black Terror* was released into the swift current shortly before midnight on February 25.

Below Vicksburg, a party of engineers worked tirelessly on the *Indianola*, trying to repair the rudder and other damage caused by her battle with the Confederate gunboats. Every man knew this vessel would play a key role in the Confederate defense of the river if they could refloat her before any other Union boats arrived. Work suddenly stopped when the firing of heavy guns upriver broke the nighttime silence. The men recognized the sounds of the Vicksburg batteries, and grew jittery at the thought that Federal gunboats might be coming downriver to rescue what remained of *Indianola*. Adding to the noise were the whistle blasts of a steamboat. Peering into the darkness of the river, they were surprised to see the *Queen of the West* rushing south at full speed. She had been tied up near Vicksburg when the *Black Terror* began her run safely past the batteries, and rushed south to warn the repair party.

The mock ironclad drifted under the batteries with little or no damage. Rebel gunners pounded the river in an attempt to sink her, and were surprised when the large and seemingly powerful craft failed to return their fire. The river current did its duty for the Union.

The *Black Terror* continued downriver in what appeared to the Confederates to be an attempt to reach the *Indianola*.

The Confederate officer commanding the work parties and the soldiers guarding them cannot be faulted for the actions he took when word of the giant ironclad reached him from several sources. These included a telegram from local army headquarters, and the *Queen*, which stopped just long enough to give the alarm, then fled downriver. The telegram compounded the error made by those who mistook the wooden craft belching black smoke for a warship by claiming two such ironclads had run the batteries and were steaming southward. Fearing the vessel would be recovered by the approaching enemy gunboats, the officer detailed a party to blow up the *Indianola* where she lay. Porter's ruse to cause damage to the Vicksburg battery cannons had inadvertently prevented the Confederates from putting a powerful ironclad to use in their effort to remain in control of the river from Vicksburg to Port Hudson.

The loss of both the ram *Queen of the West* and the much-heralded new ironclad *Indianola* was a blow to Porter. In a rare instance of candor, he wrote the Navy Department, describing what had happened as "the most humiliating affair that has occurred during the rebellion."

When word of the loss of the *Queen of the West* and the *Indianola* reached Farragut at New Orleans, he was furious. He wrote Undersecretary Fox that he was "grieved" that Porter had sent his boats below the Vicksburg batteries one at a time instead of in large enough numbers to destroy the Confederate boats operating between Vicksburg and Port Hudson. He expressed surprise that the *Indianola* had been captured without loss of life among her crew. "I never thought much of ironclads," he told the undersecretary, "but my opinion of them is declining daily." The admiral was in the habit of telling all who would listen, "Give me wooden ships and iron hearts," because he believed they were as good as any ironclad.

After weeks of waiting for the army to act, he decided he could wait no longer. Impatient to move against Port Hudson, Farragut swung into action. He informed Captain Jenkins of the disasters upriver, and told him, "The time has come; there can be no more delay. I must go—army or no army." Recalling Commodore Bell from blockade duty off the Texas coast, the admiral told his friend, "Porter has allowed his boats to come down one at a time, and they have been captured by the enemy, which compels me to go up and recapture the whole, or be sunk in the attempt. The whole country will be up in arms if we do not do something."

"Doing something" meant passing the Port Hudson batteries and taking back control of the river between that bastion and Vicksburg. Burning with new determination, Farragut pressured and cajoled Banks into action. The general agreed to make a diversionary attack against Port Hudson's rear in order to draw some of its guns away from the river. The army would also keep the nearly twenty thousand Confederate troops stationed there busy while Farragut's ships steamed past.

Farragut remained short of ships. The majority of his squadron was still on blockade duty in the Gulf. Since his goal was to get as many large warships north of Port Hudson as possible, Farragut hoped that Bell, aboard the *Brooklyn*, would arrive in time to join his expedition. Some relief on this score was provided by the arrival of the *Monongahela*, a screw-driven sloop-of-war.

Responding to Farragut's pressure, New Orleans was stripped of most of its Federal defenses by General Banks, who assigned twelve thousand men to Baton Rouge, increasing that city's garrison to over twenty thousand Federal troops. Leaving behind a few gunboats to keep the peace, Farragut steamed upriver with a squadron of four large warships: the sloops *Hartford*, Captain James S. Palmer; *Richmond*, Commander James Alden; and *Monongahela*, Captain J. P. McKinstry; and the side-wheeler *Mississippi*, Captain Melancton Smith. Two gunboats and several mortar frigates accompanied them. Arriving at Baton Rouge on March 11, they were greeted by Commander H. B. Caldwell of the ironclad gunboat *Essex*. Caldwell had under his command two more gunboats and several mortar boats waiting for the admiral.

Earlier the same day, Banks had left Baton Rouge with his force of more than twelve thousand men, including the first Negro regiments to engage in combat, the First and Third Louisiana Native Guards. The former comprised free blacks from New Orleans, many of whom were educated and possessing some wealth. Their officers were also all black. The latter were mostly freed slaves who had been trained and were led by white officers. Banks's force also included nine companies of cavalry and several units of light artillery.

The *Monongahela*—a fearless wooden ship. Courtesy of Anne S. K. Brown Military Collection, Brown University Library.

While they waited for the army to get into position, the sailors aboard Farragut's little fleet stripped their ships for battle. Rigging was removed and stowed, nets to catch splintered wood flying through the air were hung, chains were suspended over the sides to protect the hulls and boilers, and buckets of sand were placed near gun positions to help soak up the blood that was sure to be spilled.

After weeks of waiting, the activity and the coming engagement revived Farragut. Men who had been with him for a long time recognized the renewed spring in his step as he moved about the *Hartford*, checking on all details, great or small. Older crewmen started referring to him as "Daring Dave" once more.

Perhaps recalling the incident when the *Brooklyn* had failed to pass the Vicksburg batteries because of a misunderstanding, Farragut made his instructions extremely clear for passing the Port Hudson batteries. "Bear in mind that the object is, to run the batteries at the least possible damage to our ships, and thereby secure an efficient force above, for the purpose of rendering such assistance as may be required of us by the army at Vicksburg; or, if not required there, to our own army near Baton Rouge. If they succeed in getting past the batteries, the gunboats will proceed up to the mouth of Red River, and keep up the police of the river between that river and Port Hudson, capturing everything they can. Whoever is so fortunate to get through, will proceed to carry out the views contained in the General Order, that is, stop the communication between Red River and the rebels on the eastern bank of the Mississippi River, and communicate with the army and fleet above, and, if their services are not required to assist in reducing Vicksburg, return to the mouth of Red River and keep up the blockade until the want of provisions and coal makes it necessary to return to Baton Rouge. Nurse your coal with all possible care."

"Supplies of coal and provisions may probably be obtained from the fleet and army above. As long as supplies can be obtained, the vessels above Port Hudson will remain there."

A few minutes after 4:00 P.M. on Friday, March 13, Farragut's fleet left Baton Rouge and steamed upriver for about fifteen miles. It was a crisp, clear afternoon, and the cool breeze refreshed the men working on the decks. Anchors were dropped and the crews given a brief respite before proceeding. Before dawn on Saturday, they were under way again, and arrived at a small piece of land in the river called Prophet's Island at 8:00 A.M. Two hours later, all boat commanders and senior officers attended a war council on board the *Hartford*. The strength of the river current and the sharp turn above the batteries were major concerns of all in attendance. The river was running at about five knots, meaning that the sloops would be slowed by the current to a speed almost equal to that of a walking man. Exacerbating the challenge was the one-hundred-degree turn to the west just above the batteries. Because of a large shoal at the bend, there was only a narrow channel with sufficient depth to allow the larger ships to pass. Its width was barely enough for the passage of one ship at a time.

To compensate for the drag of the current, and to help the sloops maneuver at the bend, Farragut ordered that each of the three sloops have a gunboat secured to her port side. This would also help protect the gunboats from the shelling of the batteries, which were on the starboard side of the ships. It also provided emergency power to the larger ships, should their boilers suffer damage. Lashed to the side of the *Hartford* was the gunboat *Albatross*, Lieutenant Commander John E. Hart; to the *Richmond* was attached the powerful *Genesee*, Commander W. H. Macomb; and to the *Monongahela* was affixed the *Kineo*, Lieutenant Commander John Watters. Only the *Mississippi* remained alone. Her configuration, with large paddle wheels on either side, prevented a gunboat from joining her. The order of battle was *Hartford, Richmond, Monongahela,* and *Mississippi.* Each ship was to remain slightly starboard of the one ahead, allowing free use of bow guns. Five mortar boats were tied up along the eastern bank about a half-mile below the first batteries, and shielded from the sighting of rebel gunners by the thick woods that ran to the edge of the river. Protecting the mortar boats from attack were the gunboats *Essex* and *Sachem*, with orders to remain below the batteries. Farragut had instructed the mortar boat skippers to hold their fire until firing was commenced by either the ships or the batteries. Although he was aware that Confederate lookouts had been watching their progress, he wanted to keep the moment of movement of the fleet as secret as possible. Early attack on the batteries by the mortars would only serve to give the enemy advance warning that the ships would soon be under way.

When the officers left the *Hartford* to return to their own vessels, each must have recalled the admiral's admonition, "I think the best protection against the enemy's fire is a well-directed fire from our own guns, shell and shrapnel at a distance, and grape when within four hundred or five hundred yards."

As the day migrated toward its end, the crews of the Union ships and boats made every possible preparation for the coming battle. Decks were whitewashed so that obstacles could more easily be seen in the dark, and shot was made ready for quick loading. On board the *Hartford*, Fleet Surgeon J. M. Foltz asked Farragut to assign Loyall to work with him belowdecks. Foltz said that since the Admiral's son was not in the service, "and had nothing to gain, but everything to lose, by exposure on the quarter deck," he should be in a more protected part of the ship. Farragut responded that such a suggestion would not do. Although Loyall was not in the service, and was aboard the flagship only as a visitor, he would remain on deck, acting "as one of my aids, to assist in conveying my orders during the battle." Farragut and his only child would "trust in Providence and la fortune de la guerre."

When the sun disappeared and the night grew darker, a deathly silence fell over the river. In the afternoon a message had arrived from General Banks that his troops would be ready to attack Port Hudson from the rear. Farragut sent word back that he hoped to be north of the batteries before midnight. If the army was to be of any assistance, it would have to launch its diversionary attack before then. The obviously slow pace of Banks's force must have caused Farragut to wonder if the diversion would actually take place.

A few minutes before nine o'clock, following a light supper, Farragut stood on the quarterdeck listening to the silence. There was no breeze, and the air was heavy with moisture. He turned to Loyall and quietly told him to go below and inform Captains Palmer and Jenkins that he was ready to get under way. The signal, two red lanterns hung at the stern, was given, and crewmen set about preparing the ship to move as quietly as they could. The admiral and the two captains watched astern as the *Monongahela* and the *Mississippi* were evidently experiencing difficulty in weighing anchor.

Suddenly a screeching whistle from downriver broke the silence, and flares waved wildly in the darkness. Greatly annoyed by the attention it had brought to his ship, Farragut watched as the army tug *Reliance*, its high-pressure engines puffing loudly, approached the *Hartford*. It brought word that General Banks would be at the crossroads east of Port Hudson at midnight, at which time he would begin his diversionary attack. Banks had halted his army five miles from Port Hudson, and would ultimately serve no useful purpose in diverting the attention of Confederate commanders from the Union ships. Farragut read the message and handed it to Captain Jenkins with the remark, "He had as well be in New Orleans or Baton Rouge for all the good he is doing us."

Some dispute arose afterward concerning the timetable for passing the batteries. Banks claimed that Farragut had originally planned to make his run in the predawn hours of the following day. Based on this, Banks said he had not been in position to launch his diversionary attack when Farragut started upriver. Although the admiral did not enter the fray over this, his supporters insisted that Farragut had informed Banks of the change early in the day, when the general's messenger had informed Farragut that the army was in place. They accused Banks of being reluctant to attack the fortifications from the rear because he believed a Confederate disinformation campaign that the rebel garrison now numbered between twenty and thirty thousand men. The Confederate force was actually about equal in size to that Banks had brought. In any event, the massed Federal troops played no role in the operation, but instead remained, as one army officer said, "little more than spectators and auditors of the battle between the ships and the forts."

By ten o'clock, each ship was in line and under a head of steam. Quietly they slid upstream, the sloops' screws beating like hearts in a distant body. The whooshing of the two great paddle wheels of the *Mississippi* sounded like surf crashing on a beach.

High on the bluffs, the Confederate gunners were ready. The pounding of the steam engines in the river below had alerted them to coming action. The arrival of the noisy little army tug had also told them on board which vessel the fleet's commanding officer was located. The rebel soldiers waited in silence as they watched the darkness that consumed the river below, looking for a sign of the enemy ships. On the river, the air was still, with no breeze at all, hanging heavy with a humid mist. The ships moved so slowly against the current that their forward motion produced very little air movement that might help relieve those on the decks.

Shortly before 11:20 P.M., the *Hartford* was opposite the most southerly of the batteries when a Confederate lookout on the west bank of the river fired a signal rocket that soared into the black sky over the ships and burst into a starlike light before falling into the river. It was quickly followed by another. Even before the flares extinguished themselves in the water, the enemy's southernmost batteries, commanded by Lieutenant Colonel Paul F. de Gournay, opened fire. The first shot was fired by Battery 9, its eight-inch shell exploding in the air above the *Hartford* and the *Albatross*. The first shells fired by the batteries were the signal for the mortar boats to begin their deadly work of driving the rebel gunners from their weapons and reducing the enemy's ability to fire down into the ships. The *Essex* and the *Sachem*, guarding the mortar boats from possible infantry attack, also began shelling the batteries, although their guns did not have the height range of the mortars. On board the *Hartford*, the only gun that could be brought to bear on the bluffs above was the Sawyer on the forecastle. She quickly began firing at the muzzle flashes of the enemy guns. The Union gunners were virtually blind to the enemy positions in the dark.

Suddenly the river around the flagship lit up in a kind of false dawn. On the west bank, a group of Confederate soldiers had put the torch to several huge piles of pitch pine that had been prepared for this purpose. As the fires roared to life, large reflectors mounted behind them threw their light onto the flagship, making it a clear target for the gunners high on the east bank. The *Hartford* fired a few broadsides into the fires that scattered the wood and returned the river to darkness.

Farragut had prepared his gun crews for fighting in the dark with instructions to hold their fire until they saw the flash of an enemy gun, then use that as their target. Both sides were working in a condition of near blindness, with the black of the night broken only by the explosions of shells. Compounding this disability was the amount of smoke created by the firing. This was a minimal hindrance to the *Hartford*'s gunners, but became progressively worse for each of the following ships, as the smoke from the *Hartford*'s guns blew back into the faces of the *Richmond*'s gunners, then combined with the *Richmond*'s gunsmoke to make the situation even worse for the men aboard the *Monongahela*. Suffering worst from the thick smoke that lay on the river from the firing of ships' guns was the last in line, the *Mississippi*.

As shells burst around the *Hartford* and her gunboat consort, the Union sailors returned fire so rapidly that gunnery captains repeatedly had to order them to slow down before the heat damaged their own guns. The Confederate gunners, eighty feet above the river, were unable to depress their guns sufficiently to direct their fire at the flagship with great accuracy. Most of the shells burst either above or far

"Attack on Port Hudson," from a painting by A. R. Waud. Courtesy of the Hastings (N.Y.) Historical Society.

to the port side of the ship. Only a few actually found their target. In the midst of the battle, as his ship virtually crawled through this gauntlet of explosions, Farragut stepped back for a better look and accidentally stepped onto a tarpaulin covering a gangway. Only the quick reaction of Loyall and a nearby sailor saved him from a dangerous fall.

Farragut had prepared for the buildup of blinding smoke that lay on the top of the water. His pilot, Thomas R. Carrell, was stationed in the mizzentop, where Farragut had ordered a speaking trumpet tied. From this vantage point, Carrell could be expected to see over the smoke. The trumpet and its long tube allowed him to shout instructions to the wheelhouse with some hope of being heard over the noise of the battle.

Except for brief moments of light from the explosions, no one on either side could see much of anything. The deafening blasts of the naval guns and enemy cannons filled the night air close around the ships, and the deep, hollow roar of the mortars thumped in what sounded like the distance. Bursts of light dotted the darkness in a grand pyrotechnic display that was as deadly as it was awe-inspiring. Loyall wrote later that the "magnificent" display was a sight "not often witnessed in a life-time." From the relative safety of a trench behind the bluffs, a Confederate soldier from Tennessee described the scene as "full of the screaming, exploding heavy bombs. The man who would say he could look with complacency and ease on such a scene has no regard for the truth. It was terrific."

The roar of the mortar guns and the spectacle of their flashing projectiles climbing high into the air, slowly arcing as their speed slowed to a stop, then quickly picking up velocity as they plummeted to earth, mesmerized more than one witness. At a plantation four miles away, several women stood at a second floor window, listening and watching. One equated the scene to the bombardment of Baton Rouge, claiming the latter was "child's play compared to this." She said the house shook with every explosion of a mortar shell. For miles around, people reported shattered windows and fallen objects as the earth itself trembled from the pounding of the mighty guns.

But to all this beauty was added death. Shells did hit the ship, and their blasts injured and killed men. Watching all this, the admiral remained unruffled as he quietly walked around the quarterdeck, issuing orders to his young aides in a calm voice and sending them off to deliver his instructions around the ship.

Above the smoke, the pilot, who was used to steering river craft through these waters under peaceful conditions, must have been terrified by the death and destruction he witnessed, and the explosions that rocked the mast that was his perch.

Through all the noise and chaos, the *Hartford* and the *Albatross* moved ahead at a pace so slow it belied the power of their engines. From his roost above the ship, Carrell called down to Farragut that the layer of smoke had risen so high he could no longer see anything. Farragut immediately ordered the ship's guns to cease firing. It was not a moment too soon, for the *Hartford* had been gently swung around by the current, and was heading toward the shore below the bluffs. Suddenly the sound of the ship's hull scraping the bottom told all aboard that she was in danger of grounding.

For a brief few moments it appeared the flagship would fall victim to the river, but Farragut's quick response helped save the day.

Through his hailing trumpet he shouted at the *Albatross*, "Back, back!" Instantly the screw driving the gunboat stopped and began spinning in reverse. Her engine-room crew poured liquid combustibles into her fires to increase steam pressure quickly for additional power. It worked, and not a moment too soon. Confederate infantry officers thought the ship had touched the shore on purpose and was preparing to land marines. In response they sent a company of sharpshooters to the scene. The rebel riflemen arrived just as the two ships began to back away, but were able to fire several volleys at the figures visible on the decks. The ships, lashed together, rocked for a moment as the larger was already partially grounded. Then the smaller, with great effort, backed them both off. The *Hartford* and her partner slowly turned north and in a few minutes were beyond the range of the enemy's guns.

Next in line was the *Richmond*. She struggled not only with the night, as the flagship did, but had the added burden of the smoke generated by the guns and engines of the *Hartford* and the *Albatross* to abet her blindness. As she approached safety at the northern end of the line of batteries, her pilot prepared to make the turn he was still unable to see in the dark and thick smoke. Enraged by the successful run of the *Hartford* and the *Albatross*, a Confederate gun crew rolled their weapon out to the very edge of the northernmost bluff. Using ropes to secure it, they tipped the gun over the edge so it faced almost directly down into the river. Suddenly, from high above them, a shot plunged down through the *Richmond*'s decks and destroyed her steam safety valves. Escaping steam scalded engine-room crewmen and filled the lower decks of the ship. Vapor extinguished the port fire. The sloop quickly lost pressure and slowed almost to a halt. Four seamen entered the steam-filled engine room at great personal risk in an attempt to restart the port furnace by carrying fire to it from the starboard furnace. Their daring efforts earned all four, First Class Firemen Matthew McClelland, Joseph E. Vantine, and John Rush, and Second Class Fireman John Hickman, the Congressional Medal of Honor.

Crippled and unable to move under her own power in spite of the courageous efforts of her crew, the *Richmond*'s guns blazed away at the unseen enemy, while rebel canister and grape tore through her. As the gunboat *Genesee*, lashed to her side, tried desperately to drive herself and the larger ship to safety upriver, the *Richmond* remained for several minutes a stationary target for the Confederate gunners and sharpshooters. According to the ship's journal, "We were, for a few minutes, at the rebels' mercy; their shell were causing great havoc on our decks; the groans of the wounded and the shrieks of the dying were awful."

Among the wounded was the executive officer, Lieutenant Commander A. Boyd Cummings, who lost a leg to a rebel round shot. As sailors and officers ran to his aid, Cummings cried out, "Quick, boys, pick me up, put a tourniquet on my leg, send my letters to my wife, tell them I fell in doing my duty." Taken below where doctors were treating the wounded, Cummings ordered that men more seriously hurt than he be attended to first.

Confederate shells, canister, and grape riddled the *Richmond* as she stood virtually still in the rain of death and destruction. A shell entered the forward starboard gun port and exploded beneath the gun. The exploding metal and wood ripped one arm and both legs from the body of the boatswain's mate. He died within minutes, but not before exhorting his shipmates not to give up the ship. More shells smashed through the numbers 8, 11, and 12 gun ports, killing or wounding over a dozen sailors and marines. The *Richmond*'s gunners were almost helpless in their ability to fire back, since most of her guns could not be raised high enough to return effective fire. Many of their shells drove harmlessly into the mud below the crest of the bluffs.

Meanwhile, the *Genesee,* the most powerful of the gunboats attempting to run the Port Hudson batteries, finally pulled the larger ship free. She struggled to make progress against the current and join the *Hartford* beyond the river bend. Despite her best efforts, however, the ships lost ground, and when the current caught the *Richmond*'s bow just right, both vessels began to swing around in the river. Giving up the effort, the gunboat's captain, Commander W. H. Macomb, continued turning both ships around, and headed back downriver.

On deck, the gunners, who were still blinded by the night and the ever-thickening smoke, were unaware of the change in direction. When they saw what appeared to be flashes from enemy guns, they fired several shots before they were stopped. Unfortunately, the flashes they saw were from the guns of the *Mississippi*. The two ships passed each other in the middle of the river, with neither knowing the other was so close.

Belowdecks, when Lieutenant Commander Cummings was informed of the direction change, he cried, "I would rather lose the other leg than go back. Can nothing be done?" Nothing could be done. The *Richmond* and the *Genesee* continued downriver until they were out of the enemy's range, where they dropped their anchors at about 1:00 A.M. The *Richmond* had been engaged with the enemy for over one hour, and had suffered such heavy damage that many believed that if the swift gunboat had not been lashed to her side, she would have been destroyed by the enemy batteries. Cummings succumbed to his wounds four days later.

Next in line were the *Monongahela* and the *Kineo*. Both made it almost to the river bend, when the gunboat's rudder was disabled by several rifle shots from the western bank. The *Kineo* returned the fire and either killed or drove off the rebel soldiers. As she prepared for the turn, having to move from the center of the river closer to the eastern bank, the big sloop suddenly grounded, with such force that the lines securing the sloop to the gunboat snapped. Because she was unable to free herself without the help of the *Kineo*, new lines were run between them. All this took over twenty minutes to accomplish. During that time rebel gunners took advantage of the *Monongahela*'s predicament, and poured shells and canister into her at an alarming rate. In the hail of fire the ship's bridge collapsed, killing three men and severely injuring Captain McKinstry, rendering him unconscious.

As sailors fought to reunite the two vessels, one grounded, the other unable to maneuver properly because of rudder damage, they were exposed to enemy fire. Screaming men fell along the entire main deck, where the flow of blood made it nearly impossible to secure a foothold. Finally, success was achieved, and amid the continuing bombardment, the gunboat pulled her companion free. The *Monongahela*'s executive officer, future admiral and Spanish-American War hero, Lieutenant Winfield Scott Schley, ordered both vessels to continue upriver, and they both attempted to restart their voyage. Unfortunately, the lines that had been hastily run between both vessels were only temporary, and once again they snapped. Unable to continue north without the use of her rudder, the *Kineo* drifted

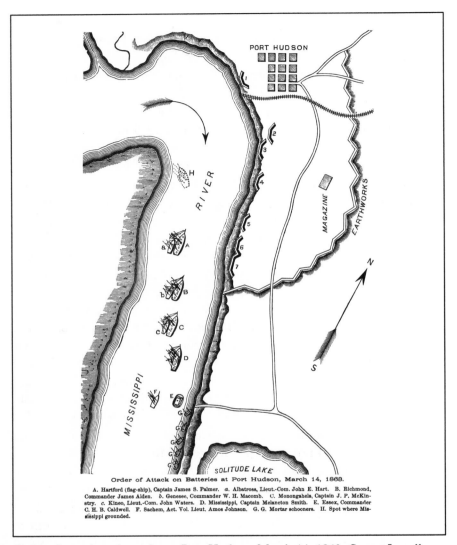

Order of Attack on Batteries at Port Hudson, March 14, 1863.

A. Hartford (flag-ship), Captain James S. Palmer. a. Albatross, Lieut.-Com. John E. Hart. B. Richmond, Commander James Alden. b. Genesee, Commander W. H. Macomb. C. Monongahela, Captain J. P. McKinstry. c. Kineo, Lieut.-Com. John Waters. D. Mississippi, Captain Melancton Smith. E. Essex, Commander C. H. B. Caldwell. F. Sachem, Act. Vol. Lieut. Amos Johnson. G. G. Mortar schooners. H. Spot where Mississippi grounded.

Order of attack on batteries at Port Hudson, March 14, 1863. *Source:* Loyall Farragut, *The Life of David Glasgow Farragut* (New York: D. Appleton and Co., 1879).

helplessly downriver with the current. She returned as much fire as she could while she passed beneath the batteries. As with the other vessels in the force, her guns could not reach the bluffs, so her crew concentrated their fire on the Confederate infantry and cavalry that had massed along the western bank.

The *Monongahela* almost made it to the safety of the river bend alone, when her engines suddenly stopped. A crank pin, overheated and damaged during the efforts to free the ship from the grounding, cracked. Unable to regain power, the ship drifted back downriver, powered only by the current. Once again she was subjected to a severe pounding as she swept below the batteries.

Last in line was the *Mississippi*. Because Farragut felt that the old side-wheeler had the least chance of successfully running the batteries, he had positioned her at the end of the line, where, if she failed to make the passage, she would not interfere with the other ships.

As the *Mississippi* began her passage, she was completely enveloped by the smoke caused by the ongoing battle of the ships ahead of her. Her executive officer, Lieutenant George Dewey, reported that his ship passed the *Monongahela* while she was grounded without ever seeing her. "Both Captain Smith and myself," Dewey later wrote, "felt that our destiny that night was in the hands of the pilot. There was nothing to do but to fire back at the flashes on the bluffs and trust to his expert knowledge. It was a new experience for him, guiding a heavy-draught oceangoing ship in the midst of battle smoke, with shells shrieking in his ears."

As had her predecessors, the *Mississippi* took a pounding from the Confederate guns. The smoke was so thick by now that men literally choked on it. The rumble of cannon fire, the blasts of exploding shells, and the deep booming of the mortars made most men deaf to shouted orders.

Straining to see through the smoke and keep control of his fear at the same time, the civilian pilot watched for some sign indicating the ship had reached the point in the river where it would have to make a sharp turn in order to negotiate the river bend. Suddenly he realized the ship had reached the place he sought, and shouted as loud as he could, "Starboard the helm! Full speed ahead." The huge paddle wheels rapidly gained speed and drove the ship high up on a sandbar. The pilot had been mistaken, and ordered the turn before actually reaching the river bend. The officers and crew reacted quickly and professionally to the grounding. Dewey attributed this to their weeks of training while stationed in the Gulf, and the fact that most of the crew had been aboard when the ship ran Forts Jackson and St. Philip the year before.

The *Mississippi* had just begun to gain momentum when she struck the bar. This helped drive her farther on the sandbar than might otherwise have been the case. Smith immediately ordered the paddle wheels reversed at full speed. The ship did not move. She began to list badly to port, so the port guns were run in to attempt to balance the weight and help right her. Nothing seemed to be going well. "Every precaution to meet the emergency was taken promptly," according to Dewey, "and there was remarkably little confusion."

For thirty-five minutes the crew struggled in vain to free their ship. Orders had to be shouted two and three times so they could be heard above the barking of the ship's guns, the pounding of the big wheels against the sandbar, and the throbbing of the straining engines. Offered another stationary target, gunners on the nearby bluffs soon found their range and began splintering the fine old ship that had seen such glorious duty in the Far East. Several shells hulled her, and a fire broke out in the flammables storeroom, which is normally protected from enemy fire because it is usually below the water line.

Standing on deck amid the noise and smoke, Captain Smith, a man known for his calm deportment, used a flint to light a cigar. Looking around at the death and destruction, he was heartbroken over the thought of losing so many crewmen, and the real possibility of losing his ship to enemy fire. As Lieutenant Dewey approached, he said, "Well, it doesn't look as if we could get her off." Quietly Dewey replied, "No, it doesn't."

Around them the noise continued at its deafening rate. Sand and water splashed onto the listing ship from shells that missed, and wood and metal splinters flew through the air from those that did not miss. "Can we save the crew?" Smith asked, to which his executive officer answered, "Yes, sir!" The order to abandon ship was given. Despite this, the gunners on the starboard side kept up their firing as if they expected to be victorious.

The lifeboats on the starboard, facing the bluffs, had all been destroyed, so the wounded were brought on deck and placed in the three port boats. Several trips to the nearby shore had to be made by the boats. Dewey realized that if the men who took the boats to shore failed to return, those left on board were sure to die, so he jumped into one of the boats and went to the shore with it. As the boats emptied of men, Dewey ordered four men to remain to row the boat he was in back to the crippled ship. Each man thought the order was for another, and all abandoned him, except the *Mississippi*'s black cook, who remained to help. Shamed that the white sailors who had been trained to fight had left their officer alone, with only the black cook voluntarily remaining, several men returned and rowed back to the ship. A second boat joined the return trip after an acting master's mate named Chase used his revolver to force four crewmen back into his boat.

While the last remaining crew members boarded the waiting boats, Smith and Dewey searched the ship for survivors. Having found only one, a young ship's boy partially buried under a pile of dead bodies, they set several fires. Smith was determined that no rebel flag would ever fly over his ship. As the fires spread and became visible to those high on the bluffs, a loud and sustained rebel yell of victory exceeded even the sounds of the shells exploding.

As the boats rowed away and got caught in the current, the *Mississippi* burst into flames. Soon, water rushed into the lower decks and began to lift her off the bar. Flames leapt into the air from a dozen places, as the vessel slowly regained the water. Turned around by the powerful current, she began drifting downriver. As she passed the enemy batteries, her port guns, which had been loaded in case they were needed, began firing when the flames reached their primers. As Dewey and the others watched, she became "a dying ship manned by dead men, firing on the enemy."

Watching his ship drift off into the night in flames, Captain Smith removed his sword and pistols and dropped them into the river. "I'm not going to surrender them to any rebel," he told Dewey. Smith's act was a bit premature, for those on board the boat were soon rescued by the *Richmond*, which was at anchor downriver.

Meanwhile, upriver, unable to see anything of what was happening beyond the river bend, Admiral Farragut waited with intense anxiety for the arrival of his ships. The first sign of disaster came with the explosions and flames that destroyed the *Mississippi*. The cannon fire slowed and eventually ceased. Farragut realized the rest of his fleet was not coming. Several signal flares were fired into the night sky, but they elicited no response. The *Hartford* and the *Albatross* were the only Union vessels to make the run successfully, and now they were alone in the Confederate-dominated section of the river.

9

"The Father
of Waters . . ."

T HE LAST ECHOES OF NAVAL GUNS and shore batteries died away. Word soon reached General Banks that Farragut had maneuvered two vessels north of Port Hudson. Having taken virtually no part in the battle, and seeing no purpose in remaining, Banks ordered his troops to withdraw. Rumors quickly spread among the reserve units that the front-line troops had fought a desperate battle and had been defeated. Dreading their fate in enemy hands, these units, consisting of two infantry brigades, some artillery, and the quartermaster's wagon train, began withdrawal in what rapidly escalated to a panicked retreat. Overcome by the heat and humidity, many threw their equipment and ammunition onto the roadsides. The front-line troops, who knew firsthand they had engaged in no real battle, withdrew slowly. Many of them were angry over not seeing action after their tedious march from Baton Rouge. As Banks rode past these men, he was greeted by a sullen silence. Only a day earlier the same troops had cheered him when they thought he was leading them into battle.

On the river below Port Hudson, the Union fleet made a "melancholy spectacle." The decks of the *Richmond* were covered with blood and body parts. Laid out wherever space could be found were the survivors of the ill-fated *Mississippi*. The *Monongahela* looked as if she were made of Swiss cheese. At least eight shots had passed completely through her hull. As sailors struggled to wash the decks of the remains of their shipmates, doctors cared for the wounded, and carpenters quickly hammered coffins together.

North of Port Hudson, Admiral Farragut spent a sleepless night wondering what fate had befallen the remainder of his fleet. The following day, Sunday, March 15, 1863, the sun rose bright in the morning sky. The officers and men aboard the flagship busied themselves with the same chores that occupied the crews of the Union ships below Port Hudson. The decks had to be washed of blood, the wounded cared for, and temporary repairs made to the ship herself. Lookouts watched the river above and below them for enemy activity. Occasionally they would catch sight of Confederate cavalry moving about on either side of the river. A few of the more brazen of these rebel soldiers actually rode to the edge of the river and watered their horses in full view of the Union sailors.

The presence of mounted enemy units on both shores precluded any possibility that Farragut could send word of his position to the fleet by an overland route. Although the river was quiet all morning, the rebel troopers remained nearby. It was obvious that they intended to fire at anyone attempting to land from the enemy warship. The thick woods at the bend in the river made it impossible for the *Hartford* to catch sight of the rest of the fleet, even when she moved down almost within range of the Port Hudson batteries. Unable to communicate his safe passage, he had a message nailed to a launch, which was then set adrift to be carried downriver by the current.

Farragut was concerned that the failure of the rest of his ships to pass the batteries might be viewed as a military disaster. The following day, as the *Hartford* and the *Albatross* cautiously steamed upriver in search of enemy vessels, he wrote his report of the action to Secretary Welles. It began, "It becomes my duty to report disaster to my fleet. . . ."

Welles saw the entire affair differently from the way his admiral did, stranded as he was alone on the enemy's river. The following month he wrote Farragut, "The Navy Department congratulates you and the officers and men of the Hartford upon the gallant passage of the Port Hudson batteries, and also the battery at Grand Gulf. Although the remainder of your fleet were not successful in following their leader, the Department can find no fault with them." The great naval theorist Alfred T. Mahan studied Farragut's actions at Port Hudson, and concluded, "Thus analyzed, there is found no ground for adverse criticism in the tactical dispositions made by Farragut on this memorable occasion."

Secretary Welles's response to the operation, in which three-fourths of the vessels Farragut hoped to get past the Port Hudson batteries failed, was typical throughout the Union. To a nation used to reading of immense numbers of casualties in the great land battles of the war, the loss of three dozen men to close the Red River seemed a small price. Farragut's fleet reported 113 casualties, of which thirty-five were killed and seventy-eight wounded. While the numbers belied the ferocity of the battle, many in the North viewed it as an acceptable price to pay to get a great warship like the *Hartford*, and her gunboat consort, to the mouth of the Red River. An effective blockade would stop the flood of supplies that fed the Confederate forces throughout the South.

No one regarded the battle at Port Hudson as a failure for the Union, least of all the Confederate government or the rebel forces at Port Hudson itself. When Farragut passed their fortifications, the troops at Port Hudson had less than two weeks' worth of rations in their storehouses. Major General John C. Pemberton, Confederate commander of the Department of Mississippi and East Louisiana, which included both Vicksburg and Port Hudson, wrote the War Department in Richmond, "The Mississippi is again cut off, neither subsistence nor ordnance can come or go." Six days after Farragut had passed beneath Port Hudson's guns, Pemberton wrote to the commanding officer of the District of Western Louisiana, Major General Richard Taylor, son of former president Zachary Taylor. It was through Taylor's district that supplies passed before they crossed the Mississippi River to reach the Confederate armies. Pemberton emphasized the dangerous position of the troops stationed at Port Hudson by reminding Taylor that "Port Hudson depends almost entirely for supplies upon the other [west] side of the river."

Actually, the condition at Vicksburg was almost identical to that at Port Hudson. Nearly surrounded by Grant's armies, Vicksburg depended almost entirely for her supplies on steamers coming down the Red River and heading north on the Mississippi. Confederate control of this section of the Mississippi was itself dependent on keeping the Red River open. Farragut presented the only danger to keeping the

Red River open, since the *Indianola* had run the Vicksburg batteries a month earlier and been captured by rebel gunboats.

Hundreds of thousands of pounds of bacon and other provisions were at that very moment moving down the Red River, en route to Port Hudson. One Confederate officer responsible for getting supplies down the Red River into the Mississippi responded in this way: "Great God! How unfortunate. Four steamers arrived today from Shreveport (with supplies intended for Port Hudson). One had a load of 300,000 pounds of bacon, three others are reported coming down [the Red River] with loads. Five others are below with full cargoes designed for Port Hudson, but it is reported that the Federal gunboats are blockading the river." The presence of the *Hartford* sent all these steamers scurrying back up the Red River long before they reached the Mississippi and the blockading Federals.

The distance from Port Hudson north to Vicksburg is over two hundred miles. Two Union vessels alone could not control the entire length of the river between these strongholds, but they could do something even more consequential: they could close the Red River to enemy traffic. This was Farragut's reason for risking his ships in running the Port Hudson batteries. The admiral's instructions to the captains of his fleet had been clear. Any ship surviving the run past the batteries was to steam to Vicksburg and offer its services to the Union forces operating against that city. If not required there, they were to "proceed to the mouth of Red River, and keep up a police of the river between that river and Port Hudson." Farragut intended to follow his own orders.

Just as dawn broke over the river on March 16, two men emerged from the woods on the west bank and, waving their arms and calling, paddled out into the river in a small dugout canoe. Taken aboard the *Hartford*, they identified themselves as crewmen of the *Queen of the West* who had survived her grounding and capture on the Red River and made their way to the Mississippi, where they had waited for the appearance of a friendly vessel. From these men Farragut learned of the final fate of the ironclad *Indianola*. The daring attack on the Union ironclad by rebel gunboats served as a warning to him to keep a vigilant guard at all times. He also took special precautions to protect his ship against attack from Confederate rams. Heavy chains were hung over the sides. Huge cypress logs were cut from the woods along the riverbanks and tied just above the waterline to act as buffers, should a ram attempt to penetrate the ship's wooden hull.

Later that day the two Union vessels dropped anchor near the mouth of the Red River. News of Farragut's passing of the Port Hudson batteries had traveled fast up the river. Hours before the great masts of the *Hartford* could be seen by curious onlookers who had been drawn to the spot where the rivers joined, Confederate transports and gunboats had turned tail and scattered. Most had sped up the Red River, where they expected to be safe from the warship's powerful guns.

Early on the morning of March 17, the *Hartford* and the *Albatross* weighed anchor and headed north. The level of the Mississippi was rapidly rising as a result of the spring thaws farther north. She was beginning to expand her banks, causing the yearly flood of the plains along her route. The water rushing down from the mountains far beyond the horizon also increased the speed of her current. This condition made the going rough, and it was not until late in the afternoon that Farragut arrived at Natchez, Mississippi. Just below the town, a party of sailors from the *Hartford* went ashore and cut the telegraph line south to Port Hudson in several places.

The arrival of the tall ship, enemy or not, drew a crowd to the Natchez waterfront. Farragut dropped anchor opposite the town and sent a boat with a party of men to locate the town's mayor. Led by Captain Jenkins, they delivered the following message to the mayor:

Sir:

I trust that it is unnecessary to remind you of my desire to avoid the necessity of punishing the innocent for the guilty, and to express to you the hope that the scene of firing on the United States' boats will not be repeated by either the lawless people of Natchez or the guerrilla forces; otherwise, I shall be compelled to do the act most repugnant to my feelings, by firing on your town in defense of my people and the honor of my flag.

I shall be most happy to see his honor the Mayor on board.

Very respectfully, D. G. Farragut, Rear-Admiral

Although such communiqués to local officials along the river were not uncommon, they were usually preceded by reports of gunfire aimed at Union vessels. In this case there was apparently no such report. Even Farragut's son, Loyall, who was still aboard the *Hartford* at the time, and described the ship's arrival at Natchez, did not report any such firing. The note was most likely intended to convince Natchez officials that the Federal vessels planned on remaining at their city for at least several days. As loyal Confederates, they could be counted on to pass this intelligence along to nearby military commanders, which they evidently did. Farragut's invitation to the mayor to visit him aboard the ship, something that could not take place until the following day because of the lateness of the hour, further supports the belief that the whole affair was a subterfuge designed to convince rebel authorities upriver that the two vessels posed no immediate threat to their positions.

Before dawn the following day, both vessels were under way. They continued their passage north toward Vicksburg, where Farragut hoped to contact Major General Ulysses S. Grant, who was preparing his second campaign against that rebel stronghold.

The night of March 18 was spent in the middle of the river just below Grand Gulf, which is thirty miles south of Vicksburg by land, but sixty miles by boat. During the previous spring and summer, Confederate forces had erected an earthwork fortification on the high bluffs at Grand Gulf. It was now occupied by a strong gun battery that, like those at Port Hudson and Vicksburg, had a dominating view of the river. The position at Grand Gulf formed the extreme left, or southerly, flank of the Vicksburg defenses.

On the morning of the nineteenth, Farragut watched the eastern shore as his two vessels neared Grand Gulf. What drew his notice was a group of blacks who were waving their arms in the air, trying to draw the attention of the Union sailors. Once they were sure they had succeeded, they began pointing in the direction of the high bluffs the ships were at that moment approaching. The men and women along the shore were doing their best to warn the vessels of the presence of a battery of rifled fieldpieces that awaited them atop the Grand Gulf cliffs. As the ships came within range, the battery fired a round, then the guns disappeared behind the pile of earth forming their protection.

Farragut signaled the gunboat *Albatross* to close in under the *Hartford*'s port side for protection. The two vessels then ran under the bluffs with a full head of steam while the flagship's starboard guns returned the enemy's fire. Unfortunately, against the river's current, full speed was not fast enough to prevent the deaths of two men and the wounding of six others aboard the *Hartford*. And the return fire did little damage to the battery, owing to the elevation of the bluffs. While the *Albatross* was undamaged by the fire, the *Hartford* suffered several shots into her hull, and sections of her rigging were cut away.

Just as she reached the extremity of the enemy's range, Captain Jenkins, who was standing near Farragut on the quarterdeck, turned to him and said, "Admiral, this ship goes entirely too slow." Seconds later an enemy shell exploded in the water almost below the quarterdeck. Farragut watched the eruption of water rise into the air above him, and crash back into the river. "I should think she was," he replied calmly, "just at this moment."

Once they were far enough from the rebel batteries, the two vessels stopped to assess the damage to the flagship and begin making repairs. As was the custom, the bodies of the two dead sailors were laid in a place of honor on the quarterdeck. Each was covered with an American flag. Returning from an errand, Loyall found his father pacing back and forth near the corpses, "not ashamed to show his deep emotion." The men who sailed under Farragut knew that the admiral suffered personally at the loss of every life aboard his ship.

After setting carpenters to work repairing the damage caused by the Grand Gulf batteries, the two Union vessels continued up the Confederate river. Closer to Vicksburg, they came upon what was first believed to be the wreck of the Federal gunboat *Indianola*, but on closer inspection proved to be the mock ironclad *Black Terror*, resting quietly where it had run aground along the eastern bank of the river. The logs that had served as her "guns," and the stacked pork barrels that were her "funnels," brought laughs to the crews of the *Hartford* and the *Albatross*. Forgetting for a moment that they were deep within rebel territory, the men joked about the damage done to the enemy by the abandoned vessel's imitation guns.

It was almost four o'clock in the afternoon of March 19 when the *Hartford* and her gunboat companion dropped anchor. They were twelve miles below Vicksburg, and three miles below the village of Warrenton. Farragut brought both vessels in close to the Mississippi side of the river, where a stretch of high cliffs reached out over the river. They served as protection from riflemen who might be moving along the shore looking for convenient targets.

Soon after their arrival, a small boat approached from the western bank, carrying several Union soldiers. Among them was the commanding officer of the southernmost pickets on guard duty protecting the right flank of the Federal army facing Vicksburg. Farragut was overjoyed at meeting these men, since it meant he had achieved his objective of making contact with General Grant's forces. The officer informed Farragut that the main body of the Federal army was on the opposite side of the river, along the peninsula facing Vicksburg known as Young's Point. It was at Young's Point during the previous year that General Williams had struggled gallantly and in vain to dig a canal across the peninsula. Large portions of Grant's army were bogged down in a quagmire of mud that covered almost the entire peninsula. The river had risen above the long-neglected levees that protected the low peninsula, and the muddy waters were pouring in at hundreds of sites. Dry land was a premium few of the Union soldiers enjoyed.

That evening, Farragut took advantage of the lull in activity to send a telegram to Secretary Welles advising him of his arrival below Vicksburg. He also wrote a letter to his wife, the first since running the Port Hudson batteries. "We came through in safety," he told Virginia. "Your dear boy and myself are well." Then, explaining how it was that *Hartford* alone among the big ships had passed Port Hudson, he told her, "You know my creed, I never send others in advance when there is a doubt and being the one on whom the country has bestowed its greatest honors, I thought I ought to take the risks which belong to it; so I took the lead. I knew they would try to destroy the flag ship and I was determined to follow out my idea that the best way to prevent it was to hurt them the most." The admiral concluded his letter with the heartfelt comment that one of his "greatest troubles on earth is the pain and anxiety I inflict upon one of the best wives and most devoted of women. Oh, that it yet be in my power to compensate you for the pain I have caused you."

Early on the morning of the twentieth, Farragut moved the vessels upriver, intending to tie up at the deserted village of Warrenton. From there he hoped to facilitate communications with the Federal forces above Vicksburg. Unfortunately, the village was not as deserted as it appeared. As soon as the *Hartford* came within range, Confederate gunners manning a casement battery in the center of Warrenton opened fire. They were quickly dispersed by a broadside from the great ship. Neither the *Hartford* nor the *Albatross* suffered any damage from the attack. Wishing to avoid another such ambush, Farragut had both vessels drop anchor near the western shore, and Captain Jenkins and a party of marines rowed across the river to conduct a reconnaissance of the village. They returned with news that preparations for additional batteries were being made by Confederate forces. The rebels evidently intended to fortify the village. This intelligence gave the admiral the idea that a force of Federal infantry could feasibly be ferried across the river under the protection of his guns. They could capture Warrenton with little effort, since only a small number of Confederates were in the village at the time. Grant would then have a foothold on the Mississippi side of the river, south of Vicksburg.

That day, Farragut sent his secretary to Grant's headquarters with news of his arrival. He told Grant the reason he had run the Port Hudson batteries was to close the Red River to enemy traffic and attempt the recapture of the two Federal boats lost on the Mississippi, the *Queen of the West* and the *Indianola*. He offered to assist Grant and Porter. The latter commanded naval forces north of Vicksburg, and was operating in cooperation with Grant, in whatever way possible. Farragut requested a supply of badly needed coal to power his vessels, and the loan of one ironclad gunboat and two rams to assist with the Red River blockade.

When Farragut's communiqué arrived at Union headquarters, Porter was away on an expedition aimed at Yazoo City, so Grant replied on both their behalfs. While unable to supply the gunboat or rams, he could provide Farragut with coal.

The following night a large coal barge was set adrift in the river. Writing back on the twenty-second, Farragut expressed his gratitude for the fuel, and told Grant of the situation at Warrenton, suggesting that the place be taken before a larger rebel force arrived. Grant decided to take advantage of Farragut's offer of transporting troops from Young's Point to Warrenton, and ordered two regiments from the far side of the peninsula to march immediately across the marshy stretch of land and await Farragut's instructions to embark and attack the village. Unfortunately the troops were too late. By the time they arrived, a large and heavily armed force from Vicksburg had arrived and taken control of Warrenton.

Desperate for news of the remainder of his fleet, Farragut had to wait until March 25 before he learned of their fate. Writing home, he told his wife, "You can imagine the pleasure I have received today by a New Orleans paper which gives an account of the fleet below—to learn that Alden and Smith escaped unhurt. McKinstry, it is said, will lose his leg. I sincerely hope not. Poor Cummings, they say, is mortally wounded; he is a fine fellow and a noble officer. The list of killed and wounded was small, compared to what I imagined."

Before preparing to steam down the Mississippi to the mouth of the Red River, Farragut decided it was time Loyall returned to New York and his mother. He sent him to Porter's headquarters via the Young's Point route. To Virginia he wrote, "I am too devoted a father to have my son with me in troubles of this kind. God grant that he may be as great a comfort all the days of your life as he has been to me."

Meanwhile, Porter was stuck with a force of ironclads and mortar boats in a Mississippi waterway called Steele's Bayou, where he was under attack by rebel snipers. With Federal troops trailing along behind, his objective had been to traverse the bayous into the Big Sunflower River, then into the Yazoo River. Once there, he planned to attack and capture a place known as Hayne's Bluff. From this vantage point, Union forces could launch an attack against Vicksburg's rear. It was a good plan, but failed to take into account how easily even a small group of rebel soldiers could trap the boats. They accomplished this by felling numerous trees and dropping them across the waterways, effectively closing the bayou to Porter. Sailors who struggled to remove the trees were constantly harassed by sniper fire. Felled trees even prevented Porter from backing out to safety. When word reached Porter that Confederate infantry units were rushing toward him with a battery of artillery, he knew his fate was almost sealed. It was only the quick action of General William Tecumseh Sherman that saved Porter's expedition from capture. Sherman rushed his troops through the swamps in the middle of the night to beat off the enemy before they were able to organize themselves for a concerted attack on the boats. Finding it impossible to advance or turn around,

Porter's gunboats took three days to back out the thirty miles they had traveled up Steele's Bayou.

Hearing of Admiral Farragut's request for two rams, Brigadier General Alfred Ellet, commander of the Marine Brigade and the Ram Fleet, visited Farragut on board the *Hartford* and offered to send two of his army rams below Vicksburg. Farragut was pleased with the offer, but expressed concern that Ellet should first clear his intentions with Porter, trapped in Steele's Bayou. Although Ellet was an army officer, and his troops and ram crews were all army soldiers, they were a component part of Porter's Mississippi Squadron. Neither Ellet nor his officers were happy to be taking orders from navy officers, and as a result, Ellet's relationship with Porter was strained at the best of times.

General Ellet asked Farragut if having two of his rams below Vicksburg would "benefit the country and the cause." Farragut answered "certainly," but again expressed reservations concerning Porter. He was unsure of the relative positions of Porter and Ellet, and did not want to do anything that might give the appearance he was undermining Porter's command. Ellet apparently waved off the concern. Before leaving, Farragut gave Ellet, probably at the general's request, a letter saying, in part, "I have written to Admiral Porter to the effect that I am most desirous of having an ironclad gunboat and two rams below Vicksburg to maintain control of the river between this place [Vicksburg] and Port Hudson. I am unwilling to interfere with [Porter's] command in any way, but I feel sure that if he was here he would grant the assistance I so much need to carry on this object. I beg to assure you that nothing would be more gratifying to me than to have two of your rams."

General Ellet left the *Hartford* after assuring Farragut that he would send two rams downriver after dark. The crews on board both the *Hartford* and the *Albatross* waited that night for the sound of the Vicksburg batteries opening fire, a sure sign that the rams were coming down, but nothing happened.

When Ellet had returned to his headquarters above Vicksburg, he had ordered that two rams, the *Switzerland* and the *Lancaster*, be prepared to run the batteries. His attempts to get the navy to assign an ironclad to join his boats failed. Because Porter was still beyond the reach of normal channels of communication, the ranking naval officer in Porter's command decided it was prudent to await his commander's arrival before taking any action.

The rams were delayed until nearly daybreak by coaling operations and the loading of extra provisions. As was the habit with the entire Ellet clan, the general decided against the prudent course of waiting another day, and sent the rams down as soon as they were ready. He may have been provoked to this action because he feared Porter would arrive at any moment and stop him. It proved to be a disastrous decision.

It was already daylight when the rams reached the northern limits of the Vicksburg batteries. This meant they had to make the six-mile-long run past the batteries in full view of enemy gunners. As the batteries opened fire, the rams counted on their speed to get them safely through the rain of shot and shell. The *Lancaster,* an old boat in poor condition, was hit at least three times. Her steam drum was burst, her steering mechanism destroyed, and a large portion of her bow blown off before she sank. Most of the crew managed to escape in small boats or by clutching cotton bales that floated them to the western shore.

The *Switzerland* fared better. Her boilers were disabled, but she managed to drift with the swift current until she was out of range of the batteries. She would have drifted right past the waiting Union ships, had it not been for the timely work of the *Albatross* in getting lines to her and taking her in tow. After four days of hard work, the ram's boilers were repaired and she joined Admiral Farragut's river navy.

When Porter finally arrived back at his headquarters several days later, he was furious with Ellet over the incident. The general exacerbated matters when he informed Porter that the Marine Brigade would prefer to serve under army command. Porter exploded in a rage and ordered Ellet's arrest. Ellet was forced to withdraw his request before Porter would order his release. The loss of the two rams from his command, and the impudence of Ellet in requesting a transfer, was the last straw for Porter. He banished General Ellet and the entire Marine Brigade to Tennessee to combat rebel guerrillas operating there. It was as far away from his headquarters as he could send them.

Soon after, Porter and Farragut began a correspondence that lasted several days. Farragut asked for one or two ironclads to help blockade the Red River and patrol the Mississippi. Porter, whose letters were a little defensive because of the ram incident, declined the request, claiming he had none to spare. He did, however, promise to send a force of ironclads and rams down the Bayou Macon, which runs parallel to the Mississippi several miles to the west, as soon as he could. Bayou Macon empties into the Red River a short distance north of the point where that river enters the Mississippi. If such a force could reach the Red River, all enemy traffic would cease immediately.

In the predawn hours of March 28, the flagship *Hartford*, accompanied by the gunboat *Albatross* and the ram *Switzerland*, left the Vicksburg vicinity and headed downriver to take up station at the Red River. Passing Warrenton, the vessels came under fire from several new batteries the Confederates had located in the village. The *Hartford* returned the fire with a broadside, but Farragut expected that it caused little damage to the hidden enemy.

Of much greater danger to Farragut's vessels were the batteries at Grand Gulf. In anticipation of the *Hartford*'s return, three heavy guns had been moved down from Vicksburg. The Confederates had full intentions of sinking the ship and perhaps even capturing America's first rear admiral. During the night of March 31, the three Union vessels sped down the river under the Grand Gulf bluffs. The *Hartford* fired several broadsides at the enemy, and succeeded in forcing a number of gun crews to cease fire and seek cover. The flagship was hit by one shell, which caused little damage to the vessel, but killed one sailor. The ram *Switzerland* was hit by two shots, but suffered only minor damage. The *Albatross* got through unscathed, even though her speed was reduced by the coal and provisions barges she had in tow.

On April 2 the three arrived at the mouth of the Red River. Along the way they had sunk a large number of Confederate flatboats loaded with supplies of various description, and had burned stacks of provisions awaiting transportation at several levees. Anxious for news of his fleet below Port Hudson, Farragut left the gunboat and the ram on blockade duty and steamed downriver to Port Hudson. He arrived within sight of the formidable bluffs on April 6.

Several attempts were made to establish contact with the Federal vessels below the batteries. Signal flags were hoisted to the *Hartford*'s mast during the day, to no avail. Timed gunfire also failed to elicit a response, as did signal rockets launched during the night. Despairing of making contact, Farragut reluctantly agreed to an idea put forth by his daredevil secretary, Edward C. Gabaudan, a man who had previously demonstrated his dauntless spirit. After arriving below Vicksburg, Farragut had sent Gabaudan across the Young's Point peninsula with instructions to deliver a letter to Porter. Discovering that Porter was not at his headquarters, Gabaudan had borrowed a horse and ridden through miles of rebel-infested country to reach Porter at Steele's Bayou.

Now the secretary proposed to hide himself inside a narrow dugout canoe resembling a log, and, covered with branches and twigs, float downriver until he reached the Federal fleet. Such sights were common on the river, and it was hoped that rebel gunners would not decide to use this particular "log" for target practice. The admiral gave him several dispatches for the fleet and one for General Banks. Accompanied by an escaped slave who had also volunteered for the mission, Gabaudan was concealed inside the "log" and set adrift in the current. The voyage appeared to be going well until the dugout was swept too close to the east bank, where it attracted the attention of several soldiers on guard duty. Although unable to see, Gabaudan and his companion could clearly hear the men discussing the unusually large object floating nearby. Several rebels pushed a small boat into the water and rowed close to Gabaudan, who clutched his pistol close to his chest, determined to fight if discovered. Luckily the soldiers quickly tired of the venture and called to those waiting on the shore that it was "only a large log." Two hours later the two men pushed the concealing branches into the water and revealed their presence to the first vessel they saw. To their surprise, they had actually drifted past the Federal gunboats patrolling the river below Port Hudson and floated all the way down to Baton Rouge. The ship that hauled them in was the *Richmond*. Several hours later the *Richmond*'s boats uncovered a similar fake log with two former slaves aboard, bearing additional dispatches from Farragut. They had left the *Hartford* a little over a half hour after Gabaudan. Two signal rockets fired from several miles below Port Hudson were the prearranged sign that the manned "logs" had survived their journey.

The next day the *Hartford* steamed up the Mississippi and returned to blockading the Red River. Along the way, the sloop gave chase to two Confederate steamers found attempting to cross the river. Although one escaped capture, the other was driven directly at the *Albatross*, which was on routine patrol. Found aboard the captured steamer, the *J. D. Clarke,* was a Major Howard, who was assigned to the Confederate Army Commissary Department. A few days later a rebel boat carrying mail was taken. Among the official Confederate government documents found was information about a plan to attack the *Hartford* with several small boats and board her. Farragut immediately ordered additional steps to increase the measures he had already taken to fend off boarders. Logs and chains hung from the *Hartford*'s side made it virtually impossible for an enemy boat to get within twenty feet of her.

Farragut had arranged with Gabaudan to meet him at the same place in which he was set adrift, north of Port Hudson, on April 15. Dropping anchor within sight of the Port Hudson bluffs, Farragut found that the west bank had been cleared of all Confederate troops by General Banks's actions on that side of the river. The *Richmond* had moved upriver and anchored just out of range of the batteries. By placing a small platform atop the sloop's gallantmast, signal officer Eaton was able to communicate with the *Richmond.*

The admiral's secretary soon arrived, with four army officers and the former slaves who had floated downriver with him. The following day, five men trekked across the marshy land to bring Farragut and his crew the mail they had been holding for them. Following a conference with the army officers, Farragut once again returned to the Red River, where he remained for the following two weeks. The Red River was now effectively closed to enemy shipping, although it was impossible for Farragut to control any sizable length of the Mississippi with only three vessels. By constant patrols, numerous rebel steamers were destroyed, and tons of supplies and provisions were prevented from reaching the Confederate troops at Port Hudson, where hunger became their biggest enemy.

While Farragut had been conducting his business within sight of Port Hudson, Navy Secretary Gideon Welles was growing increasingly irritated with Acting Rear Admiral David Porter. Glowing reports crammed with useless information appeared at times to be compensating for his lack of aggressive action, or the failure of some of his actions, such as the Steele's Bayou expedition. Both Welles and Fox were anxious to get Farragut back to New Orleans, where he could resume personal command of the Blockading Squadron. Washington had been receiving intelligence that Confederate admiral Franklin Buchanan might any day burst out of Mobile Bay with his new ironclad fleet and attack the wooden Federal ships on blockade duty.

The U.S. Navy Department was not about to forget that Buchanan had been the captain of the ironclad *Virginia* (the rebuilt Union ship *Merrimack*) on March 8, 1862, when she swept into Hampton Roads and destroyed two Federal warships, the frigate *Congress* and the sloop *Cumberland*. A serious wound had prevented Buchanan from remaining in charge of the ironclad when she fought the Union ironclad *Monitor* the following day. Both Welles and Fox knew that if Buchanan attacked the blockading ships outside Mobile Bay with his new ironclads, that waterway, so vital to the Confederacy, would open to commerce runners like a floodgate. Farragut had to get out of the Mississippi River and back in personal command of the blockade, but he could not leave until Porter got below Vicksburg and took command of the entire river to New Orleans.

Welles believed the reason Porter had not yet moved below Vicksburg was his "great vanity and great jealousy" concerning command. While he remained above Vicksburg, the commander of the Mississippi Squadron was the senior naval officer on the scene. Such men as Grant and Sherman were obliged to deal with him in all matters requiring navy participation. Once he went below that Confederate bastion, Farragut, the hero of New Orleans, would be senior naval officer. Judging by his later actions, especially his self-serving history of the war, Welles was probably correct. What Porter failed to take into consideration was that Farragut was anxious to get out of the river as quickly as possible, and leave the entire region north of New Orleans to Porter. New Orleans itself had been designated as the base of the blockading squadron, and would therefore remain under Farragut's naval command.

On April 15, 1863, Welles sent a secret telegram to Porter with instructions to move below Vicksburg "so that Admiral Farragut may return to his station." The shove from Welles was not needed, for General Grant had already obtained Porter's agreement to take a number of his boats below Vicksburg. The following day, Porter moved seven ironclad gunboats, one ram, one tug, and three empty troop transports south as part of Grant's new plan to capture Vicksburg. The rest of his squadron remained north of the city to protect army communication lines.

Convinced that Vicksburg would never be taken from the north, Grant decided to march down the Louisiana side of the river, opposite Vicksburg, recross the river to the Mississippi side, and attack the city from the south. The army would be forced to sever all communications with its supply bases north of Vicksburg, and live off the land. Credit for this maneuver is usually given to Grant himself, although some historians claim it was first suggested by his chief of staff, General John A. Rawlins.

The plan called for first sending a large body of troops down the western side of the river with equipment and tools to repair roads and rebuild bridges destroyed by the retreating Confederates. This would permit the bulk of Grant's army to march unimpeded as far south as New Carthage, Louisiana, twenty-five miles south of Vicksburg, from which point Porter's troop transports, protected by his gunboats, all of which were to run past the Vicksburg batteries, would ferry them to the Mississippi side of the river

Shortly after 9:00 P.M. on the sixteenth, Porter's boats left their moorings just below the mouth of the Yazoo River and began steaming down the Mississippi toward Vicksburg. General Grant, along with his staff, his wife, and their children, watched as the line of boats slowly steamed past them. The army commander had a front-row seat for what proved to be an impressive fireworks display. Porter had prepared his boats well for the trip. Logs and bales of cotton were tied to every available space to reduce damage from enemy shelling. Knowing that the waters opposite Vicksburg were swept by eddies from the western shore that caused whirlpools and other hazards to navigation, he ordered the boats to travel at slow speed below the batteries. While this might make them better targets for enemy gunners, it would help their pilots maintain control over the vessels. Since Porter intended to come as close to the Vicksburg side of the river as possible, hoping to be too close for many of the higher batteries to fire down at them, control of the boats was paramount. The last thing he wanted was for his boats to lose control in the swirling eddies and begin crashing into each other. Each transport and gunboat was to maintain a fifty-yard gap between itself and the preceding boat. Except for the gunboat carrying Porter's flag, each gunboat and transport had a coal barge tied to her starboard or "off" side, leaving open to her guns the port side, facing Vicksburg. Each barge was loaded with ten thousand bushels of coal to help maintain the fleet while it operated below Vicksburg.

First in line was Porter's flagship, the *Benton*. Because she was a rather sluggish vessel, the sixteen-gun ironclad had the tug *Ivy* lashed to her starboard side. Behind her came the brand-new eight-gun ironclad *Lafayette*, with the ram *General Price* lashed to the off side of her coal barge. Fifty yards behind was the twelve-gun *Louisville*, followed by the *Mound City* with fourteen guns, then the *Pittsburg* with thirteen guns, and the *Carondelet* with eleven guns. Next came the transports *Silver Ware*, *Henry Clay*, and *Forest Queen*. Empty of troops, they were loaded with supplies for the army and fodder for its horses. Last in line was the new five-gun *Tuscumbia*. Her commander, Jim Shirk, an officer with long experience, was responsible for helping keep the transports, manned by green volunteer crews, safely in line.

Just before ten o'clock, as they neared the bend above the first batteries, the *Benton* flashed two lights, the signal for all boats to cut their engines. Porter's plan called for the little fleet to drift downriver in silence until discovered by the enemy. They drifted quietly, until someone on shore spotted them and set signal fires to alert the gunners.

Once the enemy knew his boats were passing, Porter gave the signal to restart their engines, and the noisy ironclads clanged to life. The boats moved only a little faster than they had when powered solely by the current, since the coal-laden barges dragged heavily on them. The *Benton*, with Porter on board, was the first to come under fire. The ironclad's bow gun returned fire first with percussion shells, followed quickly by broadsides of grape and shrapnel. The *Benton* first targeted enemy guns in the lower batteries with her broadsides. Once she was opposite the town itself, she poured nearly eighty shells into Vicksburg, doing considerable damage to numerous buildings, including the Washington Hotel. In the process she took four direct hits, and was spun completely around once by the rushing eddies.

The *Benton* was followed by the small fleet, each boat in turn receiving enemy fire. The transport *Henry Clay* was set ablaze by rebel shelling and had to be abandoned. In the confusion of fire and smoke, vessels were turned first in one direction and then another by the water rushing from the eddies. At one point the crews of the two remaining transports, finding their vessels swung around with their bows facing north, attempted to flee the scene for safety. Aboard the *Tuscumbia*, Commander Shirk, conscious that the success of the campaign rested on getting the transports below Vicksburg, used the bow of his ironclad to nudge the two reluctant transports around and shove them back into line.

Once out of range of the enemy's guns, the boats dropped anchor to assess their damage. A few coal barges had broken loose during the battle, but they had been recovered. Except for the *Henry Clay*, the fleet had suffered no significant damage. No lives were lost, including those aboard the sunken transport, who were all rescued. Fourteen sailors were wounded, including two aboard the *Benton*, each of whom lost a leg to a rebel shot that pierced her armor.

Cheered by Porter's passing of the batteries, Grant sent six more transports downriver on the night of April 22, five of which survived the passing. The Mississippi River was now completely in the hands of the Union, with Federal naval forces steaming on patrol its entire length. "I regard the navigation of the Mississippi River as shut out from us now," wrote General John C. Pemberton.

Grant planned to ferry thirty thousand men across the river. But with only a handful of transports, this operation would take too long, allowing Confederate forces to attack troops as they disembarked on the Mississippi side of the river. What he needed was a place on the eastern shore where the men could disembark and quickly establish a defensive perimeter against possible attack. When New Carthage offered no such opportunity, Grant marched farther south to Hard Times, Louisiana, five miles above Grand Gulf, Mississippi, on the opposite shore.

Grant and Porter met at Hard Times on April 28. After reviewing other options with Porter, Grant decided that Grand Gulf, a busy river port during peacetime, was an ideal place to which he could ferry his troops. Before that could be done, however, the rebel batteries there had to be silenced. Farragut had passed Grand Gulf twice that year, once steaming up to Vicksburg with only the *Hartford* and the *Albatross*, and again returning to blockade the Red River, with the ram *Switzerland*. The Confederates, anxious to remove the *Hartford* from the river, had greatly reinforced the Grand Gulf batteries in anticipation of her making another pass upriver. Farragut, however, saw his primary mission as sealing up the Red River, so he never returned to Grand Gulf. It was Porter who received the brunt of the improved rebel batteries.

General Grant asked Porter to reduce the Grand Gulf batteries so that the troops could cross the river at that place. On the morning of the twenty-ninth, Porter's gunboats attacked the batteries, but were severely damaged in the battle that ensued. The reinforced batteries now comprised one one-hundred-pounder, two sixty-four-pounders, two seven-inch rifled guns, three thirty-pounder Parrott rifles, two twenty-pounders, and one ten-pounder Parrott rifle. The battle raged for nearly five hours. Porter himself was wounded, the *Benton*'s steering mechanism was severely damaged, and she was swept downriver, spinning like a top until her crew could regain control. The *Tuscumbia*'s engines were so badly damaged that she was forced out of the battle and drifted downriver until her crew could force her aground on the Louisiana shore.

Porter returned to Hard Times, where Grant had been watching the battle from the deck of the tug *Ivy*. They both agreed that the batteries were too high up to be effectively attacked from the river. Grant ordered his troops to continue their march south, deciding to cross the river below Grand Gulf. Porter was able to bring his gunboats and the transports below the batteries that night with minimal damage. Shortly after dawn on April 30, Federal troops began crossing the mighty river from Louisiana to the undefended town of Bruinsburg, Mississippi. Porter used his gunboats as transports to help ferry the men across as quickly as possible.

The move across the river south of Grand Gulf caught the Confederate forces by surprise. The wily Grant had planned a number of actions, both upriver of Vicksburg and to her rear, that served to draw the attention of rebel commanders away from the troops marching south on the Louisiana side of the river. Once across the river, Grant's force, now effectively cut off from all communications with the north, and without supply lines, fought its way north. First to fall was a small Confederate garrison at Port Gibson, a few miles south of Grand Gulf. When word reached Grand Gulf of the approach of such a large Federal force, the garrison was abandoned. And so began the campaign that led to Grant's victory at Vicksburg. After failing to take the heavily fortified city by storm, Grant settled down to a protracted siege on May 22. Sealed off from the outside world, the twenty thousand Confederate troops and the city's civilian population were reduced to disease and starvation. Daily bombardment from army artillery and Porter's boats forced many to spend days inside caves or bombproofed basements. Finally, with no hope of escape or relief, General Pemberton was forced to surrender Vicksburg "unconditionally" to Grant on July 4, 1863.

Meanwhile, Farragut kept the Red River closed to enemy traffic, sinking an occasional boat that attempted to break his blockade. By remaining on station, he prevented food and supplies from reaching both Port Hudson and Vicksburg, contributing to their ultimate collapse. He also prevented reinforcements from Mississippi coming to the assistance of Confederate General Richard Taylor's army fighting in western Louisiana.

During the second week of April, Banks crossed the Mississippi from New Orleans, and began a campaign against rebel forces there. Accompanying him along the numerous bayous that crisscross that part of Louisiana were four of Farragut's vessels. Under the command of Lieutenant Commander Augustas P. Cooke, the light gunboats *Estrella*, *Arizona*, *Calhoun*, and *Clifton* fought their way along Bayou Teche and the Atchafalaya River, all the way to the Red River.

On the evening of the same day that Porter had completed ferrying Grant's men across the river so they could begin their march north, lookouts on the *Hartford* had spotted a steamer coming down the Red River. The alarm was given, and all hands prepared for battle. When the approaching vessel signaled her presence, the men aboard the flagship realized it was the *Arizona*, and gave a roaring cheer of welcome. A few hours later *Estrella* arrived with Cooke aboard. Cooke carried a dispatch from General Banks requesting assistance in preventing Confederate forces from reinforcing Alexandria, Louisiana, which Banks intended to capture. The general feared that enemy troops were to be transported to the city from the north by way of the Black River. The following day Farragut sent the *Albatross*, the *Arizona*, and the *Estrella* to close the Black River, which they did.

After ferrying Grant's army across the river, Porter would have preferred to return to Vicksburg to participate in the large, victorious campaign that was sure to draw the nation's attention from the big battles being fought in the East. Instead he was instructed by Welles to move south, relieve Farragut of his command of the river above Port Hudson, and support General Banks's campaign by sailing up the Red River.

On May 4, Porter arrived at the mouth of the Red River with several of his gunboats. Two days later, Farragut wrote to Secretary Welles, "Feeling now that my instructions of October 2, 1862, have been carried out by my maintenance of the blockade of Red River . . . I shall return to New Orleans as soon as practicable, leaving the *Hartford* and *Albatross* at the mouth of Red River to await the result of the combined attack upon Alexandria, but with orders to Commodore Palmer to avail himself of the first good opportunity to run down past Port Hudson."

On the morning of May 8, Admiral Farragut left his flagship in the hands of Palmer, and boarded a gunboat for the long, roundabout journey up the Red River, through a series of bayous, and finally to his destination, New Orleans. Crew members aboard the *Hartford* crowded the decks and climbed into the rigging to watch Farragut leave. In a spontaneous demonstration of their affection for the man who had commanded them through so much, they cheered until they were hoarse. There were few dry eyes among those brave sailors, for many wept openly and unashamedly at his departure.

Farragut's arrival at New Orleans on May 11 was greeted with great surprise by the population, many of whom had hoped he would be trapped above Port Hudson forever. That day and the following, he wrote long letters to his wife. "You say you think I am getting too ambitious," he wrote in reply to one of her letters. "You do me great injustices in supposing that I am detained here a day by ambition.

I am much more apt to lose than win honors by what I do. My country has a right to my services as long as she wants them. She has done everything for me, and I must do all for her. The worst of it is, that people begin to think I fight for pleasure. I shall go to church tomorrow and try to return suitable thanks for the many blessings that have been bestowed upon me.

"I hope Port Hudson will soon fall, and that will finish my river work. As soon as Mobile and Galveston are away, I shall apply to be relieved. But it is difficult to get off, as long as the country demands my services."

Farragut returned to Port Hudson on May 23, 1863, using the sloop *Monongahela* as his temporary flagship while the *Hartford* remained above the enemy batteries. He wanted to help make his hope of the town's fall a reality by keeping up a steady bombardment of the rebel positions. The Union ships engaging in this action, in addition to the *Monongahela*, were the *Richmond*, the *Essex*, the *Kineo*, the *Genesee*, and four mortar boats. General Banks arrived the same day, and prepared to assault the Confederate fortifications in the mistaken belief they were nearly abandoned. The attack on May 27 failed to capture the Confederate stronghold. With the Confederates completely surrounded by his fourteen thousand troops, Banks settled down for a siege. By the end of June, the seven-thousand-man garrison, under Major General Franklin Gardner, was forced to eat mule and horse meat, and some men even resorted to killing and cooking the large rats found near the camps. Farragut's ships supported the siege by sealing off the river side of the town, and by bombardment of the defenses. Offered an opportunity to surrender, Gardner refused, claiming his duty "requires me to defend this position."

When word that Vicksburg had fallen reached the besieged rebels, Gardner sent a message to Banks asking for confirmation. Provided with the proof he requested, Gardner felt he had done his duty to the best of his ability, and surrendered Port Hudson on July 9, 1863. The *Hartford* and the *Albatross* steamed downriver once the Port Hudson batteries had been silenced. Eight days later the merchant steamship *Imperial* arrived at New Orleans from St. Louis, demonstrating that the mighty river was now truly in the possession of the Federal government.

On July 10, Undersecretary of the Navy Fox wrote Farragut, "You smashed in the door in an unsurpassed movement and success above [Vicksburg] became a certainty." A joyful President Lincoln wrote, "The father of waters again goes unvexed to the sea."

When Porter arrived at New Orleans on August 1, Farragut turned command of the entire river north of New Orleans over to him, and steamed out of the Mississippi River aboard his beloved flagship. He was going home.

10

Mobile Bay: The "Brilliant Achievement"

REAR ADMIRAL DAVID FARRAGUT arrived at the Brooklyn Navy Yard, across the East River from New York City, on August 12, 1863. The *Hartford*, the *Brooklyn*, and the *Richmond* were all in dire need of repairs. The flagship, which was the least damaged of the three, had been hit 240 times by enemy shot and shell during her nineteen months of service.

Virginia and Loyall journeyed from Hastings-on-Hudson to meet Farragut. It was a tearful yet happy reunion for the couple, after so many months of absence and anxiety. The occasion was made even more joyful when Farragut was informed that Loyall had passed the entrance examinations for West Point and had received his appointment to the military academy. He was scheduled to enter on September 1, less than three weeks away.

Farragut was hailed as a hero everywhere he went. The country was in a better mood than it had been in a long time. A month earlier a Confederate army under General Robert E. Lee had been badly defeated in a three-day battle at Gettysburg, Pennsylvania, and General George Meade's successful Union army had chased Lee all the way back into Virginia. As a result of this stunning victory, New Yorkers were especially anxious to welcome home a true hero of the war. The Northern press had been reporting on Farragut's activities up and down the river for over a year, and many people wanted a glimpse at him.

Describing Farragut's campaigns on the Mississippi River, one New York newspaper bestowed the title "American Viking" on him.

It said that he had earned a name for himself equal to "the naval commanders of any nation." A proud Navy Secretary Welles telegraphed a welcome home, and told Farragut he deserved a "respite from the labors and responsibilities which have been imposed upon you and which you have borne so heroically under difficulties and embarrassments which only the Department can know and appreciate." The secretary said Farragut could report to him whenever he felt like traveling to the nation's capital.

Eighty-one of New York City's leading citizens signed a letter exalting Farragut. In it they exclaimed, "The whole country, but especially this commercial metropolis, owes you a large debt of gratitude." The Chamber of Commerce called the passing of the lower river forts and the capture of New Orleans "one of the most celebrated victories of any time."

A week after Loyall left Hastings for West Point, Farragut reported to Secretary Welles in Washington. Following a dinner party at which the admiral was the guest of honor, Welles wrote in his diary, "The more I see and know of Farragut the better I like him. He has the qualities I supposed when he was selected. The ardor and sincerity which struck me during the Mexican War when he wished to take Veracruz, with the unassuming and the unpresuming gentleness of a true hero."

Anxious to return to the Gulf and plan his attack on Mobile Bay, Farragut wrote his great friend, Commodore Bell, who remained with the blockading ships off the Texas coast, "I am run to death with the attention of the good people, but I am beginning to give out, as I am not able to bear my honors. I have not been able to have a day at home in a week."

The first of Farragut's warships prepared to sail was the *Richmond*. The admiral informed Welles that he could steam to the Gulf in her and wait there for the *Hartford*. However, the secretary asked him to remain in the North until repairs to his own flagship were completed. The names Farragut and *Hartford* had become synonymous in the minds of the public, and Welles evidently didn't want one to sail without the other.

During his stay in New York, Farragut had occasion to dine with Russian rear admiral Lessovski, commander of two fleets, one wintering at New York, the other at San Francisco. The two rear admirals had met years earlier in the Mediterranean, and had become friends. When Farragut asked Lessovski why he was anchored at American ports in relative idleness, the Russian explained that he was "under sealed orders, to be broken only in a contingency that has not yet occurred." He then confided that he was under orders from the Czar to break the seals if the United States became involved in a war with a foreign power during the current rebellion. The implication was clear that the Russian Czar, Alexander II, planned to support the United States actively if it was attacked by either France or England. These two great European powers had more than once demonstrated their support for the Confederacy. Before the fall of New Orleans, it had been widely rumored that Napoleon III was anxious to enter the Civil War on the South's side in return for Confederate recognition of his hegemony over Mexico. In London, Queen Victoria made little effort to conceal her personal attachment to the Confederate cause.

In all the hubbub of social and official activities, Farragut never lost sight of his next objective, Mobile Bay. He repeatedly asked Welles and Fox to send ironclads and shallow-draft gunboats to the Gulf area so they would be available for use when he attacked the forts guarding the bay. On learning that several new *Monitor*-type ironclads had been added to Porter's river fleet, he asked Fox to send some of them to New Orleans.

By mid-December the *Hartford* was ready to sail, but because there were not enough crewmen available, the departure was delayed. Things dragged on, as they did whenever Washington was involved, even when the nation's highest-ranking naval officer was trying to get back to the war. What finally lit a fire under the Navy Department was an erroneous intelligence report that Admiral Franklin Buchanan was preparing to burst out of Mobile Bay in what many believed was the most powerful ironclad ram afloat, the *Tennessee*. After reading this report, Welles immediately ordered the transfer of the required number of seamen from another ship to the *Hartford*.

On the afternoon of January 5, 1864, Farragut left New York harbor during a fierce snowstorm. Twelve days later his flagship dropped anchor in the Gulf, off Pensacola. The "American Viking" was ready for action, and every officer and sailor on blockade duty in the region was glad to have him back.

Farragut made a brief visit to New Orleans, where rumors that several huge rebel ironclads were preparing to attack the city had infected local Federal officials with "ram fever." The *Hartford* then anchored among the ships blockading Mobile Bay, and the admiral immediately began preparations for his long anticipated attack on the Confederacy's last important Gulf port.

Before the war, Mobile, Alabama, had been the second most important port on the Gulf of Mexico, following New Orleans. Located near the northwest corner of Mobile Bay, some thirty miles from the Gulf, the city of Mobile was a center for both rail and river traffic. Two important rivers, the Alabama and the Tombigbee, joined together thirty miles above the city to form the Mobile River. The city was built along the Mobile River's banks as it emptied into the bay, providing Mobile ready access to the interior. Further supporting Mobile as an important commercial center was the Mobile & Ohio Railroad. The longest railroad in the Confederacy, the M&O ran all the way to Columbus, Kentucky. In addition, Mobile had developed its own manufacturing base, something that was in dangerously short supply in the Confederacy.

Mobile Bay is a wide and shallow body of water—so shallow that most of the larger ships transporting cargo to and from the city had to anchor in the lower part of the bay. Their cargoes were transferred between city wharves and ships by a fleet of shallow-draft lighters. There were two means of passage for ships entering or leaving Mobile Bay. The first, Grant's Pass, connected the bay with the Mississippi Sound to the west. This entrance was guarded by an earthwork fort called Fort Powell, located on a small island in the center of the channel. Grant's Pass was usually not deep enough for large ships, but was easily accessible for coastal vessels.

The main shipping route into Mobile Bay ran through a much larger opening at the bay's southern end. This channel was bordered on the east by a long finger of land called Mobile Point. At the very edge of Mobile Point stood the strongest of the bay fortifications, Fort Morgan. Three and one-half miles to the west, built on Dauphin Island, stood Fort Gaines. Most of the water between these two forts was too shallow to allow oceangoing ships to pass, except for a quarter-mile-wide channel close to Fort Morgan.

The tip of Mobile Point was first fortified by French troops in 1699. In 1818, on the same spot, the United States Army began construction of a brick fort that was eventually completed in the early 1830s. Named for a Revolutionary War hero, General Daniel Morgan, Fort Morgan had been captured by Alabama state troops sent by Governor Andrew B. Moore on January 4, 1861. Seven days later the delegates to a state convention voted for secession. Fort Gaines fell to the rebel state forces two weeks later, on January 18, 1861. Both forts had been primarily occupied by engineering troops who were strengthening their defenses when the rebels took possession.

Shortly after his arrival, early in January 1864, Admiral Farragut wrote to both David Porter and Navy Secretary Welles. By then Porter had been promoted to rear admiral, following the capture of Vicksburg, in which his squadron had played a role. Farragut asked each man to assign him at least two ironclads to use against Mobile. Porter responded that he could not spare any vessels at the time because they were all engaged in river campaigns. Welles said he could not make any of the newly constructed monitors available, since they were already committed to the siege of Charleston.

Like many of the older ship captains, Farragut had disliked the ugly "stinkpots" from their inception. However, he had soon recognized the military value of adding ironclads to his fleet. This was especially true when he learned that the Confederate Navy was building a fleet of extra-large and powerful ironclad rams with the stated purpose of attacking his wooden hulled ships blockading Mobile Bay. Such an offensive by well-armed rams could annihilate much of his fleet. It was a dramatic change for the man who, less than a year earlier, had written Undersecretary Fox that the capture of the *Indianola* by rebel gunboats without the loss of a single life had "astounded me. I never thought much of ironclads, but my opinion of them is declining daily. At any rate, I am willing to do the little fighting left to me, as I told you before, in the wooden ships."

On January 20, Farragut transferred his flag temporarily to the double-ended gunboat *Octorara*, and, in company with the gunboat *Itasca*, conducted a personal inspection of the defenses around the entrances to Mobile Bay.

From this close reconnaissance, Farragut developed his final plan of attack. To Welles he wrote, "We must have about two thousand, five hundred men in the rear of each fort, to make regular approaches by land, and to prevent the garrison's receiving supplies and reinforcements; the fleet to run the batteries, and fight the flotilla in the bay." When he learned that the *Tennessee* was not yet ready for battle, that her reputation had preceded her actual commissioning, he told Welles that if he had only one ironclad in his fleet, "I could destroy their whole force in the bay, and reduce the forts at my leisure, by co-operation with land forces." The naval force inside the bay was little more than a squadron of river steamers that had been converted to gunboats, some of them too hastily converted for their intended use. The admiral was anxious to get into the bay before the giant ram arrived.

Farragut closed the ring around Mobile Bay as tightly as possible, while he waited for the arrival of at least two ironclads and a sufficient number of troops to enable him to run the forts and enter the bay. The troops were vital to his plan for two reasons: first, they could launch attacks against the rear of both Fort Morgan and Fort Gaines as his fleet ran past, diverting some of the enemy's attention and firepower from his vessels; second, it was important to take possession of the forts immediately after his fleet was in Mobile Bay. This strategy would prevent the forts from being reinforced and his fleet trapped inside the bay.

During a visit to New Orleans, Farragut learned from General Banks that Major General William Tecumseh Sherman was preparing what would become his famous campaign through Georgia, aimed at capturing Atlanta. Sherman's plan was to push from Tennessee into Georgia with three Federal armies: the Armies of the Cumberland, the Tennessee, and the Ohio. With this force, numbering more than one hundred thousand men, he hoped to drive the defending sixty-thousand-man Confederate Army of Tennessee, under General Joseph E. Johnston, into southern Alabama so he could capture Atlanta. Although there was no naval role in this objective, Farragut hoped to aid Sherman by distracting some Confederate forces away from his line of march. He decided he could accomplish this by a minor subterfuge in which he would launch an attack against one of the smaller forts at Mobile Bay and perhaps fool the enemy into thinking he was preparing to enter the bay and capture Mobile itself. If the ploy was successful, the Confederate troops in and around Mobile, rather than being reduced in number to supply men and material to General Joseph E. Johnston's Army of Tennessee, would be forced to remain where they were. The more rebel soldiers Farragut could keep at Mobile, the fewer would be sent against Sherman.

Farragut launched his attack against Fort Powell in Grant's Pass on February 16. He had intended to begin three days earlier, but a severe drop in temperature, along with heavy winds, had delayed the action. Six mortar boats were towed within range of the fort, and opened a steady bombardment. They were protected against possible enemy attack by four gunboats that all but sealed the entrance to the pass. The bombardment did little real damage to the fort. The officers' quarters were hit several times and destroyed, but little else suffered. In the words of Farragut's newly appointed fleet captain, Percival Drayton, "We are hammering away at the fort here, which minds us about as much as if we did not fire."

Prior to the start of the bombardment, Farragut allowed word that he was planning a major assault on Mobile to reach Major General Dabney H. Maury, the Confederate commander of the District of the Gulf, which included Mobile Bay. Three days before the mortars began firing, Maury requested an additional six thousand men to bolster the ten thousand defending Mobile. Maury was convinced that Farragut intended to enter the lower bay and lay siege to Mobile. The ploy had worked. In a report to Confederate Secretary of War James Seddon, Maury gave a pessimistic appraisal of the defenses of Mobile Bay. He told Seddon that both Grant's Pass and the main ship channel between Forts Gaines and Morgan could probably be forced by a strong and resolute fleet.

Help did arrive in the form of army engineers who strengthened the walls of the main channel forts to protect their masonry from the more accurate and destructive shelling of rifled guns. Maury did not receive the additional troops he requested; however, the forces under his command around Mobile remained in place and were not used against Sherman. Although he eventually realized the attack on Fort Powell was a feint, Maury continued to believe that Farragut intended to send shallow-draft boats through Grant's Pass in an effort to occupy the southern section of the bay. So convinced was he of this that he gathered together a large group of sharpshooters from among his forces and organized them into a single unit with the purpose of firing into any boats attempting to gain entry to the bay.

On February 22, Farragut and Captain Drayton scrutinized the bombardment of Fort Powell from the deck of the side-wheel gunboat *Calhoun*. They found the water so shallow that the mortar boats could get no closer to Fort Powell than four thousand yards. Even at that range, several of the boats were over a foot deep into the mud. At one point, Farragut's own gunboat became stuck and had to be pulled free by two of the gunboats guarding the mortar vessels. The admiral knew the attack would never accomplish anything in terms of reducing the fort, but he hoped again that it would distract local Confederate authorities from the coming campaign against Atlanta, which it did. He decided to keep up the attack until intelligence reports indicated the enemy was no longer deceived.

Following another visit to Grant's Pass, Farragut reported that the fort had periodically returned fire with its half-dozen rifled guns. One of the mortar boats, the *John Griffiths*, was hit four times in succession by one-hundred-pound shells, but all failed to explode. Damage aboard the schooner was limited to the wounding of one sailor.

Meanwhile, 150 miles up the Alabama River, the ironclad ram *Tennessee* was finally commissioned on February 16. She left the makeshift navy yard at Selma, Alabama, and began her journey downriver to Mobile Bay and into history. Throughout the war, the Confederacy had a perpetual shortage of naval machinery. This was nowhere more apparent than in the large ironclad ram on which a disproportionate portion of the defense of Mobile Bay rested. Her power plant and much of her related machinery had been recovered from a river steamer that the war had left stranded in the Yazoo River. It was only by a contrived arrangement of gears and chains that this equipment was adapted for use in the ram. The river steamer's engine was a poor substitute for one that might have been designed for the warship herself.

The *Tennessee* was launched prior to the completion of her construction. Like more than a dozen other ironclads being built in the mostly shallow and muddy waters of the lower Confederacy, she had to be launched when the river was high enough to float her. Her construction would be completed once she reached Mobile Bay. The ram was 209 feet long, with an unusually wide beam of forty-eight feet, and drew fourteen feet of water. She had been framed with thirteen-inch-square yellow pine timbers, covered first with five-inch-thick pine planks laid horizontally, then four inches of oak laid vertically on top of that. Her stern and sides were shielded by four-inch-thick boiler plate, and her forward with six inches of plate. All the plate was fastened to the wood with one-and-one-half-inch bolts. Tiller chains enabling the river steamer's power plant to be used were placed in open channels at her stern, exposing them to enemy fire. The most serious defect in this mighty ship was her power plant. Built to power a wooden riverboat, it strained under the weight of the big ram, managing to drive her at a speed of no more than six miles per hour when the *Tennessee* was fully loaded.

The ram's armament consisted of six Brooke rifled guns. Two had seven-inch bores, and four had 6.4-inch bores. They were powerful and accurate weapons, but of little use until the vessel could be brought into the lower portion of the bay. As protection against enemy rams, the *Tennessee*'s armor plating was extended into the water for eight feet, at the same downward angle as her casement.

To get to her destination, the *Tennessee* had to pass over the Dog River Bar. Even at high tide there was only nine feet of water at the bar, much less than required by the ram's fourteen-foot draft. Special devices, called "camels" or "caissons," had to be built to lift the vessel high enough to pass over the bar. These wooden caissons were fitted around the base of the ram to form a temporary undercarriage. Once secured in place, the water in them was pumped out and they rose higher in the water, raising the ram at the same time. Finally, on May 18, after several failed attempts, the ram was raised as high as possible, then pulled across the bar by a steamer. The *Tennessee* at long last was in the lower and navigable portion of Mobile Bay.

Four days later, after the caissons had been removed and the coal and provisions had been loaded, Admiral Franklin Buchanan raised his flag on the *Tennessee*. Buchanan, and the ram's captain, James D. Johnston, had worked hard to get the vessel completed before Farragut launched his expected attack. Buchanan had threatened reluctant workers and slow contractors, conscripted striking laborers and placed them in the charge of naval officers, hounded Richmond for experienced sailors and officers, and been personally responsible for the ram's completion. Now he would take her to war.

Born in 1800, Franklin Buchanan had become a midshipman in the United States Navy when he was fifteen years old. A ship's captain in the Perry expedition to Japan, he had been appointed the first Superintendent of the United States Naval Academy. As secessionist fever swept the South, Captain Buchanan, expecting his home state of Maryland to follow her Southern neighbors, resigned from the navy. When it became apparent that despite widespread sympathy for secession, Maryland would not leave the Union, he attempted to have his resignation withdrawn. Navy Secretary Welles, a man who had little patience for those he considered traitors, refused to allow the resignation to be withdrawn, and made matters worse for Buchanan by having him officially dismissed from the service.

At first Buchanan tried to remain neutral, but found this position impossible. With few options open to him, he enlisted in the Confederate Navy as a captain. Already widely respected as a fighting officer, Buchanan enhanced his reputation when he commanded the rebel ironclad *Virginia*, formerly the *Merrimack*, in her first battle against blockading Federal ships at Hampton Roads on March 2, 1862. Seriously wounded in that battle, he was compelled to relinquish command prior to the ironclad's world-famous battle against the Union ironclad *Monitor* the following day.

Known to his former friends throughout the Union navy, including Rear Admiral David Farragut, as "Old Buck," Buchanan was prepared to defend Mobile against the increasingly powerful enemy fleet standing offshore.

While Buchanan was preparing the *Tennessee* to defend Mobile Bay, Farragut spent his time engaged in the monotonous work of blockade duty, with occasional visits to Pensacola and New Orleans. A great amount of his time was devoted to official and unofficial correspondence. His failing eyesight often forced him to rely on another officer to read the letters aloud. Farragut's physical inactivity took its toll on his body. During this sedentary time his weight increased to 150 pounds, twenty pounds over his normal weight. In April he inspected the ships along the Texas coast, and found them, like most of his fleet, in need of repairs. With few replacements and such a long coast to guard, few ships could be sent in for repairs at any given time. The condition of many of his ships made him thankful that blockade duty on the Texas coast was less important now that the Mississippi River was in Federal hands.

When he learned that Buchanan had gotten the *Tennessee* across the Dog River Bar, Farragut rushed back to his fleet. He expected "Old Buck" to attack the blockaders almost immediately. Buchanan, however, had no intention of rushing out of the bay until he had given his new vessel some trial runs. He was complaining that

"Everybody has taken it into their heads that one ship can whip a dozen and if the trial is not made, we who are in her are damned for life, consequently the trial must be made. So goes the world."

The *Tennessee*'s first real test came on May 22, when she prepared to put out to sea. Rough weather grounded her before she even left the bay. In the process of grounding, she took in so much water that her boilers were extinguished. After inspecting his flagship, Buchanan realized that the ram would never survive the rough seas of the Gulf, much less a pounding by enemy ships on the open seas. This most aggressive senior officer of the Confederate Navy resigned himself to fighting a defensive action against Farragut's fleet when the latter decided it was time to attack. His little squadron took up position just inside the bay, near Fort Morgan. In addition to the hulking ram, Buchanan had three wooden gunboats, the *Gaines*, the *Morgan*, and the *Selma*. A fourth vessel, the *Baltic*, was an old, worm-eaten steamer with a thin covering of iron plate. The hope of Confederate officials in Richmond, to build a fleet of powerful ironclads that would break the Mobile blockade and recover New Orleans from enemy occupation, had floundered and died on the rivers of the South. More than sixteen ironclads were in various stages of construction, but owing to a multitude of problems, including a shortage of iron plate, and Sherman's destruction of the railroads, only one ever saw duty, and that one was incapable of leaving the protective waters of Mobile Bay. She would now serve as a ram and a slow-moving floating battery to attack enemy ships as they entered the bay.

The dreariness of blockade duty dragged on for Farragut. At one point he wrote, "I am tired of watching Buchanan and Page, and wish from the bottom of my heart that Buck would come out and try his hand upon us." The Page he refers to was Brigadier General Richard L. Page, commanding officer of the outer defenses of Mobile Bay, with headquarters at Fort Morgan.

Farragut kept up a constant barrage of requests for ironclads and troops. His plan was as simple as the one he had successfully used in the lower Mississippi. He would force his way past the forts guarding the main channel, and use the ironclads against the rebel fleet inside the bay, which he expected to contain several ironclad rams similar to *Tennessee*. The troops would attack the forts from the rear, effectively cutting them off from supplies and reinforcements. Once totally isolated, they would have to surrender eventually, just as had Forts St. Philip and Jackson on the Mississippi River. But the requests for more ironclads remained unfulfilled.

Early in the evening of May 24, 1864, Farragut and Drayton took the gunboat *Metacomet* in close to Fort Morgan, to get a better look at the Confederate fleet. In addition to the ram and her consorts, they watched a group of small boats busily laying torpedoes in the main channel. Two types of torpedoes, which today would be called mines, were then in use by the Confederates at Mobile Bay. The more popular of the two was the Fretwell-Singer. Invented by two Texans, Dr. J. R. Fretwell, and gunsmith E. C. Singer, a cousin of the sewing machine manufacturer, this deadly "infernal machine" was a floating tin cone that was two-thirds full of powder. Its firing mechanism was a spring-loaded iron plunger that, when released through contact with a ship's hull, smashed a percussion cap, setting off the explosion. Such torpedoes were usually anchored or tied just below the surface of the water to make them as invisible as possible. The second type, the Rains Keg, was a wooden beer keg with conelike tin ends that was also set off by contact with a ship.

Closer inspection of the obstructions the rebel forces had installed in the gap between Fort Morgan and Fort Gaines revealed how dangerous attempting to enter the bay would be for the Federal fleet. A long finger of sand reached out from Dauphin Island, on which Fort Gaines stood, toward the fort at Mobile Point. Where this sand diminished to a level that might permit a ship to pass, a series of pilings had been installed, which acted as an additional block to passage. From the far edge of the pilings to the start of the shipping channel, three lines of torpedoes were anchored. Each line was staggered behind the one in front of it, in order to prevent a boat of any size from squeezing through. Left open was the narrow channel, through which pilots would carefully bring in blockade runners. The entire channel was covered by the guns of Fort Morgan.

When word reached Washington that Buchanan had finally gotten his large ram into the Bay and might attack the blockade fleet at any time, Welles suddenly found the ironclads that Farragut had been requesting. The monitor *Manhattan* was instructed to leave New York and proceed "with all possible dispatch" to Mobile Bay. Rear Admiral Porter was instructed to send two of his new ironclads to the Gulf

USS *Hartford*. Courtesy of the U.S. Naval Academy Museum.

to join Farragut. Porter was reluctant to do so, possibly because he had suffered a humiliating defeat at the hands of the rebels during the Red River campaign, and did not want his adopted brother to continue to outshine him. Once again he had gotten his boats stuck up a river, and had to be rescued by army engineers. Ignoring Porter's claims that the two vessels he wanted sent to Farragut could not survive in the waters of the Gulf, Welles ordered Porter in no uncertain terms to send the *Chickasaw* and the *Winnebago* to Mobile immediately. They left Mound City, Illinois, on June 30.

Then, in March, President Lincoln took a step that drastically improved Farragut's ability to carry out his plan for Mobile Bay: he promoted Army General-in-Chief Henry W. Halleck to the newly created post of army chief of staff, replacing the brilliant but overly cautious Halleck with one of his most successful field commanders, Ulysses S. Grant. As supreme army commander, Grant could now approve a plan that would permit army troops to support Farragut's fleet against Mobile Bay, something he had wanted to do even before Vicksburg fell to him. Grant's attempts to win Washington's support for a campaign against Mobile had repeatedly failed, as he later documented in his memoirs.

In early June, General Sherman asked Major General Edward R. S. Canby, who had replaced General Banks as district commander, to prepare an attack against Mobile in coordination with the naval forces there. Suddenly things were looking up for Farragut. The ironclads and the army troops he had requested were on their way.

On June 17, Canby visited the *Hartford* off Mobile Bay. The general and the admiral laid plans for a combined army-navy attack on the bay forts. On July 5, Farragut celebrated his sixty-third birthday. The weariness of waiting for something to happen must have made him begin to feel his age, for the following day he wrote his wife, "Would to God this war was over that I could but spend in peace with you all the few remaining years of my life. . . ."

Two days later the ironclad *Manhattan* arrived at Pensacola. In need of repairs, she had been towed south by a steamer. No matter what her condition, Farragut was glad of her arrival and anxious to get her off Mobile along with his other ships. The same day, July 8, Major General Canby returned. This time he was accompanied by Major General Gordon Granger, who was to command the troops Canby was sending to aid Farragut. Canby also brought news that two monitors had arrived at New Orleans from Porter's squadron, and would shortly join the fleet. Soon after, Farragut learned that a fourth monitor, *Tecumseh*, was heading south along the Atlantic coast, destined for Mobile Bay.

As things began to warm up, Farragut regained the energy the long wait had sapped from him. On July 12, he issued his General Order No. 10. The admiral's own excitement about the coming battle is evident in the tone of this order. "Strip your vessels for the conflict. Send down all your superfluous spars and rigging. Trice up or remove the whiskers. Put up the splinter nets on the starboard side, and barricade the wheel and steersmen with sails and hammocks. Lay chains or sandbags on the deck over the machinery, to resist plunging fire. Hang the sheet chains over the side, or make other arrangements for security (from ramming and shelling) that your ingenuity may suggest."

View from Fort Gaines. On the day of the battle, the horizon was full of Union warships. Courtesy of Dauphin Island (Ala.) Park and Beach Board. Photo by Michael H. Henderson.

In typical Farragut fashion, leaving nothing to chance, the order detailed how the forts would be run. The ships would pass beneath the guns of Fort Morgan in pairs. The *Hartford*, with the gunboat *Metacomet* lashed to her port side, would lead the way. The ships were to maintain a distance between themselves close enough to form a tight line, but far enough to allow the stern guns of the forward ship and the bow chase guns of the next ship to fire without danger of hitting each other. The four monitors were to form a second line, in single file, and run past the fort on the starboard side of the fleet between the large ships and the fort itself. The lead monitor would be the large *Tecumseh*, armed with two fifteen-inch guns in her single revolving turret.

Fourteen wooden ships and four monitors were to push their way past Fort Morgan, enter Mobile Bay, and engage the Confederate flotilla in battle. Other ships of Farragut's fleet were to remain outside, causing as much damage to the fort as they could by firing into it from the Gulf side. They would also be responsible for preventing any Confederate ships that might come along from entering the bay. Confederate raiders continued to sail the Gulf and the Caribbean Sea, and Farragut did not want any of them entering the fray from behind him.

Before the battle began, several ship captains persuaded Farragut to place his flagship in second place, behind the *Brooklyn*. This was not an easy thing for them to accomplish, since it was always Farragut's opinion that a commanding officer should lead his ships into battle. While their true motive was to lessen the danger to the admiral, they used as their argument the fact that the *Brooklyn* had four bow guns compared to the *Hartford*'s two, and she had a torpedo-sweeping device attached to her bow. Both of these advantages would serve the fleet better if the ship bearing them were in the front of the line. Farragut reluctantly agreed to exchange the position of the two ships, a decision he would regret.

It was Farragut's goal to get as close as possible to Fort Morgan before opening fire. However, as soon as the fort fired at them, he ordered that the ships were to return fire immediately. "Use short fuses for the shell and shrapnel," he told the gunners, "and, as soon as within 300 or 400 yards, give them grape." He pointed out that in the past, when firing at elevated batteries, they had fired too high, "but, with grape-shot, it is necessary to elevate a little above the object, as grape will dribble from the muzzle of the gun."

He then ordered that each ship should strap guns down to its highest elevated locations, such as the poopdeck. This raised the guns higher than usual, allowing them to reach higher into the fort. But, he reminded his captains, if the rebels fired grape, the crews manning these raised guns were unusually vulnerable, and should be moved to the guns below "until out of grape range."

The mood of the men and officers of the fleet was lifted throughout the month of July. The arrival of additional ships, including the long-awaited monitors, the word that General Canby was sending soldiers to attack the forts from the rear, and the general preparations a fully armed fleet must make before going into battle, raised everyone's spirits.

One spirit not lifted, at least not too high, was that of Acting Rear Admiral Theodorus Bailey, who, aboard the gunboat *Cayuga*, had led the fleet past Forts Jackson and St. Philip. Bailey wanted to take part in Farragut's entry into Mobile Bay. "Nothing will please me more than to hoist once more the square red flag, and lead the van of your squadron into Mobile Bay," wrote Bailey. Unfortunately, it was not to be. Bailey's East Gulf Blockading Squadron had been struck with an epidemic of yellow fever that had even Bailey laid low. It was thought wiser to keep the ships of these two fleets as far apart as possible for obvious reasons. Instead of Mobile Bay, Bailey was sent home to regain his health.

Because of other pressing needs, the army could not provide enough troops to attack both forts; only two thousand men were available for the Mobile Bay operation. It was agreed between Admiral Farragut and Major Generals Canby and Granger that these troops would concentrate on Fort Gaines, leaving Forts Morgan and Powell for later. Their landing on Dauphin Island would be protected by Farragut's gunboats, including five sent to keep Grant's Pass closed.

While the Federal fleet was readied for the coming battle, the Confederate forces in the forts and on the bay were making preparations of their own. The *Tennessee* made several runs around the lower bay, engaging in target practice. On at least one occasion, Farragut watched as Buchanan put his slow ironclad through its paces. The wooden gunboats generally remained anchored slightly to the rear of Fort Morgan, where they could train their guns on any enemy ship trying to force its way into the bay. The men waiting aboard the big ram suffered terribly from its poorly designed interior and insufficient ventilation. The navy surgeon aboard the *Tennessee* described life aboard her as "desperate." Daily rain turned her into a high-humidity oven that was so hot men couldn't sleep inside, much less engage in strenuous work for any period of time. Although they dreaded fighting the powerful fleet that was preparing to attack them, all the sailors on board the ram looked forward to the coming battle with a "feeling of relief."

Inside Fort Morgan, Brigadier General Page, commander of the outer defensive forts, watched the gathering of the enemy fleet. The fort's garrison of roughly five hundred men came mostly from Alabama, although there were also two companies from the First Tennessee Heavy Artillery. Her armament at the time consisted of twenty-two thirty-two-pound smoothbore cannons, four ten-inch columbiads, three eight-inch rifled guns, four 5.82-inch rifles, and two thirty-two-pound rifles. Morgan was the principal defense fort, and was a formidable obstacle barring entry to the bay.

Across the mouth of the bay, Fort Gaines was home to about four hundred men under the command of Colonel Charles D. Anderson, who was subordinate to Page. His troops were all from Alabama regiments, including two companies from an artillery battalion. Gaines had twenty-seven guns, the majority of which were obsolete thirty-two-pounders built around 1839. Farragut selected Fort Gaines as the target of the army landing because it offered the best opportunity for success. Once its guns were silenced, and the lower bay in Union hands, all land and naval forces could concentrate on the bigger fort without fear of attack from the troops at Fort Gaines.

Fort Powell, guarding Grant's Pass, contained 140 men, again mostly Alabamians, except for a portion of a South Carolina battery. Commanded by Lieutenant Colonel James M. Williams, Fort Powell had four smoothbores of various sizes, and two seven-inch Brooke rifles.

The only fort that would play a direct role in Farragut's passage was Morgan. Fort Gaines was too far away, the main channel being out of range of its guns. Fort Powell was shelled by gunboats to keep its forces from attempting to participate in the defense against the fleet, but it too was too far away to play any role.

On July 29, Farragut issued his General Order No. 11, in which he addressed specific questions that had arisen, or might arise, among the ship commanders. One concerned the actions to be taken by a disabled ship. The admiral's chief concern was to prevent a damaged ship from stopping in the channel, or in some other way preventing the following ships from completing their passage. This was followed by instructions concerning the torpedoes the enemy had planted near the channel. Flag Lieutenant John C. Watson, whom Farragut cared for like a son, made several late-night excursions into the mouth of the bay to examine the torpedoes. He found that many had become inoperable, either because of the long period they had been in the water, or as a result of the nesting of sea worms around the detonator pins. He also identified the buoys that marked the locations of torpedoes, especially the one at the start of the shipping channel. Farragut identified this all-important buoy in his general order, and reminded his captains to keep their vessels on the starboard side of it. Once inside the bay, the smaller gunboats would be cast off from the larger ships so they could pursue the rebel gunboats and destroy or capture them.

On August 1, General Granger arrived with 2,400 troops aboard several ships. That evening, over dinner with Farragut, the two laid out their plan of action. Granger's troops were to attack Fort Gaines from the rear and capture it as quickly as possible. Army signalmen were stationed on each of Farragut's large ships to facilitate communications between the ships and the troops once the forts had been passed. Farragut planned to launch his attack at the same time, hoping to force the enemy to divide its attention and resources.

All was ready, with the exception one of the large monitors, which had not yet arrived. The *Tecumseh*, commanded by one of the admiral's old friends, Commander T. A. M. Craven, whose brother had commanded the *Brooklyn* when the fleet had passed the lower Mississippi forts and captured New Orleans, had been delayed in Pensacola. Farragut sent the *Richmond* and the *Metacomet* to hurry her along. Now he waited impatiently for the arrival of three ships.

During the morning of August 4, 1,500 Federal troops landed on the rear of Dauphin Island and began to make their way across the island to Fort Gaines. Most of these men were infantry, although there were some dismounted cavalry, engineers, and four batteries, two light and two heavy. The accompanying gunboats successfully conducted a shore bombardment to clear the landing site of Confederate pickets. The pickets returned to the fort and reported what they had seen, but there was little that Lieutenant Colonel Williams could do to stop the landing. Instead he moved several of his batteries so they would face inland and oppose the invaders. In addition, he sent skirmishing parties out into the woods to harass and slow the Federals as best they could. To make matters worse, several of Farragut's gunboats and monitors engaged in a bombardment of the fort itself.

By midnight the invading force had reached a point about midway across the island, where it stopped to rest. It was with great effort that they had managed to struggle through the deep, sandy soil, dragging their artillery with them. The rebel skirmishers withdrew, but another enemy soon appeared in the form of thousands of mosquitoes, sand fleas, and biting flies. The men spent an unbearable night, getting little of the rest they badly needed.

Williams, unaware of the size of the invading force, surmised that its intention was to capture the fort before the Federal navy entered the bay. He sent an urgent request to General Maury at Mobile for

Reenactment of the defense of Fort Gaines. Courtesy of
Dauphin Island (Ala.) Park and Beach Board. Photo by Michael
H. Henderson.

reinforcements to drive the invaders back into the sea. Maury
rounded up every man he could, and sent them to Dauphin Island.
Except for a handful of marines, these reinforcements proved more
of a hindrance than a help. Most of them were either old men of the
Home Guard or members of the Pelham Cadets, who were as young
as thirteen. They contributed little to the fort's fighting capability.
However, they raised its garrison to over eight hundred men, more
than the fort could protect from enemy shelling.

Meanwhile, news of the landing reached Farragut, and he grew
even more impatient. The army had engaged the enemy at the appointed time, but the navy had been unable to synchronize the attack, so the enemy would no longer be taken by surprise. Because of
the invasion of Dauphin Island, every Confederate soldier and officer
expected the Federal ships to come at any moment.

In the early evening of August 4, the three vessels Farragut had
been waiting for arrived. Word was passed throughout the fleet that
the attack would be made the following morning, before dawn. In the
solitude of his cabin, the admiral wrote what he obviously thought
might be his last letter to Virginia.

"My Dearest Wife: I write and leave this letter for you. I am going into Mobile Bay in the morning, if God is my leader, as I hope

He is, and in Him I place my trust. If he thinks it is the proper place for me to die, I am ready to submit to His will, in that as all other things. . . ."

Shortly after three o'clock the following morning, Friday, August 5, 1864, the quiet was broken by the shrill sounds of boatswains' whistles aboard the ships and boats of the Federal fleet anchored off Mobile Bay. The "all hands" signal was soon followed by "up all hammocks." Farragut and Drayton left their breakfast and walked out on deck to check weather conditions. It had rained during the night, but the sky was clear now, and a slight breeze was blowing from the southwest. The breeze must have brought a smile to the old admiral's face, for it meant that the smoke of the battle would be blown into the eyes of the Confederate gunners.

After a quick breakfast for their crews, the ships and boats maneuvered into their prescribed positions, and the process of lashing vessels together began. In each case the smaller vessel was on the port side of the larger, where she would be protected from enemy shelling. The large ships had taken the precautions against enemy fire mentioned earlier, such as sheet chains hung over their starboard sides. The gunboats had no similar protection, so it was Farragut's plan that the large craft would protect the smaller whenever possible.

The first five starboard-side ships were all steam sloops with powerful broadside batteries. The last two were large gunboats. The lead ship, the *Brooklyn*, Captain James Alden, was tied to the double-ended gunboat *Octorara*, Lieutenant Commander Charles H. Green. Next came the flagship, Flag Captain Percival Drayton, with the *Metacomet*, Lieutenant Commander James E. Jouett. Third was the *Richmond*, Captain Thornton A. Jenkins, and alongside it was the *Port Royal*, Lieutenant Commander Bancroft Gherardi. The final sloop was the *Monongahela*, Commander James H. Strong, with the *Kennebec*, Lieutenant Commander William P. McCann. Bringing up the rear were the matched gunboats *Ossipee*, Commander William E. LeRoy, and *Itasca*, Lieutenant Commander George Brown. Last were the *Oneida*, Commander J. R. Madison Mullany, with the *Galena*, Lieutenant Commander Clark H. Wells.

As the column formed, the four monitors took up their positions. Standing to the right or starboard side of the column, where they were closer to the fort and better able to attack the enemy fleet once inside the bay, they formed their own line. The first, the *Tecumseh*, was abreast of the *Brooklyn*, so they could be expected to enter the enemy's field of fire simultaneously. She was under the control of Commander T. A. M. Craven. Following was the *Manhattan*, Commander J. W. A. Nicholson, then the *Winnebago*, Commander Thomas H. Stevens, and finally the *Chickasaw*, Lieutenant Commander George H. Perkins. The remainder of the fleet was divided among the six gunboats that had supported the army landing on Dauphin Island, and that now conducted a steady bombardment of Fort Powell, and six others that remained off the coast near Fort Morgan. These last six, the gunboats *Pinola*, *Tennessee*, *Genesee*, *Pembina*, *Bienville*, and *Sebago*, engaged in some minor shelling of the fort, but for the most part were out of effective range. Their primary duty was to prevent enemy vessels from entering or escaping the bay.

At five-thirty, as he was finishing a cup of coffee with Fleet Captain Drayton and Dr. James C. Palmer, the fleet surgeon, Farragut was informed that the fleet was prepared. The sea just outside the entrance to Mobile Bay was bristling with warships. The battle flags flying from each vessel snapped in the morning breeze. As daybreak began to spread a misty, dull light over the scene, anyone watching from the nearby fort could not help but be stirred by the sharp flapping of the oversized American flags, even if they were the enemy's. Quietly turning to the flagship's captain, Farragut put his cup down and said, "Well, Drayton, we might as well get under way."

Within minutes the fleet was moving, slowly and deliberately, like a mighty wrestler who approaches his opponent with the confidence that he need not rush to prevail. Aboard every ship the men stood at their stations, waiting for the opening shots, as they gradually approached the massive enemy fort. At 6:47 the first monitor, *Tecumseh*, fired two shots from her mighty fifteen-inch guns to test the range. Neither shell struck the fort. A few minutes later, anxious Confederate gunners returned the fire.

Aboard the ram *Tennessee*, stationed behind the fort, Admiral Buchanan was awakened to the news that the enemy was under steam and preparing to pass the fort. He ordered Captain Johnston to get under way and head for the lead vessels of the enemy fleet. He planned on engaging each vessel in turn as it passed before him.

In a more or less straight line behind the ram were the other vessels of Buchanan's little flotilla, all wood, and of small value against such a powerful enemy. Directly behind the *Tennessee* was the *Morgan*, Commander George W. Harrison. His vessel had been built as a gunboat, but the haste of her construction was obvious in the use of unseasoned wood and a power plant much too small to be effective. She carried two seven-inch rifles and four thirty-two-pounders. The *Morgan* was followed by the *Gaines*, Lieutenant Commander J. W. Bennett. Except for her armament, which consisted of one eight-inch rifle and five thirty-two-pounders, she was identical to the *Morgan*, suffering the same problems inherent in her construction. Finally, there was the *Selma*, an open-decked river steamboat that had been impetuously refitted into what passed for a war vessel. Her armament fit her condition. She carried three obsolete eight-inch shell guns and one ancient smoothbore thirty-two-pounder that someone had rather clumsily attempted to rifle. Her weapons were so unreliable that her own crew feared for their lives when they fired them.

Meanwhile, Farragut's fleet moved into the entrance to the bay in what one sailor aboard the *Galena* described as "grand style, slowly and calmly." The glowing morning sun began lighting up a cloudless sky as the bows of the first Union ships, the *Brooklyn* and the *Octorara*, cut through the deep blue waters and came within range of Fort Morgan's guns and the guns of her lower water batteries. It was a few minutes before 7:00 A.M. when the batteries and the fort's guns opened fire on the pair. The *Brooklyn* quickly returned fire with a roaring broadside. Within five minutes the *Hartford* and the *Metacomet* also received enemy fire. The flagship, with the admiral's blue pennant standing taut in the wind, came in for the special attention of the rebel cannoneers. She also returned the fire, from both her starboard broadside and the one-hundred-pound Parrott rifle on her forecastle.

From Fort Gaines, on the western end of the entrance to the bay, far out of range, Colonel Anderson watched as the Union ships slowly moved through the shipping channel. The air around them was filled with the smoke of battle, and the explosions of dozens of cannons firing as rapidly as their crews could reload. To his rear, Federal troops, entrenched about eight hundred feet from the fort's western wall, had isolated her from the rest of the island. A few minutes after the battle between Farragut's fleet and Fort Morgan began, General Granger's forces began an artillery barrage of Fort Gaines. With devastating accuracy, they soon disabled or dismounted every gun in the fort.

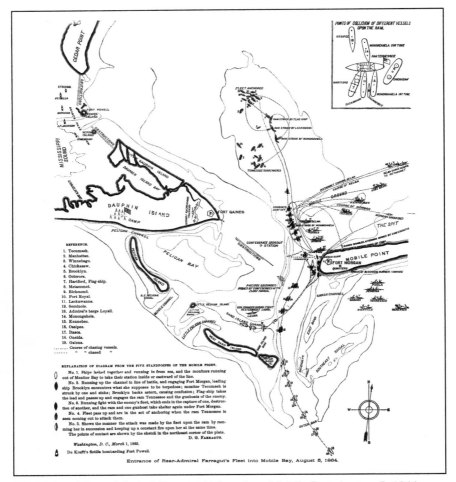

Entrance of Rear Admiral Farragut's fleet into Mobile Bay, August 5, 1864.
Source: Loyall Farragut, *The Life of David Glasgow Farragut* (New York: D. Appleton and Co., 1879).

On board the *Hartford*, where the enemy gunners appeared to be aiming with great effect, the decks were awash with blood and body fragments so thick "that it was difficult to stand on the deck."

As the fleet made its slow progress, the firing filled the channel with thick, acrid smoke. Unable to see what was happening, Farragut began climbing the flagship's rigging until he had reached a point some forty feet above the deck. From his perch he could shout to his pilot, Freeman, who was also high up in the rigging. Using the same voice tube Farragut had installed at Port Hudson, the pilot could communicate with the ship's commander, Captain Drayton. By shouting, the admiral could issue orders to Lieutenant Commander Jouett, who stood atop the *Metacomet*'s wheelhouse.

Captain Drayton watched as his sixty-three-year-old admiral climbed higher and higher, until he was almost obscured by the smoke. Fearing for his safety, for he easily could have been thrown overboard or flung to the deck if the ship suddenly shuddered, as often occurred under heavy fire, the captain could watch no more. He called Quartermaster Knowles to his side and pointed out Farragut's position. Drayton told him to find a way to secure the admiral to the rigging. "I went up with a piece of lead line," Knowles later wrote, "and made it fast to one of the forward shrouds, and then took it around the admiral to the after shroud, making it fast there. The admiral said: 'Never mind, I am all right'; but I went ahead and obeyed orders, for I feared he would fall overboard. . . ."

Two army signal officers had been stationed aboard the *Hartford*. At Farragut's orders, they were to remain belowdecks, out of harm's way, until required. They were instructed by the ship's executive officer, Lieutenant Commander Lewis A. Kimberly, to provide whatever assistance they could to the ship's medical staff while they were below. One of the officers, Lieutenant John C. Kinney, later described what it was like waiting belowdecks while the battle raged above their heads. "Presently one or two of our forward guns opened, and we could hear the distant sound of the guns of the fort in reply. Soon the cannon-balls began to crash through the deck above us, and then the thunder of our whole broadside of Dahlgren guns kept the vessel in a quiver."

Over the roar of the guns and the explosions of enemy shells, the cry was heard, "Send up an army signal officer immediately, the *Brooklyn* is signaling." Kinney sprinted up the ladderway and was on deck in an instant. The army officer made his way through the noise, chaos, and death of the deck toward the forecastle, where he was able to read the signal being sent by one of the signal officers stationed aboard the *Brooklyn*, despite the ever-thickening, acrid smoke that was quickly engulfing the ship.

From the sloop just ahead came the message that the monitors were almost directly in front of the great wooden ship, and that she could not proceed without passing them. The original plan called for the speedy monitors to pull ahead of the fleet and engage the enemy vessels, especially the ram *Tennessee*. This would give the line of ships greater safety in entering the bay. The message was relayed to Farragut, who sent a reply that the *Brooklyn* should proceed into the bay, regardless of what the monitors did. Farragut feared that the *Brooklyn*, which was already slowing down because of the monitors, would block the passage of the following ships, leaving the entire line of vessels motionless under the guns of Fort Morgan. As stationary targets, they would surely face destruction from enemy gunners who would quickly find the correct range and elevation.

Meanwhile, Admiral Buchanan's small rebel flotilla steamed out from behind the fort and proceeded to execute the classic naval maneuver of "crossing the *T*." In this instance, the Federal fleet formed the upright portion of a capital T, while the Confederate vessels formed the crossbar. By this tactic the Union ships, which were in a more or less straight line, would come under fire from the rebels one pair at a time. All the Confederate vessels would then be able to concentrate their fire on one pair of enemy ships, and receive return fire from only that pair. In such a stratagem, a smaller enemy could engage a larger fleet without fear of being outnumbered at any point, since most of the following enemy vessels were unable to fire at them until the preceding vessels were out of the way. Farragut's plan called for the monitors to attack the rebels when they crossed the *T*. If successful, the monitors would sink or scatter at least the gunboats, leaving the *Tennessee* alone to face the entire fleet.

As the monitors drew closer to the enemy flotilla, the officers and men of the leading ships could see the captain of the double-turreted *Winnebago*, Commander Thomas H. Stevens, calmly walking back and forth between the turrets, giving orders to the gun crews inside.

And then suddenly it happened, the worst nightmare of every sailor.

On board the first monitor, the *Tecumseh*, Captain Craven watched as the giant ram moved across the entrance. Fearing that the *Tennessee* was about to escape, Craven ordered the pilot to cross the channel from the eastern side to the western and pursue the enemy. The monitor quickly picked up speed and a few moments later crossed the edge of the minefield. She was on the wrong side of the signal buoy. Almost instantly a great roar filled the air. It was louder than

"The Battle of Mobile Bay," from a painting by J. O. Davidson. Courtesy of Anne S. K. Brown Military Collection, Brown University Library.

any of the guns then firing, and was heard by every man on both sides. Thinking that the monitors had struck the *Tennessee* a fatal blow, Federal gunners stopped firing at the fort and gave a loud cheer. In the smoke they were unable to see that the roar had come from the *Tecumseh.* Having struck an enemy torpedo, the monitor stood virtually on end, with her bow straight down. From the turret of the following monitor, *Manhattan,* comes this description of the fate of the *Tecumseh:* "[Her] stern lifted high in the air with the propeller still revolving, and the ship pitched out of sight like an arrow twanged from a bow."

Within seconds the monitor had disappeared from view into the over sixty feet of water in the channel. On board the *Tennessee,* gunners, who had been prepared to fire at the monitor seconds before, stopped and gazed silently through their gun ports at the frightful sight. Every man knew that a similar fate awaited him should his own vessel strike a torpedo. Being enclosed inside the iron vessel was as near as many wanted to get to being inside a coffin. Now, before their eyes, an entire ship's company of men were about to die, locked alive inside their own coffin.

Aboard the sinking vessel, Captain Craven pushed the pilot, John Collins, through an escape hatch in the turret, but failed to follow. Inside the iron vessel, ninety-three officers and men lost their lives. Of the twenty-one who somehow managed to escape the downrushing ship, four swam to shore below the fort and were taken prisoner, and seven climbed inside of one of the *Tecumseh*'s boats that had broken lose from the ironclad and managed to stay afloat. The remaining ten were rescued by a boat sent by Admiral Farragut.

From his perch high above the action, Farragut watched in disbelief as the monitor vanished in less than thirty seconds. He shouted an order down to Lieutenant Commander Jouett to send a boat to rescue survivors. Rapidly, one of the *Metacomet*'s boats was lowered and, under the command of Acting Master Henry C. Nields, made its way through the smoke to the scene of the disaster, some 500 yards from the flagship.

High above them, General Page saw the small boat on its mission of mercy, and quickly ordered Fort Morgan's gunners not to fire on her. Aboard the *Tennessee*, the same order was passed down the line, although it was not necessary, because every man watching the scene knew he might be awaiting just such a rescue boat any minute.

The explosion that sank the *Tecumseh* so stunned everyone, Yankee and rebel, that the firing slackened slightly for a few moments, but it quickly resumed its intensity.

Stunned by the sinking of the monitor, less than one hundred yards away, Captain Alden slowed the *Brooklyn* to a crawl, and then reversed engines. He feared suffering the same fate as the *Tecumseh*, and was determined to avoid coming too close to the minefield. He was unaware that the monitor had actually passed on the port side of the signal buoy and entered the danger area. As the *Brooklyn* slowed, the morning current sweeping into the bay caught her stern and swung the ship around, so that her bow faced toward Fort Morgan. Farragut, who had earlier feared that the *Brooklyn* would stop the entire fleet when she first slowed down, realized the sloop was about to accomplish the same. She was now blocking a large portion of the channel.

In an attempt to turn his ship back around, Alden reversed engines. The *Brooklyn* immediately began to straighten and back toward *Hartford*. "What is the matter with *Brooklyn*?" Farragut asked pilot

Freeman, who was just above him. "She must have plenty of water there." Watching the *Brooklyn* swing back toward them, Freeman replied, "Plenty to spare, Admiral."

Looking around the channel, Farragut saw that his entire fleet was quickly bunching up behind him. Such a state of confusion was developing that captains of great warships had no idea what was going on ahead of them. Meanwhile, the gunners of Fort Morgan kept up their deadly firing into the ships. Had it not been for Farragut's instructions to run in close to the fort and keep up a rapid fire of grape and shrapnel, the fleet would have been decimated. Only the firing of broadsides loaded with grape and shrapnel could drive the rebel gunners away from their guns and into safety.

For Admiral Farragut, the moment of monumental decision had arrived. Should he go on despite the beating his ships were taking, or should he signal them to turn and run? Like so many other great battlefield commanders before and since, he knew the only decision was to go forward. Although it might cost him several ships and, more important, hundreds of lives, if he could get enough ships into the bay, Mobile would be closed forever. Later he said that he had calculated he might lose some of his ships, but that he couldn't lose them all. He would go forward, and true to his own beliefs, he would lead the way. If another ship was to suffer the fate of the *Tecumseh*, he was willing to allow that ship to be the one flying his flag.

Reaching up, he grabbed the pilot's foot and tugged. "I shall lead," he shouted to Freeman. The order was passed via the speaking tube. The engine room poured in the coal, and the *Hartford* quickly moved forward. Behind her, the rest of the fleet did likewise. Farragut was no longer sure about the location of the enemy torpedoes, but he decided that most of them had probably been in the water so long that they were harmless. It was a gamble, but a gamble he believed worth taking, even if losing meant the end of his own life.

As the flagship passed on the port side of the *Brooklyn*, Farragut shouted down to her, "What's the trouble?" "Torpedoes," was the shouted reply.

"Damn the torpedoes," responded Farragut.

Then, calling down to the captain of his flagship, he shouted, "Four bells, Captain Drayton."

Then he bellowed to the commander of the gunboat lashed to the flagship's side, "Go ahead, Jouett, full speed."

Time eroded Farragut's orders to simply, "Damn the torpedoes, full speed ahead." It became a naval battle cry that has stirred sailors on to battle for over a hundred years.

The *Hartford* swept beyond the *Brooklyn* as the latter struggled to right herself. Those below the *Hartford*'s decks could hear the primers snapping off the torpedoes beneath them as the flagship crossed the corner of the minefield. Not one exploded. Farragut's gamble that they were disabled by too long a time in the water had paid off. Within minutes the entire fleet, including Captain Alden's errant vessel, was inside Mobile Bay, beyond the reach of Fort Morgan's guns. The *Tecumseh* was the only vessel lost in the passage, although most, especially the larger ships, had suffered badly. The *Oneida* had suffered a shot that disabled her engine, causing her cohort, the *Galena*, to drag her along, which she did with great success.

Aboard the *Tennessee*, Buchanan saw the admiral's blue pennant flying from the *Hartford*, and aimed his ram directly at her. Unable to gain sufficient speed to ram the wooden sloop, the ram turned, and the two vessels passed alongside each other, exchanging a raking fire. The remaining rebel vessels kept up a terrible fire, until Farragut ordered the *Metacomet* cut loose, and she rushed at the enemy with her guns ablaze.

The *Tennessee* attacked each of the following pairs of Union vessels, causing damage to several, and killing a large number of sailors. Each in turn fired broadsides and chase guns at the ram, which, due to its weak power plant, was unable to ram any of them. When the three remaining Federal monitors, which had been covering the passage of the wooden ships, joined the action against the *Tennessee*, Buchanan withdrew from a battle that was leading his ship into a trap surrounded by the enemy.

Meanwhile, the *Metacomet* chased down the rebel gunboat *Selma*, and sank her. Soon the remaining Federal gunboats, freed from their positions lashed to the larger ships, entered the battle against the two remaining rebel gunboats. The *Itasca*, the *Kennebec*, and the *Port Royal* fired into the enemy. The *Gaines* received two shots below the waterline, causing her to begin sinking. Fearing for the lives of his crew, Lieutenant Commander Bennett ran his vessel onto the beach behind Fort Morgan and ordered his men to abandon her. Pursued by a

Admiral David G. Farragut and General Gordon Granger
meeting at Fort Gaines to discuss strategy for the attack on
Fort Morgan, scheduled for August 22, 1864. Courtesy of Anne
S. K. Brown Military Collection, Brown University Library.

relentless enemy, Commander Harrison took the *Morgan* to safety under the guns of the fort.

Later that night the *Morgan* slipped away and rushed past several
Union gunboats. She sped across the shoals and returned to Mobile.

The *Tennessee* had also sought the safety offered by Fort Morgan's
guns. Admiral Buchanan surveyed the situation, and while his crewmen took a brief break to eat hardtack and take great swallows of
warm water to slake their universal thirst, he planned his next action.
The ram had less than six hours of coal to burn, and Buchanan knew
that once darkness blinded the fort's gunners, Farragut's monitors

would attack and quite likely destroy her. He was determined not to be forced to surrender without putting up the best fight he could.

Grim-faced, the Confederate admiral watched as the enemy fleet gathered together three miles inside the bay. He decided he would do as much damage to them as possible, even though his chances of victory were nonexistent. Turning to Captain Johnston, he quietly ordered, "Follow them up, Johnston, we can't let them off that way." It was a few minutes after 9:00 A.M.

Buchanan's estimate of Farragut's plans had been correct. The Federal admiral told Captain Drayton that he planned to move his flag temporarily to the monitor *Manhattan* after dark, take the three monitors in under the fort's guns, and attack and possibly board the *Tennessee*. He realized that the costly victory his fleet had attained would count for little if the mighty ram was left to help Fort Morgan defend against attack.

As the two officers watched the ram, it began to move forward. At first, Drayton thought it might be heading out of the bay to attack the gunboats stationed offshore. "No," replied Farragut, watching through his glass. "Buck's coming here. Get under way, we must be ready for him." The signal was sent from ship to ship, "Run down the ram!"

Suddenly, anchor chains clanged and smoke belched from smokestacks, and virtually every ship in the fleet sprang to life. Everyone wanted his ship to be the one that sank or captured the infamous ram. The first to reach the approaching *Tennessee* was the *Monongahela*. The sloop struck the ironclad amidships with such force that most of the men on both vessels were knocked off their feet. But the ram suffered no visible damage. Instead, the *Monongahela* had her reinforced iron prow torn completely off. She then fired a broadside as the ram passed, but her shells simply rolled off the rebel's casement. Buchanan was heading for the *Hartford*, and had little time or patience with other ships, so, except for a few shots that penetrated the sloop's hull above the water, he ignored her.

Next came the *Lackawanna*. She too rammed the *Tennessee*, and also suffered damage to her forward section, again doing little damage to the enemy. In the collision, both ships were swung around so they were side by side. Rebel gunners opened their ports and began calling obscenities at the Union sailors. The insults brought a round of small-arms fire. Sailors without handguns or muskets simply picked objects up off the deck and threw them at the enemy. These included a holystone and a spittoon. The former struck a taunting Confederate square in the face, knocking him to the deck. As the two vessels drew apart, they began firing directly into each other. A small fire was begun on the wooden ship, but was quickly brought under control. The *Tennessee* suffered a damaged gun port, which prevented that gun from being used. Still the ram continued on in an almost straight line for the *Hartford*. The monitors began to close in and fire, although they had to be especially careful, because so many Federal ships were now steaming around the ram that they might hit one of their own.

Finally, in the midst of wild firing and ramming, the *Tennessee* reached her target. Suddenly it became a battle of the two admirals. The *Hartford* turned on her attacker and sped up with full intention to ram her. The *Tennessee*, unable to get up much speed to begin with, was slowed even more by several debilitating shots to her smokestack. The two flagships faced off, and for a few seconds it looked as if they would meet head-on, a collision in which both ships would go down. At the last second, Buchanan turned ever so slightly to starboard. The two vessels scraped alongside each other, their guns almost touching as they fired broadsides into each other. Fortunately for the Federal ship, the Confederate gunners suffered a string of bad primers, so most of their guns were unable to fire. Even with all the noise and screaming around them, the surprised Union sailors could hear the loud clicking sounds as the primers snapped and failed to blow. Farragut jumped into the rigging and swung out to get a better view. At one point he was actually standing above the enemy ram, and could have stepped down onto her if he had been moved to do so.

Small-arms fire and flung objects landed on the enemy ships. One Union sailor was stabbed by a bayonet jabbed at him by a Confederate engineer, who was shot in the shoulder by another sailor for his trouble.

The chaos and confusion of this short but horrendous battle is exemplified by the accidental ramming of the *Hartford* by the *Lackawanna*. Both ships suffered damage in the collision. An irritated Farragut turned to an army signal officer standing nearby and asked "Can you say 'For God's sake' by signal?" When the man responded in the

"Battle of Mobile Bay," from a painting by Xanthus Smith. Courtesy of the U.S. Naval Academy Museum.

affirmative, the admiral told him to signal the *Lackawanna*, "For God's sake, get out of our way and anchor!" The signal was either never received or ignored in the heat of the battle.

Life inside the ram, taking shells and ramming from all directions, was reaching the breaking point. Two monitors moved in for the kill as the *Tennessee* and the *Hartford* parted. The *Manhattan* fired her huge fifteen-inch guns at close range, doing considerable damage to the ram's iron plate. The *Chickasaw*'s Lieutenant Commander Perkins pushed his vessel right up to the stern of the ram, and fired his eleven-inch guns into her casement at from ten to fifty yards' distance. The series of rapid blows finally succeeded in penetrating the casement and brought a portion of the structure down. Among the killed and wounded from the *Chickasaw*'s pounding was Admiral Buchanan, who was discovered under a section of metal with a badly broken leg.

Unable to continue in command, he turned full authority over to Captain Johnston. Both men knew this meant the unenviable task of surrendering would fall to the captain, for there was nothing left to be done. The ram could hardly move, for her stack was now completely shot away. In addition, the exposed steering chains had been de-

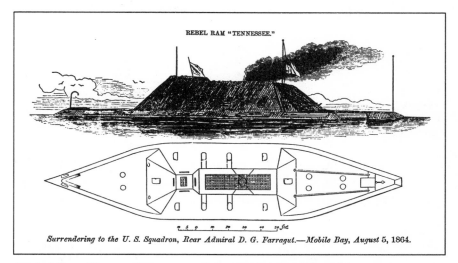

REBEL RAM "TENNESSEE."

Surrendering to the U. S. Squadron, Rear Admiral D. G. Farragut.—Mobile Bay, August 5, 1864.

"Rebel Ram *Tennessee*." Courtesy of the Confederate Naval Museum.

stroyed. The mighty *Tennessee* could no longer steer or gather any speed.

At 10:00 A.M., after taking a pounding that would have sunk any ship in the Federal fleet, Johnston had the Confederate battle flag lowered and a white flag raised in her place. The battle for Mobile Bay had ended.

The victory had cost the Union one monitor, along with ninety-three of her crew. Other losses included fifty-two killed and 170 wounded. The flagship had suffered twenty-five killed. Quartermaster Knowles was present when Farragut viewed the lines of dead sailors and officers laid out on the deck. "It was the only time I ever saw the old gentleman cry, but the tears came in his eyes, like a little child."

Epilogue

WHEN THE BATTLE FOR MOBILE BAY WAS OVER, and the prisoners and wounded had been taken care of, Admiral Farragut, weary from the day's exertions, sat down at the desk in his cabin to write a brief note to his wife, Virginia. He wanted to be sure that when she heard the news of the battle, she would be comforted by the knowledge that he had survived. "The Almighty has smiled on me once more," he wrote. "I am in Mobile Bay. The *Tennessee* and Buchanan are my prisoners. It was a hard fight, but Buck met his fate manfully."

The first information to reach Washington concerning Farragut's victory came in a telegram from General Butler, who was on the James River in Virginia. A staff officer brought him several copies of a Richmond newspaper describing the battle in some detail. Alone in his tent, the old general roared, "Three cheers for Farragut!" The three cheers that followed brought a group of his officers running in fear that something had happened to him. Butler telegraphed the news to Fox in Washington, and dashed off a note of congratulations to the Admiral.

Among the hundreds of congratulatory messages received by Farragut was a note from President Lincoln thanking him for his "brilliant success." Lincoln ordered that every navy yard, plus the Washington Arsenal, fire a one-hundred-gun salute in celebration of the taking of Mobile Bay. Soon afterward, the President issued a proclamation that he asked be read at every religious service throughout the Union on the following Sunday. In it he called on every citizen to give thanks to Admiral Farragut and General Sherman for their "glorious achievements," Farragut at Mobile Bay, and Sherman at Atlanta.

Captain Percival Drayton and Rear Admiral David G. Farragut in a photo taken shortly after the Battle of Mobile. Courtesy of the Nimitz Library, U.S. Naval Academy.

In the following three weeks the forts were taken by combined naval and army forces, and the entire lower bay was controlled by the Federal government. Farragut remained active during this time, but his health began to deteriorate.

Unaware of Farragut's condition, Welles selected him to lead a naval expedition against Fort Fischer, North Carolina, in support of Federal invasion forces. Before the actual order had been published, a letter arrived from Farragut, dated August 27, 1864. In it he told the secretary that his strength was almost exhausted and his health was giving out. "I have been down in this Gulf and the Caribbean Sea nearly five years out of six, with the exception of the short time at

Drayton and Farragut aboard the *Hartford* at Mobile Bay. Courtesy of the Nimitz Library, U.S. Naval Academy.

home last Fall, and the last six months have been a severe drag upon me, and I want rest if it is to be had."

The officers and men around him began to write home of their concern for the admiral. They, who knew him so well, could clearly see that he was in fact suffering greatly from exhaustion and ill health.

On December 12, a tired but buoyant Farragut arrived in New York aboard his flagship. He and Flag Captain Drayton were treated as the heroes they had proven to be, by thousands of officials and citizens who had turned out to greet them. Following seemingly endless ceremonies in which everyone wanted to greet and shake hands with the great naval officer, Farragut returned to Hastings-on-Hudson to spend some peaceful time with Virginia and Loyall. The latter was given special leave from West Point to greet his father.

On December 22, 1864, the rank of vice-admiral was created by Congress, and Farragut was immediately promoted. The following month he and Virginia visited Washington, where they socialized with President and Mrs. Lincoln. At the President's personal invitation, the couple attended Lincoln's second inauguration. In the summer

A dismounted gun at Fort Morgan, following the final battle. Courtesy of the Nimitz Library, U.S. Naval Academy.

of 1866, Farragut was named the first admiral of the navy, and joined President Andrew Johnson on a tour of the nation.

In June 1867, the navy regulation against wives sailing aboard navy ships was waived by President Johnson, without any request from the admiral, and Virginia joined her husband on a triumphant world tour. They sailed on board Farragut's new flagship, USS *Franklin*, a four-thousand-ton frigate with a crew of 750 men and officers, and boasting thirty-nine guns.

The Farraguts visited France, Germany, Russia, Sweden, Denmark, England, Portugal, Spain, Italy, Holland, and Greece. Everywhere they went, thousands cheered them, and heads of state and crowned monarchs greeted and entertained them. Included was Queen Victoria, whose sentiments had been with the defeated Confederacy.

During the winter of 1869, Farragut suffered several heart attacks, which limited his official activities considerably. After celebrating his sixty-ninth birthday, on July 5, 1870, he made an inspection of the Portsmouth Navy Yard. While there he found the sailing sloop *Dale*,

Admiral Farragut in an undated photo, perhaps one
of the last photos taken of him. Courtesy of the
Nimitz Library, U.S. Naval Academy.

which was laid up in the yard. Accompanied by the old sailor who was
the *Dale*'s caretaker, he paced her decks and spoke of what she had
looked like at sea with her sixteen guns blazing. Suddenly he stopped,
turned to the caretaker, and said, "This is the last time I shall ever
tread the deck of a man-of-war."

In less than a week his weakness confined him to bed. On August 14, 1870, Admiral of the Navy David G. Farragut died of a stroke.

A memorial service, held at Portsmouth, was attended by Welles,
Fox, and many of the men who had fought under Farragut during the
war. He was temporarily interred at Portsmouth. Conspicuously ab-
sent was President Grant, who, as a political statement, chose not to
attend. This was Grant's retaliation against the admiral because Farragut had declined to support him in his campaign for the presidency.

Veterans placing flags at the grave of Admiral
Farragut, Woodlawn Cemetery, Bronx, New York.
Courtesy of the Hastings (N.Y.) Historical Society.

Grant's absence from the memorial service caused such an uproar
among the public and press, who had not forgotten the old man's gallantry and deeds, that the White House was inundated with letters
and telegrams condemning the President.

Plans originally had called for interring the admiral at Annapolis,
but Virginia acquiesced to a request from the leading citizens of New
York City that they be permitted to bury him in New York. Responding to public condemnation and pressure, President Grant attended the funeral services, held on September 30, 1870, even marching in a torrential downpour along with ten thousand soldiers and
thousands of former sailors and past and present officials. It was a day
of mourning in the city, with all public buildings closed and draped
accordingly. Farragut was laid to rest at Woodlawn Cemetery in the
Bronx. Following the burial, General George Meade remarked to an-

The Admiral David G. Farragut memorial window, U.S. Naval Academy Chapel. Courtesy of the U.S. Naval Academy Museum.

other general officer, "I believe that the Admiral was more beloved than any other commander of the late war, either of the Army or Navy."

Twenty-eight years after his death, Admiral Farragut's spirit was once again at sea, standing alongside the man who would become the third admiral in the United States Navy, following Farragut and David Porter.

On the night of April 30, 1898, Commodore George Dewey sat in his quarters aboard his flagship, the *Olympia*, outside the entrance to Manila Bay, where a powerful Spanish fleet was at anchor. He reviewed the battle plans for the following day with the captains of his Asiatic Fleet. Carefully studying the plans, he asked himself, "What would Farragut have done?"

The next day, Dewey took his ships into the bay and destroyed the Spanish fleet, thus avenging the destruction of the battleship *Maine* in Havana harbor earlier that year. He did so without the loss of one American life.

When Dewey sailed triumphantly into New York Harbor to a spectacular hero's welcome on September 29, 1899, his ship flew the pennant of his personal hero, Admiral Farragut. Farragut's strategy of bypassing powerful enemy strongholds has been passed from one generation of military leaders to another. It was the strategy used by General Douglas MacArthur, when he decided to pass Pacific islands with strong Japanese garrisons in favor of more important targets. These powerful island fortresses were allowed to wither away once they were cut off from their supply bases, just as Forts Jackson and St. Philip did when New Orleans was taken.

Following his death, great statues of Farragut were erected in Washington, New York, and Boston. Hundreds of poems were written in his honor, as were dozens of songs. Although the naval part of the Civil War has not received as much attention as the great land battles of that conflict, the name David Farragut will last in our collective memory as long as those of Grant and Lee, and just as deservedly so.

Now then, your broadside, shipmates all,
   With grape well loaded down!
May garlands filled with sunshine fall
   To gild his silvered crown!
I give the name that fits him best—
   Ay, better than his own—
The Sea King of the sovereign West,
   Who made his mast a throne!

     —final stanza from "A Toast to the Vice Admiral"
     by Oliver Wendell Holmes

Bibliography

Adams, William Henry Davenport. *Farragut and Other Great Commanders*. New York: George Routledge and Sons, 1871.

Alden, Carroll Storrs. *George Hamilton Perkins*. Boston: Houghton Mifflin, 1914.

Anderson, Bern. *By Sea and by River*. New York: Alfred A. Knopf, 1962.

Armstrong, Hugh. "Full Speed Ahead." *America's Civil War* (November 1993), 8–12.

Barnes, James. David G. Farragut. Boston: Small, Maynard, 1899.

Bergeron, Arthur W., Jr. *Confederate Mobile*. Jackson, Miss.: University Press of Mississippi, 1991.

Blough, Joseph. "Iron Versus Wood." *Great Battles* (September 1991), 19–25.

Boatner, Mark Mayo III. *The Civil War Dictionary*. New York: David McKay, 1959.

Bradford, James C. *Command Under Sail*. Annapolis, Md.: U.S. Navy Institute Press, 1985.

——. *Captains of the Old Steam Navy*. Annapolis, Md.: U.S. Navy Institute Press, 1986.

Bradford, Ned, ed. *Battles and Leaders of the Civil War*. New York: Appleton-Century Crofts, 1956.

Burns, Zed H. *Confederate Forts*. Natchez, Miss.: Southern Historical Publications, 1977.

Clark, Charles E. *My Fifty Years in the Navy*. Boston: Little, Brown, 1917.

Cochran, Hamilton. *Blockade Runners of the Confederacy*. Indianapolis, Ind.: Bobbs-Merrill, 1958.

Commager, Henry Steele, ed. *The Blue and the Gray*. Indianapolis: Bobbs-Merrill, 1950.

Congdon, Don, ed. *Combat: The Civil War*. New York: Konecky & Konecky, 1992. Reprint of 1967 edition.

Cornelius, Commander George. "What Did Farragut See?" *Naval History* (July/August 1994), 11–17.

Dauphin Island Park and Beach Board. "The Battle for Fort Gaines, August 4–9, 1864." Dauphin Island, Ala., 1992.

Dewey, Admiral George. *Autobiography of George Dewey, Admiral of the Navy.* New York: Charles Scribner's Sons, 1913.

Dufour, Charles L. *The Night the War Was Lost.* Garden City, N.Y.: Doubleday, 1960.

Dupuy, R. Ernest, and Trevor N. Dupuy. *The Compact History of the Civil War.* New York: Hawthorn Books, 1960.

Ely, Robert B. "This Filthy Ironpot." *American Heritage* (February 1968), 46–49.

Faller, Philip E. "Pounding Port Hudson." *America's Civil War* (January 1994), 30–87.

Farragut, Loyall. *Life of David Glasgow Farragut.* New York: D. Appleton and Co., 1879.

Faust, Patricia L., ed. *Historical Times Illustrated Encyclopedia of the Civil War.* New York: HarperCollins, 1991.

Feuer, A. B. "Steady Boys Steady." *Military History* (August 1993), 47–88.

Fowler, William M., Jr. *Under Two Flags.* New York: Norton, 1990.

Franklin, S. R. *Memories of a Rear-Admiral.* New York: Harper & Brothers, 1898.

Frazier, Donald A. "Cottonclads in a Storm of Iron." *Naval History* (May/June, 1994), 26–32.

Green, Francis Vinton. *Campaigns of the Civil War: The Mississippi.* New York: Charles Scribner's Sons, 1882.

Guttman, Jon. "CSS *Manassas*, Guardian of New Orleans. . . ," *America's Civil War* (May 1992), 16–67.

Headley, J. T. *Farragut and Our Naval Commanders.* New York: E. B. Treat, 1867.

———. *Heroes and Battles of the War 1861–65: Our Navy in the Great Rebellion.* New York: E. B. Treat, 1891.

Headley, Phineas Camp. *Life and Naval Career of Vice Admiral David Glasgow Farragut.* New York: William H. Appleton, 1865.

Hewitt, Lawrence Lee. *Port Hudson, Confederate Bastion on the Mississippi.* Baton Rouge, La.: Louisiana State University Press, 1987.

Hill, Jim Dan. *Sea Dogs of the Sixties: Farragut and Seven Contemporaries.* Minneapolis: University of Minnesota Press, 1935.

Hoehling, A. A. *Thunder at Hampton Roads.* Englewood Cliffs, N.J.: Prentice-Hall, 1976.

———. *Damn the Torpedoes: Naval Incidents of the Civil War.* Winston-Salem, N.C.: John F. Blair, 1989.

Homans, James Edward. *Our Three Admirals: Farragut, Porter, Dewey.* New York: James T. White, 1899.

Hults, E. H. "Aboard the *Galena* at Mobile." *Civil War Times Illustrated* (April 1971), 12–21; (May 1971), 28–42.

Hunt, O. E., ed. *The Photographic History of the Civil War.* Secaucus, N.J.: Blue and Gray Press, 1987. Reprint of 1911 edition.

Jones, Virgil C. *The Civil War at Sea.* Three volumes. New York: Holt, Rinehart and Winston, 1960–62.

Kelly, C. Brian. "A City Facing Its Certain Fate. . . ." *Military History* (August 1993), 6.

Knox, Dudley W. *A History of the United States Navy.* New York: G. P. Putnam's Sons, 1936.

Lewis, Charles Lee. *David Glasgow Farragut, Admiral in the Making.* Annapolis, Md.: United States Naval Institute, 1941.

————. *David Glasgow Farragut, Our First Admiral.* Annapolis, Md.: United States Naval Institute, 1943.

Macartney, Clarence Edward. *Mr. Lincoln's Admirals.* New York: Funk & Wagnalls, 1956.

Mahan, Commander A. T. *The Navy in the Civil War: The Gulf and Inland Waters.* New York: Charles Scribner's Sons, 1883.

Mahan, Captain A. T. *Admiral Farragut.* New York: D. Appleton & Co., 1892.

Martin, Christopher. *Damn the Torpedoes.* New York: Abelard-Schuman, 1970.

Martin, David G. *The Vicksburg Campaign.* New York: Gallery Books, 1990.

Melia, Tamara Moser. *"Damn the Torpedoes": A Short History of U.S. Naval Mine Countermeasures, 1777–1991.* Washington, D.C.: Naval Historical Center, 1991.

Merrill, James M. *Battle Flags South.* Teaneck, N.J.: Fairleigh Dickinson University Press, 1970.

Miller, Edward Stokes. *Civil War Sea Battles.* Conshohocken Pa.: Combined Books, 1995.

Milligan, John D. *Gunboats Down the Mississippi.* U.S. Naval Institute, 1965.

Montgomery, James Eglinton. *Our Admiral's Flag Abroad: The Cruise of Admiral D. G. Farragut, Commanding the European Squadron in 1867–68.* New York: G. P. Putnam & Sons, 1869.

Musicant, Ivan. *Divided Waters.* New York: HarperCollins, 1995.

Nash, Howard P., Jr. *A Naval History of the Civil War.* Cranbury, N.J.: A. S. Barnes and Co., 1972.

Niven, John. *Gideon Welles, Lincoln's Secretary of the Navy.* New York: Oxford University Press, 1973.

Patterson, Gerard. "The Beast of New Orleans." *Civil War Times Illustrated* (May/June 1993), 29–66.

Pelzer, John D. "Stung by Mosquitoes," *Military History* (December 1994), 46–52.

Perry, Milton F. *Infernal Machines.* Baton Rouge, La.: Louisiana State University Press, 1965.

Pratt, Fletcher. *Civil War on Western Waters*. New York: Henry Holt, 1956.

Robinson, William Morrison, Jr. *The Confederate Privateers*. New Haven, Conn.: Yale University Press, 1928.

Sandburg, Carl. *Abraham Lincoln: The War Years*. New York: Harcourt, Brace & Company, 1939.

Sharf, Thomas J. *History of the Confederate Navy*. New York: The Fairfax Press, 1977. Reprint of 1887 edition.

Shorto, Russell. *David Farragut and the Great Naval Blockade*. Englewood Cliffs, N.J.: Silver Burdett Press, 1991.

Spears, John Randolph. *David G. Farragut*. Philadelphia: G. W. Jacobs, 1905.

Stern, Philip Van Doren. *The Confederate Navy*. New York: Bonanza Books, 1962.

Stevens, William Oliver. *David Glasgow Farragut, Our First Admiral*. New York: Dodd, Mead & Co., 1942.

Still, William N., Jr. *Iron Afloat*. Nashville, Tenn.: Vanderbilt University Press, 1971.

Suhr, Robert Collins. "Union's Hard-Luck Ironclad," *America's Civil War* (July 1993), 34–40.

Wilson, H. W. *Ironclads in Action*. London: Sampson Low & Marston, 1896.

Winters, John D. *The Civil War in Louisiana*. Baton Rouge, La.: Louisiana State University Press, 1963.

Wukovits, John F. "Decks Covered With Blood." *America's Civil War* (April 1991), 41–45.

Zebrowski, Carl. "Guardians of Mobile Bay," *Civil War Times Illustrated* (March/ April 1994), 20–65.

Index